Deleuze and the Body

D1615553

Deleuze Connections

'It is not the elements or the sets which define the multiplicity. What defines it is the AND, as something which has its place between the elements or between the sets. AND, AND, AND – stammering.'

Gilles Deleuze and Claire Parnet, *Dialogues*

General Editor
Ian Buchanan

Editorial Advisory Board

Keith Ansell-Pearson   Gregg Lambert
Rosi Braidotti   Adrian Parr
Claire Colebrook   Paul Patton
Tom Conley   Patricia Pisters

Titles Available in the Series

Ian Buchanan and Claire Colebrook (eds), *Deleuze and Feminist Theory*
Ian Buchanan and John Marks (eds), *Deleuze and Literature*
Mark Bonta and John Protevi (eds), *Deleuze and Geophilosophy*
Ian Buchanan and Marcel Swiboda (eds), *Deleuze and Music*
Ian Buchanan and Gregg Lambert (eds), *Deleuze and Space*
Martin Fuglsang and Bent Meier Sørensen (eds), *Deleuze and the Social*
Ian Buchanan and Adrian Parr (eds), *Deleuze and the Contemporary World*
Constantin V. Boundas (ed.), *Deleuze and Philosophy*
Ian Buchanan and Nicholas Thoburn (eds), *Deleuze and Politics*
Chrysanthi Nigianni and Merl Storr (eds), *Deleuze and Queer Theory*
Jeffrey A. Bell and Claire Colebrook (eds), *Deleuze and History*
Laura Cull (ed.), *Deleuze and Performance*
Mark Poster and David Savat (eds), *Deleuze and New Technology*
Simone Bignall and Paul Patton (eds), *Deleuze and the Postcolonial*
Stephen Zepke and Simon O'Sullivan (eds), *Deleuze and Contemporary Art*
Laura Guillaume and Joe Hughes (eds), *Deleuze and the Body*
Daniel W. Smith and Nathan Jun (eds), *Deleuze and Ethics*
Frida Beckman (ed.), *Deleuze and Sex*

Forthcoming Titles in the Series

David Martin-Jones and William Brown (eds), *Deleuze and Film*
Inna Semetsky and Diana Masny (eds), *Deleuze and Education*

Deleuze and the Body

Edited by Laura Guillaume and
Joe Hughes

Edinburgh University Press

Edinburgh University Press Ltd
22 George Square, Edinburgh

www.euppublishing.com

Typeset in 10.5/13 Adobe Sabon
by Servis Filmsetting Ltd, Stockport, Cheshire,
and printed and bound in Great Britain by
CPI Antony Rowe, Chippenham and Eastbourne

A CIP record for this book is available from the British Library

ISBN 978 0 7486 3864 2 (hardback)
ISBN 978 0 7486 3865 9 (paperback)

Contents

Pity the Meat?: Deleuze and the Body

Joe Hughes

The question animating this volume is simple: is there a coherent theory of the body in Deleuze, and if there is, what can we do with it? If the question needs to be asked, it is because the body has an uncertain place in Deleuze's work. It is its own kind of Erewhon: simultaneously 'now here' and 'nowhere'.

As evidence for its omnipresence we could begin by citing his writings on Spinoza. The 'properly ethical question', Deleuze tells us, is 'what can a body do?' *Nietzsche and Philosophy* takes this ethical question further, constructing a typology of corporeal forms based on each body's composition of forces. The two geneses of *The Logic of Sense* have their origin in 'corporeal depths'. The classification of images in *Cinema 1* is not an empirical, inductive classification. Rather, the categories of cinema are the categories of a body emerging from the plane of immanence. In *Francis Bacon* the meat is a lithe, acrobatic material which can enter into various characteristic relations. It is a constellation containing colors of such splendor that Bacon becomes a religious painter when he enters butcher shops.

Not only is the concept of the body nearly everywhere we look in Deleuze's work, but it has also gone on to inform some of the most influential conceptions of the body in contemporary critical debate. Elizabeth Grosz, Moira Gatens, Patricia Clough and Rosi Braidotti, to name only a few, have engaged critically with Deleuze's writings on the body.

At the same time, however, Deleuze rarely discusses the body directly, and he is wide open to Grosz's claim that Deleuze, among others, has not 'explicitly devoted himself to developing a theory of the body' or made it 'the center of focus' (1994: ix). The only way we can draw a theory of the body out of the central work in Deleuze's œuvre, *Difference and Repetition*, is by insisting that the three passive syntheses be read as a theory of corporeal drives. This may be a plausible reading, but the fact that we need to hunt for it already makes Grosz's point.

Even in those texts in which the body plays a prominent role, it is very quickly transcended. In Spinoza we ask what a body can do only to get to our power of action more quickly – which is not the body, but reason. Cinema discovers its essence in the disembodied time-image. In *The Logic of Sense*, sense must counter-actualize the corporeal depths and, like the Stoic incorporeals, shuffle off its corporeality and disavow itself of the passions. In *Francis Bacon*, the meat becomes all too quickly an object of pity, and, by virtue of the scream, it ultimately escapes from its corporeality, becoming a 'nonlocalized power'.

The theory of the body in Deleuze's work is thus a problematic site. It is not clear what kind of work the concept is supposed to do within Deleuze's corpus, and it is not immediately clear what kind of work we can do with it. The essays collected here address these issues. I have somewhat artificially separated the collection into two groups: 'Deleuzism' and 'Practical Deleuzism'. The first five essays work through the theory of the body at a more or less theoretical level, whereas the last five undertake or move toward various types of practical engagement. If the division is artificial it is because few, if any, of the theoretical pieces proceed without any consideration of practice, and each of the essays which bring Deleuze's thought to bear on an area contemporary debate ultimately ask us to rethink Deleuze in light of the conclusions drawn there.

Claire Colebrook's essay opens the collection. It represents a kind of before and after of Deleuze. The essay begins with a survey of concepts of embodiment from Husserl and Sartre through Grosz and Butler to autopoietic theories of embodied life. But, extending Deleuze and Guattari's claim that the experience of death is the essence of life, Colebrook argues that these theories of embodiment, and autopoietic theory in particular, cannot account for unbounded and disembodied life. How can we think viral life, evil and the inhuman – forms of life which 'make their way through the world without a thought of sustainability'? How can we think a life that is 'blindly active' and mutational and, assuming that we can think it, what would a viral politics look like?

John Protevi further develops the relation between autopoietic theory and Deleuze's thought. He directly addresses one of the more opaque claims of the second chapter of *Difference and Repetition*: namely, that underneath the three passive 'perceptual syntheses' there are thousands of 'little selves' – contemplative souls – carrying out 'organic syntheses'. Protevi shows that what looks like a bizarre 'biological panpsychism' here is in fact congruent with the arguments of Evan Thompson and Hans Jonas. Perceptual syntheses are always linked to organic or metabolic syntheses, a fact which is exemplified by research on *Escherichia coli*. Protevi ends, like Colebrook, with the provocative claim that to we need to move beyond focusing on adult functioning and homeostatic regulation and begin to focus on the process of ontogenesis.

Anna Cutler and Iain MacKenzie begin to account for this process of production in their engagement with neuroscience (Steven Rose and Wolf Singer) and philosophy (Merleau-Ponty and Judith Butler). While both neuroscience and philosophy have helpfully complicated the relation between the body (or brain) and the world, both tend to reinstate knowledge of the body as a constitutive moment of subjectivity and thus reinstall the 'knowing subject upon the throne of the world'. To avoid such a coup, they argue, it is necessary to develop a pedagogy of the concept. 'Learning both conditions the production of the known and is the real genesis of conceptuality itself.' In following this apprenticeship we see that bodies and bodies of knowledge, far from being two sides of an exclusive dualism, come together in a process of mutual genesis. From this point of view we can begin to think 'vital ideas' – ideas that are not abstract representations but material and real.

In my own contribution to this collection I further develop the contours of this genesis of vital ideas, arguing that film can play a role in the kind of pedagogy for which Cutler and MacKenzie. I trace the genesis of the body in *Cinema 1* through the crises in recognition in *Cinema 2* and argue that Deleuze's most basic claim in the cinema books, when he names the vocation of cinema as the production of belief in the world, is that cinema is capable of producing ideas which directly affect the body. The cinema project should be read as a new pedagogy of the image.

Nathan Widder's essay explores what should have been a formidable problem for Deleuze studies from the start. In several important passages Deleuze reaffirms the Hegelian theme that being is sense. But, in *The Logic of Sense*, Deleuze is clear that sense itself is produced. In other words, being has its origins outside of itself, and, to make such a claim even more scandalous, that origin is a 'universal cesspool', the tumultuous interaction of an unindividuated matter. What is the relation between such unstable materiality and sense, between corporeality and incorporeality? Deleuze himself charts the relation between these two poles in his account of the dynamic genesis. Widder traces this process of production in detail, showing how the body and its drives liberate sense from matter. In doing so, he helpfully clarifies both this process and the degree to which Melanie Klein's theory of childhood development informed Deleuze's thought.

If it is possible to say that the first set of essays in this collection come together under a common idea – and I am not sure that it is – the idea would be that, in thinking the body with Deleuze, we cannot separate it from thought itself. These Cartesian coordinates simply do not hold in Deleuze. Thought is always already metabolic (to use Protevi's expression), and, conversely, every thought we think is not an abstract representation but a vital idea (to use Cutler and MacKenzie's expression) which bears directly on the body. Arguably, it is this close connection between thinking and the body which unites many of the thinkers in Deleuze's aberrant history of philosophy, whether in the form of Spinoza's parallelism, Nietzsche's reactivation of Spinoza's ethical question, or in Bergson's arguments that even our most general ideas must be capable of being acted by the body (Bergson 1991: 13, 161). The essays in the second half of this collection tend to reaffirm the close connection between body and thought, and develop the consequences of such a position.

Ella Brians engages the 'techno-fantasy' of a disembodied thought in cyber and posthuman discourses, arguing instead that a Deleuzian perspective lets us articulate an embodied relationship to technology. While there has been a frequent mobilization of Deleuzian terms in cyber theory, Brians traces a tendency in the current discourse to align these terms with the dream of a disembodied consciousness. But, she argues, 'if Deleuze has anything to teach us about "virtual" bodies, it is that they have never been virtual, if by virtual we mean non-material.' She thus lays the groundwork for a convincing cyber theory which takes the body seriously.

Rebecca Coleman makes a similar argument in her analysis of the theme of self-transformation in popular culture. Traditional interpretations of the relation between images and bodies treat the image as a representation which carries an encoded ideological message. Coleman develops a Deleuzian approach to the image which breaks from the representationalist model, theorizing images instead as immediately material and affective. Images do not secretly implant an ideological RNA that we unknowingly reproduce; nor do they force us to take a position in a predetermined binary. Rather, images open up new possibilities for life with the potential to redirect becoming in one way or another. They engage us and they carry us away.

Peta Malins further complicates the relation between image and spectator. In her study of the heroin chic photography of the 1990s,

Malins avoids getting caught up in the moralizing discourse of whether, for example, the images encourage drug use or anorexia and attempts instead to isolate the becomings between image and spectator, 'becomings which constitute neither an imitation or appropriation of drug use nor an actual use of drugs, but a transformational trajectory between the two'. This trajectory reveals the 'ethico-aesthetic' potential of images, their ability to produce bodily transformations which not only break from the cliché but operate outside of the capitalist axiomatic.

Patricia MacCormack's essay explores what happens when, through body modification, we literally become-animal (by, for example, using contact lenses and implanted whiskers to become-cat or by splitting one's tongue to become-lizard). What happens when modification turns bodies into aesthetic events as such and the body emerges as teeming with art? MacCormack argues that in following these modifications we can discover a liminal body which allows us to 'navigate the plasticity' of signification.

Philipa Rothfield's essay begins where Claire Colebrook's ends; the 'self is a sick, pathological structure which has no ongoing future'. But rather than pursuing forms of life which permanently disrupt boundaries, Rothfield asks of what this sick self is capable. It is preeminently capable of dancing. If, according to Deleuze's Nietzsche, the body is a chance encounter of active and reactive forces whose temporary unity is underwritten by the will to power, nothing could make this more clear than the dancer's body in its constant negotiation of forces. Rothfield's descriptions of dance bring concrete clarity to Deleuze's conception of the body, and, conversely, from a Deleuzian perspective, Rothfield is able to rethink improvisation and virtuosity.

Is there a theory of the body in Deleuze and a corresponding practice? The great strength of this collection is that rather than closing the theory of the body into a definitive account of embodied life, it opens it up as a site for creative conceptual-corporeal experimentation. It shows that there are many theories of the body, each with multiple connections and applications, each with a different productive capacity, and each expanding what the Deleuzian body can do.

Finally, Laura and I would like to thank all of those who helped make this collection come into existence. In particular we would like to thank Ian Buchanan for his help in the early stages of the project and Carol MacDonald for her patience and support throughout. We would like to dedicate this collection to Elsa Rose Finney.

References

Bergson, H. (1991), *Matter and Memory*, trans. N. M. Paul and W. S. Palmer, New York: Zone.

Braidotti, R. (1994), *Nomadic Subjects: Embodiment and Sexual Difference in Contemporary Feminist Theory*, New York: Columbia University Press.

Braidotti, R. (2006), *Transpositions: On Nomadic Ethics*, Cambridge: Polity.

Clough, P. T. (2000), *Autoaffection: Unconscious Thought in the Age of Teletechnology*, Minneapolis: University of Minnesota Press.

Deleuze, G. (1986), *Cinema 1: The Movement-Image*, trans. H. Tomlinson and R. Galeta, Minneapolis: University of Minnesota Press.

Deleuze, G. (1989), *Cinema 2: The Time-Image*, trans. H. Tomlinson and R. Galeta, Minneapolis: University of Minnesota Press.

Deleuze, G. (1990), *The Logic of Sense*, trans. M. Lester and C. Stivale, ed. C. Boundas, New York: Columbia University Press.

Deleuze, G. (1992), *Expressionism in Philosophy: Spinoza*, trans. M. Joughin, New York: Zone.

Deleuze, G. (1994), *Difference and Repetition*, trans. P. Patton, New York: Columbia University Press.

Deleuze, G. (2003), *Francis Bacon: The Logic of Sensation*, trans. D. W. Smith, London: Continuum.

Deleuze, G. (2006), *Nietzsche and Philosophy*, trans. H. Tomlinson, New York: Columbia University Press.

Gatens, M. (1996a), *Imaginary Bodies: Ethics, Power, and Corporeality*, New York: Routledge.

Gatens, M. (1996b), 'Through a Spinozist Lens: Ethology, Difference, Power', in *Deleuze: A Critical Reader*, ed. P. Patton, Oxford: Blackwell, pp. 162–87.

Grosz, E. (1994), *Volatile Bodies: Toward a Corporeal Feminism*, Indianapolis: Indiana University Press.

DELEUZISM

Chapter 1
Time and Autopoiesis: The Organism Has No Future

Claire Colebrook

There was a critical scene that was narrated frequently in the theory-frenzied years of the 1980s, operating as an often-invoked tableau that would awaken us from our literalist slumbers. The child faces the mirror, jubilantly rejoicing in the image of his unity (Lacan 1977). This scene captured the predicament of misrecognition: the self is not the naturally bounded organism (a thing within the world), but a site of desires, relations, drives, fantasies and projections that cannot possess the coherence of a body. There is a radical disjunction between the subject, who is nothing more than an effect of its relation to an other whom it cannot read, and the self, ego or individual that we imagine ourselves to be. It is the body as bounded organism, centred on a looking face whose gaze can be returned by the mirror, that not only represses the chaotically dispersed and relational manner of our existence; it also operates as a figure of reading. We read other bodies as though they harboured a sense or interior meaning that might be disclosed through communication, and we read texts as though they operated like bodies – as well-formed wholes possessing a systemic logic the sense of which might become apparent (Felman 1987).

In this respect the Lacanian notion of Imaginary *méconnaissance* – where we live the decentred and dispersed incoherence of the symbolic order as some illusory whole – repeats a criticism of the organism that goes as back as far (at least) as Husserlian phenomenology. For Husserl it was quite natural to regard oneself as a thing among things, but that 'natural attitude' concealed the true nature of the subject: a subject who is not a thing but the condition through which things are given (Husserl 1965). Husserl, here, radicalised Kant's distinction between subject and body. For Kant, I know and experience myself as a body within the world, but I can only do so because of the transcendental subjectivity that is not itself spatial or temporal. For Husserl, Kant did not go far enough in his distinction between subject and body, for it is not only the case that the subject in itself cannot be known or experienced as a thing within this world; the subject is the very origin of the world (Fink 1970). There can be no sense, givenness, time or being outside the event of transcendental synthesis. Although Heidegger would place more emphasis on Being's disclosure, regarding the subject as a clearing for the event of revealing, he also was highly critical of mistaking *Dasein* (a disclosing relation) for *das Mann* (a psycho-physical body) (Heidegger 1996). This, indeed, was Heidegger's criticism of humanism; since the Roman understanding of *humanitas* man has been understood as an organism with an additional capacity of reason (Heidegger 1998). Taking up phenomenology in France, Sartre insisted on the radical transcendence of the ego; there is being on the one hand, which simply is 'in itself', and then the relation of difference to that being which can never (authentically) be experienced or lived other than as nothingness, as the negation of what simply *is* (Sartre 1957). Bergson, despite his difference from phenomenology, also criticised the ways in which the efficient intellect would reduce all its complex experiences into stable objects; this was perfectly appropriate for non-living beings but a disaster when turned back upon the human knower himself, who then experienced himself as just one more thing among things (Bergson 1931).

Whereas Husserl, Bergson, Sartre and Heidegger lamented and aimed to correct a history of philosophy that had mistaken the subject who was *not a thing* for the human body, psychoanalysis acknowledged that the condition of misrecognition is irreducible. There is a tendency towards 'organic thinking' captured in Lacan's notion of the Imaginary; we are oedipal in so far as we consider ourselves as self-bounded bodies lamentably subjected to a condition of difference. (Deleuze and Guattari will not challenge Lacan's reading of the tendency of the human organism towards privatisation, to regarding the world of difference and relations as a nightmarish beyond. They will, however, write a genealogy of that lure of the bounded body.) For Lacan, the yearning to retrieve the lost child who was once complete (before its submission to unreadable relations) follows from our organic dependence. The child appears to himself, in the mirror, as a unified whole – an identity. What that delightful recognition of one's bodily integrity covers over is the condition of subjection: that we speak and are, not through being one's own self, but as always situated within a system of symbolic relations of which we are only ever effects. These effects are never given as such, but always relayed through relations of enigma, misrecognition, anticipation, projection and unattainable desire (Butler 1997; Butler 2004; Butler 2005; Laplanche 1999; Mitchell 1975; Wright 1984).

This notion of the subject as formed through relation to an unreadable other has been reinforced recently by Judith Butler, who has placed less emphasis on her earlier notion of the self as effected through performance of social norms, and has turned instead towards Laplanche and his insistence that our ex-trinsic condition of existence is one in which we are always placed in a relation of reading an other who is essentially unreadable (Butler 2005). Laplanche was explicitly critical of Lacan's centring of the oedipal predicament on the phallus; yes, we are all constituted through a reading of the other, but we do not read that other as the one or other who possesses the phallic law, the power of castration. This liberation of the imaginary from the phallus would, at first glance, be an improvement. Why should a body part be privileged when we think about the ways in which we fantasise our existence? For Laplanche there is a structural truth to the oedipal complex, for every child lives its own world and history as if there had once been an integral unity that was then displaced by submission to an other, as though we were once perfectly bounded organisms who underwent subjection to an alien order. Whereas Lacan figured alienation in linguistic terms, with the imposition of speech being fantasised as submission to the law of the father who holds the phallus, Laplanche's 'enigmatic signifier' was not language in the symbolic sense but the look or gesture of the other who forces us to read their desire.

Now it might seem, today, that it is Laplanche's emphasis on the look of the other and each specific body's relation to the law that might be a more fruitful understanding of our body's relation to language *and* that this would accord, too, with Deleuze and Guattari's criticism of the tyranny of Oedipus and the 'despotism' of the signifier. But this is not so: for Deleuze and Guattari write a genealogy and diagnosis of the Oedipus complex and the privileging of the phallus. The virtue of the Lacanian critique is its ideality and inhumanity; before there is a human–human look or relation, something like the human organism has to be formed as an image. The body and its organs are historical and political phenomena. The modern man of capital does indeed live the relation among his body parts as oedipalised; he is the man of speech who must articulate his desires through language as a symbolic order, and who will also live in fear of the loss of that order. In *Anti-Oedipus* Deleuze and Guattari maintain the importance of the virtual body part (Deleuze and Guattari 1977). The body has been increasingly 'privatised', no longer living its forces collectively or intensively. Instead of the phallus being a collective totem, capable of generating the powerful spectacle of a tribal body moving in rhythmic pulsations, ears all responding to the beating tempo, the body has become folded in on itself. Modern man is a speaking animal, subject to no law other than that of articulating his desires in speech. The organs are now private: the eyes that look out on a world as so much calculable matter to be mastered by the hand that will labour to transform the world into exchangeable commodities. This privatisation of the organs means that desire can only be experienced as secret and personal, lost in its passage through collective speech, and never capable of reaching that full masterful voice of the phallic master.

Thinking about Deleuze's philosophy in relation to the body requires stepping back from a too easy dismissal of Lacan and the virtual body part. A social machine occurs when flows of desire are given relative stability: all the dancing bodies of the tribe gazing wondrously on the phallic symbol that allows for the creation of a territory. Body parts are always virtual before they are actual; the organised organism – where the eyes see the same world heard by the ear and narrated by the voice – is the result of a history of coordinations and stabilised relations. Lacan was aware that the gaze of the infant was never a virgin glance; to look at a world of speaking subjects was to take on the history of the organism. For Deleuze and Guattari politics could only begin with this organised and oedipal body, a body centred on the speaking voice submitted to the law of the signifier, always articulating a desire for a mastery and phallic dominance that is possessed by no one.

Only if one acknowledges the crucial role of the body in politics can one begin to think the body without organs. In this respect, if one thinks of the body as, say, gendered, then one buys into the phallic order. If we see bodies as receiving their identity through the imposition of social norms, then we assume a body as a whole that is then given identity and selfhood through normativity. Deleuze and Guattari take up the Lacanian challenge and ask how this dispersed collection of organs – the eye, ear, voice, brain, skin – comes to be organised as a speaking animal. Should we not ask how bodies that once existed through collectively intense organs – all eyes gazing on the cut into flesh, all ears feeling the stamping of feet, all voices screaming with the cry of a totem animal – became this point in space submitted to the laws of normativity? This means stepping back from *the* body to think the composition of organic powers, powers of organs and not the organism. Is this not what philosophy aims to do, to free the brain from the sensory motor apparatus of survival (Deleuze and Guattari 1994)? And is this not what visual arts aim to do, freeing the eye from reading, coding and recognition (Deleuze 2004)?

Let us pause, then, and look back to the theorisations of 'the body' that reinforce our sense, today, that we no longer assume the primacy of language. Judith Butler's *Bodies That Matter* of 1993, Elizabeth Grosz's *Volatile Bodies* in 1994 and then a series of 'body' readers and critical guides were not simple returns to the organism before language, so much as a recognition that the linguistic paradigm itself entailed at least some minimal image of embodiment. To say that the 'I' is an effect of language, an effect of the act or performance of speech, implies that one will at least imagine or construct some image or figure of the speaking body. Even if the subject is deemed to be effected through language, language can still create a body as constructed through a series of norms and figures. It was the status of the body *as image* that perhaps allowed for a confidence that one was no longer dealing with a literal pre-critical body; one could write about embodiment without appearing to be a vulgar materialist. Both in feminist criticism and beyond, the body was primarily a literary and rhetorical problem. Although a great deal of literary and cultural criticism turned to 'the body', this was always a consideration of how the body had been written, figured, problematised or constructed through various discourses (Kirby 1997; Wilson 1998). Even fiction (such as Jeanette Winterson's *Written on the Body* of 1993) responded to this trend of coupling writing and the body; to write or speak is to imagine oneself as a subject, but that imagined subject is always embodied, and the body is always constituted through tropes. (This idea of the body as being a 'lived schema' through which the world is mediated is sustained today across a range of disciplines including neuropsychology, linguistics and political theory (Gallagher 2005; Gibbs 2006).)

However, it was just this sophisticated post-Butler attitude of thinking of the body as other than representation through representation that precluded one from really thinking what the body might mean. Butler published *Bodies That Matter* at least partly in response to the putative linguisticism of *Gender Trouble*. If we accept the argument of the massively influential *Gender Trouble* that the 'sex' that would supposedly be represented, mediated or imagined through cultural figures of gender is actually always figured as other than gender, then we also acknowledge that any appeal to 'the' body is a negative critical manœuvre against received images and figures but is enabled only in its distance and difference from those figures. The body that matters, then, is not some brute 'in itself' that would precede cultural imagination, with cultural imagination in turn being some system that adds itself to a passive matter; for matter is just that which appears in the splitting of a seemingly prior 'before' from a no less illusory after:

To 'concede' the undeniability of 'sex' or its 'materiality' is always to concede some version of 'sex,' some formation of 'materiality.' Is the discourse in and through which that concession occurs – and, yes, that concession invariably does occur – not itself formative of the very phenomenon that it concedes? [. . .] to refer naively or directly to such an extra-discursive object will always require the prior delimitation of the extra-discursive. (Butler 1993: 10–11)

There 'is' no matter as such, no body as such, only a body that matters – a body known only in so far as it is recognised – and only a matter that is given as there for this body in its potentiality. Matter is given only as lost, as having been there for the work of culture and speech. Temporality is at once that which gives matter; for matter is that which must have been. At the same time, temporality is that which is the other of matter. We live and endure as the same bodies through time only in the re-iteration of an identity; this iteration that produces the subject as the same through time is also that which, through failure, can disturb and disrupt identity. There is always, in the subjection to identity, that which remains other than the normative matrix that recognises identity. Matter in itself would be imagined, mourned or figured as that strange non-identity beyond all relations of inside and outside, before and after.

Grosz's *Volatile Bodies* was avowedly less linguistically or – if we are not to have a narrow concept of language – less performatively oriented. Butler took up the notion of the performative as the linguistic act that constitutes its referent. But this is an act that is not grounded upon a static body; quoting Nietzsche, Butler insists that there is 'no doer behind the deed'. One should not imagine that there are speaking subjects who then come to make statements about material bodies. On the contrary, there is the act or event of speaking from which one is effected as a subject who speaks. The performative is an act that relies on and maintains relations among bodies, granting and sustaining each body in its force. I can be a body that matters, a body who matters, only if 'I' act in such a way that something like an 'I' can be recognised. For Grosz, in contrast with Butler and a series of other approaches to embodiment that were even more constructivist than Butler's careful negotiation of performance, the body was not achieved through the act of performance, even if that act was taken to be that which effected the 'I', rather than being the act of some 'I'. Nor was Grosz simply turning back to the motility of the phenomenological 'lived' body. (Recently there has been a widespread return and resurgence of interest in the lived body of phenomenology against the theories of language and cognition that paid too little attention to the organism's relation to the world. Such a return is premised upon correcting a supposedly disembodied subject that underpins Western reason and cognition (Thompson 2007).) Recognising that the very notion of the act, force, performance or utterance would require some minimal relation, Grosz's volatile bodies were poised membranes or borders, ongoing productions of an interior in relation to an exterior. Drawing on the lived body of phenomenology – that one could only act or orient oneself in a world if there were some space that would always be the space for this body with its potentialities – Grosz also noted that this underlying lived body that enabled spatiality would in turn have its own conditions. These she explained through the frequently used example of a möbius strip; the relation between interior and exterior, the establishment of a bounded body from which potentiality and motility might be thought, could not be taken for granted and was itself effected from a whole series of relations.

The most important relation, both for Grosz at this stage and for many writers working on embodiment, was the image. It is with the look towards another bounded body, taken as the sign of an impossible interior, that I might also live my own skin and physique as similarly blessed with its immanent spirit. To live my physical being and its potentialities both as mine, and as the ongoing subject of action, requires the experience of interior and exterior, the production of a bordered limit that would also be vulnerable to infraction and traumatic intrusion. What it means to be a self has therefore always been intertwined with what it means to be a body, and both these terms – self and body – have, in turn, been defined through a capacity of trauma, where trauma is imagined as the rupture of a border. What I want to do in the pages that follow is consider a series of possibilities: is it possible to think beyond that image of the bounded body? Such a possibility would be salutary today precisely because all those seeming gains in theoretical maturity that were won by posing the question of the body after the linguistic turn appear to be threatened, and threatened precisely because we can only imagine threat, trauma and non-life as other than the bounded body. That is, once it was accepted that bodies were not passive matters to be inscribed by culture, it was also acknowledged that the body's borders were the result of relations, encounters and – as Grosz so aptly demonstrated – morphologies; one can be a bounded body only with a sense, figure or image of one's limits. But this raises a problem: is life necessarily bounded and embodied life, a body of inside and outside? If we accept systems theory, body theory and the once-dominant idea of the self as constituted in relation to an other, then the answer is 'yes'.

There are, though, other forms of life beyond that of the organism.

First, one might question the decision to consider viruses as other than life, a decision that is based on the virus as parasitic and non-self-maintaining. Second, one might question the exclusion of *techne* from life; a living organism is bounded and self-maintaining, while other movements and mutations, such as computer viruses, technical evolutionary imperatives and the ways in which organs develop in response to machines behove us to consider the imbrication of bodies and machines. Third, one might ask whether it is fruitful at this point in human history to consider life primarily from the point of view of the organism; are we not being forced to encounter the ruptures of organic timelines as we become aware of the depletion of the cosmos and the decay of our milieu, even if such erosions are never experienced or lived as localisable events?

Before moving on, I would like to look back at the classic meditation on the image of the bounded body, Freud's *Beyond the Pleasure Principle,* where Freud posits that pleasure – the maintenance of a constant energy or equilibrium – may have some 'beyond' that would take the form of a dissipation of all energy (Freud 1975). The first principle of equilibrium and pleasure is still recognisable today in a series of post-Freudian observations regarding an organism's relation to life. A completely closed body that had no world would be deprived of the means of ongoing life; an absolutely open body without borders would not be a body at all, would have no ongoing identity. What is required, then, is a border or membrane that enables communion with an outside, but an outside that is always an outside *for* this bounded body, and that is managed so as to produce only the alteration or perturbation required for ongoing self-maintenance. The now widely cited and philosophically consecrated systems theory of Maturana and Varela (1987) deploys a series of terms to describe this necessity: coupling (where a body's autonomous or self-maintaining movements are established in relation to outside variables); autopoiesis (where the body does not interact mechanically with its outside but does so in a way to maintain its own balance and sameness); relative closure (so that a body at once maintains itself but also adapts to changing external perturbations); and meaning (for the outside of a body is always its own outside or world, experienced or lived in terms of a range of possible responses rather than an objective representation).

The ideal body must therefore balance two contrary requirements: completeness and self-sufficiency. A body detached from all that was other than itself would be hopelessly incomplete, divorced from the means of its own sustainability. A body must complete itself in order to maintain itself; it must not remain as some detached fragment but must be united or coupled with a world, open to what is not merely itself. (This requirement, as described by Freud, exposed the organism to contingency and the risk of loss and could lead to a destructive attack on the desired object to which the organism is subjected (Freud 1975). The erotic drive to connection and completion, depicted by Freud as two halves of a body seeking to be reunited, harboured an aggressive potential (Freud 1975). The organism desires a plenitude or non-separation that requires it to go beyond itself, abandoning its original and mythic self-enclosure of primary narcissism; but it is just this overcoming of the violent self-containment of original closure that may in turn lead to a destructive drive to destroy the object that lures the organism from its quiescence. That destruction could even be turned back upon the self, after losing the object, if mourning is not completed in a life-serving manner.)

Many writing after Freud have not regarded the organism's condition of coupling as anything other than benign, insisting on the originally world-oriented, meaning-making and other-directed dynamics of bodily life. The very logic of today's insistence on the 'embodied mind', the 'extended mind', the 'synaptic self', the 'global brain' and even the 'mind in life' blithely sails over the deep and essential contradiction of the living body (Varela, Thompson and Rosch 1991; LeDoux 2002; Bloom 2000; Clark 2008). All the criticisms of the detached and disembodied Cartesian subject that insist upon the self's primary and dynamic connectedness ignore what Freud and Lacan recognised as the imaginary lure of the body; for all the self's world-orientation and openness there is also a primary blindness and enclosure that is necessary for the very experience of oneself as embodied, bounded and located in a milieu. As alive, the body must be oriented or related to what is not itself, must desire a completion. Because such completion is always sought on the organism's own terms, always for the sake of the organism, a body is necessarily blind to those forces that lie beyond its range. The very desire for completeness that drives the organism to couple with its world will also preclude it from seeing the world in any terms other than its own.

Whereas philosophers have happily celebrated this necessity of the world always being meaningful, or always a world for me, we might suggest that such blissful enclosure in meaning precludes the very striving for completeness it is supposed to serve. The desire for completeness comes into conflict with self-sufficiency or the desire not to be exposed to contingency, risk or an influx of otherness so great that it would destroy all border and limit (and this would count as trauma). One might say then that pleasure – today's celebrated processes of equilibrium, home-ostasis and autopoiesis, or processes deemed to be synonymous with the life of the organism – is necessarily destructive of life that cannot be experienced in terms of the bounded body. Freud's second principle of a 'beyond' would not be in opposition to life; it would not simply be the death of the organism. Nor would it be a force regarded as traumatic, as that which is initially unassimilable but that could, through working and representation, be brought to coherence and sense. A genuine beyond of pleasure and a genuine beyond of the organism and its closed world of meaning would also be beyond trauma, for it could not be regarded as an infraction of the body from outside. This is precisely why Deleuze and Guattari suggest that one moves beyond death as a model – death as defined in relation to the bounded organism – to the experience of death.

> The experience of death is the most common of occurrences in the uncon-scious, precisely because it occurs in life and for life, in every passage or becoming, in every intensity as passage or becoming. It is in the very nature of every intensity to invest within itself the zero intensity starting from which it is produced, in one moment, a that which grows or diminishes according to an infinity of degrees ... insofar as death is what is felt in every feeling, what never ceases and never finishes happening in every becoming – in the becoming-another-sex, the becoming-god, the becoming-a-race, etc., forming zones of intensity on the body without organs. Every intensity con-trols within its own life the experience of death and envelops it. (Deleuze and Guattari 1977: 330)

Such an experience would shatter the bounded body, and occur not as the body's other or limit but as a pure predicate, potentiality or intensity taken away from the coordinates of the organism. If we do not begin the question of life from the point of view of the bounded organism and its world, then we are compelled to think life beyond the opposi-tion between pleasure and trauma, between boundary and infraction. Instead, one would note a necessarily self-destroying or suicidal trajec-tory immanent in life. Is this not what timelines of the inhuman now compel us to note, if not comprehend? A species can only survive by mutation and by not being itself; any species also – through that very survival – takes a toll on its milieu that might lead (as in the case of man) to the destruction of life in general. How could one define this dissolu-tion as tragic or traumatic or, more simply, undesirable if one were not to assume already the primacy of bounded self-maintaining life?

This raises two questions for the future of this body we recognise as human, a body that is facing – today – two possible traumas. Has this body so oriented itself to its own sustainability – seeing the world clearly only in terms of its own perturbation – that it has no sense of the distinct perceptions and souls that are destroying it from within, and no perception of the folds and series that are traumatising the milieu itself? Is it possible to speak of, or object to, the dissolution of the organism that we know as human?

How might we use these two notions of life – one that is bounded, embodied and open to trauma, and another that is post-traumatic – to assess what we mean by theory and thinking today? I would suggest that a certain notion of the theoretical, where theory is the look that we direct to our own acts of perception, has always been intertwined with a vital and normative account of life, and that it would be worth while considering a theory that might entertain a thought of viral or radically malevolent life. In order to pursue this counter-possibility of a life that is not defined in relation to trauma, I want to conclude by looking at the ways in which a certain image of the body has underpinned theory and its temporality.

Consider a certain diagnosis of disembodied life that is dominant, possibly necessary, in contemporary thought. In a series of disciplines, ranging from neuroscience, cognitive science, philosophy, evolutionary psychology, sociology, future studies and cultural studies, it is now common to begin with the criticism of the Cartesian intellect. I will take these criticisms in turn, and look at the ways in which a certain idea and ideal of the body-as-organism is posited as the remedy for the fall into the abstractions of Cartesian intellectualism. The word 'autopoiesis', along with 'homeostasis' and 'equilibrium', operates across all these disciplines with their inter-related diagnoses of the present inertia of thinking life.

First, neuroscience: this mode of enquiry has benefited greatly from the decade of the brain declared by President Bush in 1990, and from the accompanying technological expansion enabling new means of imaging. Although neuroscience is a diverse field, its very potentiality is marked by a single image; the neuroscientist is not concerned with finding the 'bit' of the brain responsible for a certain thought or idea, but can now look at systems of relations. A perception does not occur in some simple one-to-one correspondence between object in the world and picture in the brain, but through complex and distributed patterns of relation. We respond to the world, not as blank slates being imprinted with data, but as dynamic and self-regulating systems. Life strives to maintain itself, and does so not by 'picturing' an outside world, but through an ongoing, interactive and non-linear system of responses and adjustments. The non-linearity is crucial, even in the most simple of perceptions. There is not a self who captures the image of an object, but a body orienting itself toward (and anticipating) the world that is always given in a certain way; this dynamic engagement will enable the synthesis and relation to data, which in turn produces certain bodily relations, and these in turn allow further interaction with the world. If we want to understand thinking, according to Antonio Damasio, then we should not begin with cognition or representation – some mind housed in a body – but rather should begin with the body as a self-regulating system, a system that does all it can to maintain its own state of equilibrium, and that will ulti- mately experience such bodily emotions or ongoing adjustments as 'the feeling of what happens'. More importantly, that process of interaction can only be between organism and world if there is some boundary that distinguishes between surviving life and milieu:

> the urge to stay alive is not a modern development. It is not a property of humans alone. In some fashion or other, from simple to complex, most living organisms exhibit it. What does vary is the degree to which organ- isms *know* about that urge. Few do. But the urge is still there whether organisms know of it or not. Thanks to consciousness, humans are keenly aware of it.
>
> Life is carried out inside a boundary that defines a body. Life and the life urge exist inside a boundary, the selectively permeable wall that separates the internal environment from the external environment. The idea of the organism revolves around the existence of that boundary. (Damasio 1999: 137)

What we must remove is 'Descartes's error', or the idea of mind as something distinct from life, for life just is an ongoing dynamic process of response, interaction, adjustment, orientation and – most importantly – sense. There is no possibility of a brute event, a body encountering a force that is not always already meaningful.

This insistence on meaning need not be an anthropomorphic notion. And to see this we can turn to the broader and highly influential theory of life as necessarily autopoietic, particularly as adopted by the cognitive science of Maturana and Varela. One of the crucial features of Maturana and Varela's work is their definition of life that requires some form of boundary or membrane. Their definition allows, then, for autopoiesis and meaning. Life is autopoietic because a living being maintains its own internal relations; a living system must be able – through interaction with its milieu – to sustain itself. Living systems are coupled to environ- ments that are always defined as being what they are for that specific system; and this is how autopoiesis is tied to meaning. The environment of an organism is what it is in terms of that body's possible responses:

This basic uniformity of organization can best be expressed by saying: all that is accessible to the nervous system at any point are states of relative activity holding between nerve cells, and all that to which any given state of relative activity can give rise are further states of relative activity in other nerve cells by forming those states of relative activity to which they respond. (Maturana and Varela 1980: 22)

Further, life – unlike other non-living systems – has a certain self-productivity that is crucially defined in relation to that system's border. If a cell can live on, and even reproduce, simply by existing in its milieu, then we can call that cell a living system. Its living-on requires no intervention of any process or force other than relation to milieu. A clear contrast, of course, would be a machine or mechanism; a typewriter can produce text if connected to a human body, an ink ribbon and paper, but a typewriter placed in its milieu – sitting on a desk among papers – does nothing more than decay through time (even if that decay is particularly slow). Maturana and Varela, tellingly, draw upon the philosophical tradition of phenomenology and its criticism of Cartesian notions of disengaged mind. As long as we define mind as a closed being that may or may not encounter some external world, and as long as we see that world as being encountered through knowledge, or perception as a mode of 'picturing', then we will never understand the life of thought.

This brings us to the next discipline that draws on notions of distributed and embodied cognition, linear systems and self-production: artificial intelligence. There had been a criticism, early in the rapprochement between philosophy and artificial intelligence, that had insisted that – following Heidegger – it was the very embodied, active, worldly and practical nature of thinking life that precluded anything like an 'intelligence' that might be replicated in a computer (Dreyfus, Dreyfus and Athanasiou 1986). But those very Heideggerian insights regarding the necessarily embodied and temporally complex nature of thinking have now enabled new developments in artificial intelligence. If we want to create thinking we should abandon the Cartesian model of an information centre that would direct parts of a body-machine; instead we should begin with the response. In the beginning is the action in relation to an environment, and this action always occurs in an ongoing process of adjustments and responses. Creating a robot could be successful, not by building an information-loaded, brain-like centre, but by creating parts that were capable of adjusting and allowing feedback responses with an encountered environment. At the simplest level, for example, we would have more success in creating a walking machine if we were to begin with leg-like parts that could roll and rebalance in response to surfaces.

This in turn might tell us something about human embodied cognition; we are not picturing computing minds who happen to be placed in bodies that then have to encounter some world. On the contrary, we are originally responsive and action-oriented and also – more importantly – naturally prosthetic, taking whatever we can from the world as an extension of our already world-oriented and can-do openness to life:

> The old puzzle, the mind–body problem, really involves a hidden third party. It is the mind–body–*scaffolding* problem. It is the problem of understanding how human thought and reason is born out of looping interactions with material brains, material bodies and complex cultural and technological environments. We create these supportive environments but they create us too. We exist as the thinking beings we are, only thanks to a baffling dance of brains, bodies, and cultural and technological scaffolding. (Clark 2003: 10)

We therefore need to rid ourselves of the idea of a mind that would be pure and then use its body or supplement its body with alien materials. For matter, like the body, is always already familiar, already potentially available for the extension of our being as we make our way through life. In the ongoing striving to maintain ourselves all that we encounter may be incorporated, taken up as part of our ever-extending and constantly relational being:

> Autopoiesis in the physical space is necessary and sufficient to characterize a system as a living system. Reproduction and evolution as they occur in the known living systems, and all the phenomena derived from them, arise as secondary processes subordinated to their existence and operation as autopoietic unities. Hence, the biological phenomenology is the phenomenology of autopoietic systems in the physical space, and a phenomenon is a biological phenomenon only to the extent that it depends in one way or another on the autopoiesis of one or more physical autopoietic unities. (Maturana and Varela 1980: 113)

Evolutionary psychology has also, in a number of different projects, taken its inquiry into the emergence of mind away from attention to cognition, grammar and formal systems, and instead considered bodies in relations that are always already affective, sensually attuned, emotionally responsive and autopoietic or homeostatic (on an individual and on a 'social' level). Steven Mithen has argued that before we have language as some system for conveying information, or before we have a grammar that would synthesize and organise a perceived world, there is an originally and communally affective enjoyment of sound, that both gives each body a sense of its self in relation, and produces the social system of constitutive relations (Mithen 2006). Robin Dunbar has argued for the originality of gossip (Dunbar 1996). Against the idea that language begins as one body relaying content to another, Dunbar suggests that sound begins as a purely relational and communal phenomenon, allowing bodies to exist in community, through the feeling of sound and responsiveness.

These developments in the sciences and social sciences have led to the emergence of a narrative regarding theory and the time of theory. There was a time when, suffering from the disease of intellectualism or mind-centred (or simply centred) approaches, we examined social systems in terms of conscious agents. In so doing we adopted linear notions of causality, rather than looking at the complex, dynamic, interactive and materially distributed systems that contribute to any event (DeLanda 2006). We also, no less disastrously, suffered from the linguistic paradigm, where 'a' system was seen as the ground through which we might interpret the world, when in fact the world is a dynamic network of interacting, affectively attuned, responsive and self-maintaining bodies. Often this diagnosis of our misguided commitment to Cartesian notions of disembodied mind has been coupled with a moral programme for cultural reinvention. Recent work in philosophy has suggested that if we turn to non-Western understandings of mindfulness, where selves are not command centres but properly attuned to the world, existing as nothing more than a series of ongoing adjustments and mutual encounters, then we will be able to think more ecologically, less instrumentally and – most importantly – with far greater managerial success (Flanagan 2007).

The three concepts of autopoiesis, equilibrium and homeostasis function in all these domains: neuroscience, cognitive science, philosophy of mind, social theory and future studies. These concepts all presuppose a certain understanding of time, and suggest – as I state in the title to this essay – that the organism has no future. In itself, or if it remains in itself, the organism has no future. There can only be a time to come if we recall our embodied, relational, world-attuned being. The world within which we are situated – if we accept that 'we' are nothing other than the situated and responsive beings that we are – is always a world encountered in terms of possible responses. We exist in meaningful milieus. Our condition as embodied, as relating to the world as the beings that we are, is that the world is given as this world for us. To a certain extent, then, we are proto-ecological, originally attuned to our milieu. If we have a future, so it is argued, it cannot be one of calculation, instrumental reason and the mere continuance of ourselves in isolation. Our future could occur only if we remind ourselves of embodiment, if we recall what we really are and once again live our attunement to our milieu not as accidental but as intrinsic to our very being.

But there is another sense in which the organism has no future, and it is here that I want to turn back to the exclusion of non-bounded life from the definition of life in general. As long as we think of life as autopoietic, as that which strives to maintain itself, and as that which is necessarily attuned to a milieu, we will regard disembodied life as that which ought not to have occurred. In so doing we will also fail to account for its force, its persistence and the possible futures it presents to the organism that can only have a world of its own. Consider what needs to be excluded as long as we insist on life as that which is defined by self-maintenance: the virus, malevolent thinking and inhuman futures. I want to conclude by placing these three excluded lives in contrast with three too frequently cited normative bodies: the child, the Buddhist and the animal. In the current literature the Cartesian horror of the disembodied intellect – that is, the power of thinking that would not already be attuned to the world, that would not be affectively oriented via a permeable border – is frequently cured by reference to animal, infant or non-Western life. The animal is nothing more than orientation or potential action for the sake of ongoing life, not yet burdened by the life-stultifying questions of the intellect. Animals also provide the norm for an originally affective and praxis-oriented language; birds and monkeys use sounds as ways of creating bonds or affective relations, not as the representation of some idea in general. The same applies to infants, whose perceptions are originally less cognitive than affective – seeing the world in terms of what enhances or harms the self, and experiencing sound as a sonorous caress (not as the vehicle of information). Finally, the Buddhist: if we suffer in the West from centred, disembodied, linear and instrumental notions of mind, then we would do well to pay attention to the Eastern tradition of mindfulness.

As I have already suggested, these ideals of a body that is at once identifiable through time yet also nothing other than its ongoing attuned responses must exclude other lines of life and time that are defined less through the maintenance of a border in relation, and more in a form of rampant and unbounded mutation. A virus cannot be defined as a form of life on the Maturana and Varela model; its lack of a border or membrane means that it cannot be considered in relation to its milieu. It does not maintain itself, and is not a living system precisely because it is only in its parasitic capacity to open other life forms to variations that would not be definitive of an autopoietic relation. What might the future or temporality of viral life be? It could not suffer trauma, could not be subject to an excess of influx that would destroy its living balance precisely because a virus is nothing other than a process of invasion, influx and (to a great extent) non-relation. A virus does not have a world; it is not defined according to its potential responses that would enable its ongoing being. In one respect, then, it is only viral life that has a future: both in the sense of being able to live on (or more accurately mutate beyond itself) without its own world, and in the sense that 'our' future, our world in all its bounded and delicate attunement, is not really a future so much as the maintenance of the same through the constant warding off of a future that would be other than our own.

This brings me to the next non-bounded life, malevolence. If we are the embodied, attuned, responsive, dynamic and system-dependent beings of autopoiesis, how is it that we have acted in such a way that we have created a future that will no longer be a milieu for the organisms that we are? This, I think, suggests that we need to consider the future that this non-organic, non-relational, rigidly disembodied life has allowed to occur. If life in its bounded form is relational, mindful, attuned, responsive and dynamic (and if this life has no future), then what of the life that did not act to maintain itself, that did not respond to its milieu, that did not live with the sense of its trauma-sensitive membrane? As long as we fail to consider this life we fail to address the future. In recent attempts to deal with our future, and the malevolent damage or wilful destruction we have enacted upon ourselves, it is often implied that once we recognise our truly relational and embodied condition we will indeed have a future. If we could only see that we are not Cartesian minds contingently placed in a world that is of no concern to us, then we will recognise our originally ecological condition and once again live with a sense of the world (where sense is mindful orientation).

One concrete example of an ethics of the future, based on a recognition of our proper embodiment, is the turn to mindfulness. From philosophy to business management, it is argued that if we recall to ourselves our intrinsically embodied and in-the-world being, then we will act with respect and care (rather than destructive dominance) to what is not the self (but yet is always already constitutive of the self). Do we not, with this faith in the malleability, adaptability and possible future of this human body that could overcome its Western violence and rigidity, simply repress and belie that other viral tendency in life? That other tendency would not be self-maintaining and autopoietically relational, but blindly active and mutational. What any ethics of mindful responsiveness must do is dismiss as non-existent, or non-living, those forces of viral malevolence which have, until now, quite happily proceeded to make their way through the world without a thought of sustainability, and without a sense of the human as necessarily relational, embodied and affectively sensitive. How might we act if we acknowledged or even entertained the possibility of this viral and malevolent life, and if we considered the human not as a body coupled to a milieu, but as a series of potentialities that could branch out into territories beyond its own self-maintenance? How would we act if we recognised that, in so far as the organism's future is always the organism's own, then the organism has no future? Its time will always be determined in advance as the time of its own relations; and without the recognition of that other life that destroys such relations the organism's time will come to an end.

A molecular or viral politics that did not assume the benevolence or trauma-resisting membranes of a self-defining body would have the following features. First, an attention to mindlessness: how do unbounded, non-self-maintaining processes – processes with no sense of relation – create a political territory that is not that of the *polis* or mutually recognizing bodies? And how do those bodies that we are, with only a sense of processes in relation to our own living systems, resist all recognition and interaction with the mindless? Why do we not have the strength or force to think of a world that is not our milieu? Second, a politics of viral futures: if we accept life-potentials that are not self-maintaining but that operate as nothing more than mutant encounters, then we move beyond a politics of negotiation among bodies to a politics devoid of survival. Perhaps it is only in our abandonment of ownness, meaning, mindfulness and the world of the body that life, for whatever it is worth, has a chance. This, indeed, is the direction offered by Deleuze and Deleuze and Guattari's thought: a capacity to take intuition beyond the organism's own duration to imagine qualities as such, a desire to overcome the brain of the organized body and approach thought as such opening to the eternal, and a relation between art and philosophy that does not assimilate sensation (the sensible) to what can be thought (the sensed) but approaches their warring disjunction (Deleuze and Guattari 1994). Finally, the move beyond 'man' as isolated thinker will not be back towards the body, but forward to the 'superman' – to the inorganic potentialities that exist now only in confused and all too human composites (Deleuze 1988b).

References

Bergson, H. (1931), *Creative Evolution*, trans. A. Mitchell, New York: H. Holt.

Bloom, H. (2000), *The Global Brain: The Evolution of Mass Mind from the Big Bang to the 21st Century*, New York: Wiley.

Butler, J. (1990), *Gender Trouble: Feminism and the Subversion of Identity*, New York: Routledge.

Butler, J. (1993), *Bodies That Matter: On the Discursive Limits of Sex*, New York: Routledge.

Butler, J. (1997), *The Psychic Life of Power: Theories in Subjection*, Stanford, CA: Stanford University Press.

Butler, J. (2004), *Undoing Gender*, New York: Routledge.

Butler, J. (2005), *Giving an Account of Oneself*, New York: Fordham University Press.

Clark, A. (2003), *Natural-born Cyborgs: Minds, Technologies, and the Future of Human Intelligence*, Oxford: Oxford University Press.

Clark, A. (2008), *Supersizing the Mind: Embodiment, Action, and Cognitive Extension*, Oxford: Oxford University Press.

Damasio, A. (1999), *The Feeling of What Happens: Body and Emotion in the Making of Consciousness*, New York: Harcourt Brace.

DeLanda, M. (2006), *A New Philosophy of Society: Assemblage Theory and Social Complexity*, New York: Continuum.

Deleuze, G. (1988a), *Bergsonism*, trans. H. Tomlinson and B. Habberjam, New York: Zone.

Deleuze, G. (1988b), *Foucault*, trans. S. Hand, Minneapolis: University of Minnesota Press.

Deleuze, G. (2004), *Francis Bacon: The Logic of Sensation*, trans. D. W. Smith, Minneapolis: University of Minnesota Press.

Deleuze, G. and F. Guattari (1977), *Anti-Oedipus: Capitalism and Schizophrenia*, trans. R. Hurley, M. Seem and H. R. Lane, New York: Viking.

Deleuze, G. and F. Guattari (1994), *What is Philosophy?*, trans. H. Tomlinson and G. Burchell, New York: Columbia University Press.

Dreyfus, H. L., S. E. Dreyfus and T. Athanasiou (1986), *Mind over Machine: The Power of Human Intuition and Expertise in the Era of the Computer*, New York: Free Press.

Dunbar, R. (1996), *Grooming, Gossip and the Evolution of Language*, London: Faber.

Felman, S. (1987), *Jacques Lacan and the Adventure of Insight: Psychoanalysis in Contemporary Culture*, Cambridge, MA: Harvard University Press.

Fink, E. (1970), 'The Phenomenological Philosophy of Edmund Husserl and Contemporary Criticism', in *The Phenomenology of Husserl*, ed. R. O. Elveton, Chicago: Quadrangle, pp. 73–147.

Flanagan, O. (2007), *The Really Hard Problem: Meaning in a Material World*, Cambridge, MA: MIT Press.

Freud, S. (1975), *Beyond the Pleasure Principle*, trans. J. Strachey, New York: Norton.

Gallagher, S. (2005), *How the Body Shapes the Mind*, Oxford: Clarendon.

Gibbs, R. W. Jr. (2006), *Embodiment and Cognitive Science*, Cambridge: Cambridge University Press.

Grosz, E. (1994), *Volatile Bodies: Toward a Corporeal Feminism*, Sydney: Allen & Unwin.

Heidegger, M. (1996), *Being and Time*, trans. J. Stambaugh, Albany, NY: SUNY Press.

Heidegger, M. (1998), *Pathmarks*, ed. W. McNeill, Cambridge: Cambridge University Press.

Husserl, E. (1965), *Cartesian Meditations*, trans. D. Cairns, The Hague: M. Nijhoff.

Kirby, V. (1997), *Telling Flesh: The Substance of the Corporeal*, New York: Routledge.

Lacan, J. (1977), *Ecrits: A Selection*, trans. A. Sheridan, New York: Norton.

Lakoff, G. and M. Johnson (1999), *Philosophy in the Flesh: The Embodied Mind and its Challenge to Western Thought*, New York: Basic.

Laplanche, J.-L. (1999), *Essays on Otherness*, ed. John Fletcher, New York: Routledge.

LeDoux, J. (2002), *Synaptic Self: How our Brains Become Who We Are*, New York: Viking, 2002.

Maturana, H. R. and F. J. Varela (1980), *Autopoiesis and Cognition: The Realization of the Living*, Dordrecht: Reidel.

Maturana, H. R. and F. J. Varela (1987), *The Tree of Knowledge: The Biological Roots of Human Understanding*, Boston, MA: New Science Library.

Mitchell, J. (1975), *Psychoanalysis and Feminism*, Harmondsworth: Penguin.

Mithen, S. (2006), *The Singing Neanderthals: The Origins of Music, Language, Mind, and Body*, Cambridge, MA: Harvard University Press.

Sartre, J.-P. (1957), *The Transcendence of the Ego: An Existentialist Theory of Consciousness*, trans. F. Williams and R. Kirkpatrick, New York: Noonday.

Thompson, E. (2007), *Mind in Life: Biology, Phenomenology, and the Sciences of Mind*, Cambridge, MA: Belknap/Harvard University Press.

Varela, F. J., E. Thompson and E. Rosch (1991), *The Embodied Mind: Cognitive Science and Human Experience*, Cambridge, MA: MIT Press.

Wilson, E. A. (1998), *Neural Geographies: Feminism and the Microstructure of Cognition*, New York: Routledge.

Winterson, J. (1993), *Written on the Body*, New York: Knopf.

Wright, E. (1984), *Psychoanalytic Criticism: Theory in Practice*, London: Methuen.

Chapter 2

Larval Subjects, Autonomous Systems and *E. Coli* Chemotaxis

John Protevi

Upon first reading, the beginning of Chapter 2 of *Difference and Repetition*, with its talk of 'contemplative souls' and 'larval subjects', seems something of a bizarre biological panpsychism. Actually it does defend a sort of biological panpsychism, but by defining the kind of psyche Deleuze is talking about, I will show here how we can remove the bizarreness from that concept. First, I will sketch Deleuze's treatment of 'larval subjects', then show how Deleuze's discourse can be articulated with Evan Thompson's biologically based intervention into cognitive science, the 'mind in life' or 'enaction' position. Then I will then show how each in turn fits with contemporary biological work on *E. coli* chemotaxis (movement in response to changes in environment).

The key concept shared by all these discourses is that cognition is fundamentally biological, that it is founded in organic life. In fact and in essence, cognition is founded in metabolism. Thus fully conceptual recollection and recognition, the active intellectual relation to past and future – what Deleuze will call the dominant 'image of thought', is itself founded in metabolism as an organic process. This founding of cognition in metabolism can be read in an empirical sense, for just as a matter of fact you will not find cognition without a living organism supporting itself metabolically. But it can also be read in a transcendental sense: for our thinkers, metabolism is a new transcendental aesthetic, the a priori form of organic time and space. The essential temporal structure of any metabolism is the rhythmic production of a living present synthesizing retentions and protentions, conserved conditions and expected needs. The essential spatiality of metabolism comes from the necessity of a membrane to found the relation of an organism to its environment; there is an essential foundation of an inside and outside by the membrane, just as there is an essential foundation of past and future by the living present. We thus see the necessity of a notion of biological panpsychism; every organism has a subjective position, quite literally a 'here and now' created by its metabolic founding of organic time and space; on the basis of this subjective position an evaluative sense is produced which orients the organism in relation to relevant aspects of its environment.

Let us pause for a moment to appreciate the radicality of this notion of the biological ubiquity of subjects, what we have called a 'biological panpsychism'. For Deleuze in *Difference and Repetition*, the organism has an essential, albeit 'larval', subjectivity based in its organic syntheses, and our active intellectual syntheses are dynamically generated from this foundation. This truly radical thesis is shared by the 'mind in life' position. What is most interesting is that, try as they might to uphold a mechanistic position in which organisms are mere 'robots', the contemporary biologists we examine will also find themselves unable to avoid ascribing an essentially subjective position to single-celled organisms. Far from expecting them to experience the delight of a Monsieur Jourdain discovering his predilection for prose, we might anticipate the shock – if not the downright dismay – of these scientists at learning they too share in positing a new transcendental aesthetic, an inescapable production of a singular 'here and now' for each organism, and the inescapable subjective production of 'sense' by that organism.

In this essay I will concentrate on the temporal aspect of this new transcendental aesthetic and on the necessary subjectivity of the organism, as these are both treated in a manageably short text, the beginning of Chapter 2 of *Difference and Repetition*. Although we will treat it in passing in this essay, we will not be able to reconstruct Deleuze's treatment of the membrane and organic spatiality, as doing so would require a detour through *Logic of Sense*, as well as negotiating Deleuze's relation to Gilbert Simondon's notion of 'transduction'. In the fifteenth series of *Logic of Sense*, entitled "Of Singularities," Deleuze refers approvingly to the very rich section of Simondon's *L'Individu et sa genèse physico-biologique,* entitled 'Topologie et ontogenèse', citing Simondon on the importance of the membrane: 'the characteristic polarity of life is at the level of the membrane … At the level of the polarized membrane, internal past and external future face one another' (Deleuze 1990: 104; citing passages found at Simondon 1995: 224 and 226). And even then, once we would have laid out the Deleuze–Simondon connection, we would then have to articulate Deleuze's notion of 'sense' in *Logic of Sense* with the enaction school's notion of 'sense-making'. So we will defer grappling with the enormous difficulties of that full treatment and restrict ourselves to organic time and subjectivity.

Deleuze

Deleuze's overall aim in *Difference and Repetition* is to provide a 'philosophy of difference', in which identities are produced by integration of a differential field (or 'resolution' of a 'problematic' field; the two expressions are synonymous (Deleuze 1968/1994: 272/211)). The philosophy of difference intersects many forms of what we might call 'identitarian' philosophy, from Plato and Aristotle to Kant and Hegel and others, in which identities are metaphysically primary and differences are seen within a horizon of identity. With regard to Kantian transcendental philosophy, Deleuze attempts to replace the Kantian project of providing the universal and necessary conditions for any rational experience with an account of the 'genesis' (221/170) of 'real experience [*l'expérience réelle*]': that is, the 'lived reality [*réalité vécue*] of a sub-representative domain' (95/69). As 'sub-representative', such 'experience' is as much corporeal and spatio-temporal as it is intellectual, as much a passive undergoing as an active undertaking. For example, the embryo experiences movements that only it can undergo (321/249); these movements are 'pure spatio-temporal dynamisms (the lived experience [*le vécu*] of the embryo)' (277/215).

Deleuze provides two genetic accounts in *Difference and Repetition*, static and dynamic. To be fully differential, these genetic accounts must avoid a mere 'tracing' of the empirical; the transcendental must be differential in order never to 'resemble' empirical identities (176–7/135). The better-known of the two genetic accounts is that of Chapters 4 and 5, the static genesis that 'moves between the virtual and its actualization' (238/183). Thus instead of showing how psychological syntheses producing empirical unities are underlain by active transcendental syntheses (the categories) issued by a unified transcendental subject, Deleuze will provide a genetic account which first sets out an differential or 'virtual' impersonal and pre-individual transcendental field structured by Ideas, or 'multiplicities': that is, sets of differential elements, differential relations, and singularities (236/182). This is the mathematical notion of differentiation, which is then coupled to the biological notion of differenciation. In this latter complementary part of static genesis, intensive spatio-temporal dynamisms incarnate the Ideas; an intensive individuation process precedes and determines the resolution or integration of the differential Idea (318/247). The complex notion of different/ciation, then, is the static genetic account of real experience. Again, to reinforce the connection with the 'mind in life school', we should recall that the passive subject undergoing experience can be an embryo: 'the embryo as individual and patient subject of spatio-temporal dynamisms, the larval subject' (278/215). Following this line of thought, by implication Deleuze must be able to account for the genesis of the real experience of a single-celled organism; this will be our link to enaction and to current biological work.

Organic Time

Although a full treatment of Deleuze would require us to articulate the static and dynamic geneses, we will concentrate in this essay on dynamic genesis as establishing the a priori form of organic time and the necessary subjectivity of organic life. Chapter 2 of *Difference and Repetition* is devoted to Deleuze's work on 'repetition for itself'. The first step, on which we concentrate, is the discussion of the first passive synthesis of time, or habit, which produces the 'living present' as the a priori form of organic time. We should note that organic time, the synthesis of habit producing the living present, is only the 'foundation' of time. Deleuze's full treatment of time in *Difference and Repetition* posits a second synthesis of memory producing the pure past as the 'ground' of time, while the third synthesis, producing the future as eternal return of difference, we might say unfounds and ungrounds time.

The beginning of Chapter 2 provides part of the dynamic genetic account of real experience, restricting itself, except for a brief and 'ironic' remark about 'rocks' (102/75), to the biological register. It is 'dynamic' because instead of moving from a virtual Idea to its actualization, as in static genesis, here we move from raw actuality to the virtual Idea in a series of interdependent 'passive syntheses'. The first section deals with only the first passive synthesis of time, the most basic or 'foundational' in this dynamic genesis. To begin his genetic account, then, Deleuze must get down to the most basic synthesis; he must show how beneath active syntheses (thought) are passive syntheses (perception), and beneath passive perceptual syntheses are passive organic syntheses (metabolism). As always, the challenge is to describe passive syntheses in differential terms, so as to avoid the 'tracing' of empirical identities back to transcendental identities. So what Deleuze is trying to do is describe the differential transcendental structure of metabolism.

Part of the fabled difficulty of *Difference and Repetition* is Deleuze's use of free indirect discourse in which he acts as a sort of ventriloquist for various authors (Hughes 2009). In the first section of Chapter 2, Deleuze is working with Kant, Husserl, Bergson and Hume. From Kant we have the overall framework of transcendental philosophy (albeit in the form of a genetic account of real experience) and from Husserl we have the notion of the lived or living present (*le présent vécu, le présent vivant* (97/70)), as well as the distinction of active and passive syntheses. From Hume and Bergson we have the notion of habit.

Syntheses are needed to join together a disjointed matter or sensation, since in themselves, material or sensory instants fall outside each other: 'a perfect independence on the part of each presentation . . . one instant does not appear unless the other has disappeared – hence the status of matter as *mens momentanea*' (96/70). Deleuze goes on to distinguish three levels of synthesis of this first level of instantaneity:

1. Instantaneous presentation and disappearance: 'objectively' as matter and 'subjectively' as sensation
2. Passive syntheses (contraction or habit producing a living present)
   a. Organic syntheses (metabolism synthesizing matter)
   b. Perceptual synthesis (imagination synthesizing sensation)
3. Active synthesis (memory as recollection and thought as representation synthesizing perceptions).

Deleuze will distinguish the organic and perceptual syntheses by showing that organic syntheses have their own form of contraction or habit.[1] For Hume and Bergson, the psychological imagination moves from past particulars to future generalities; from a series of particulars we come to expect another of the same kind. Deleuze will abstract the process of 'drawing a difference from repetition' as the essence of contraction or habit and show that it occurs at the organic level as well as on the level of the passive perceptual imagination (101/73).

In order to isolate organic syntheses as prior to perceptual syntheses (themselves prior to active intellectualist syntheses), Deleuze radicalizes Hume and Bergson. These two 'leave us at the level of sensible and perceptive syntheses' (99/72). But these syntheses refer back to 'organic syntheses', which are 'a primary sensibility that we *are*' (99/73; emphasis in original). Such syntheses of the elements of 'water, earth, light and air' are not merely prior to the active synthesis that would recognize or represent them, but are also 'prior to their being sensed' (99/73). So, each organism, not only in its receptivity and perception, but also in its 'viscera' (that is, its metabolism), is a 'sum of contractions, of retentions and expectations' (99/73). Here we see the organic level of the living present of retention and expectation. Organic retention is the 'cellular heritage' of the organic history of life and organic expectation is the 'faith' that things will repeat in the ways we are used to (99/73). So Deleuze has isolated a 'primary vital sensibility' in which we have past and future synthesized in a living present. At this level, the future appears as need as 'the organic form of expectation' and the retained past appears as 'cellular heredity' (100/73).

Before we resume our treatment of the text, we can now briefly sketch the overall movement of the passage. Contraction or habit in organic syntheses is a 'contemplative soul' in which we find an expectation that the next element of the same kind it has experienced will arrive. This temporal synthesis, a living present of expectation and retention, is the transcendental structure of metabolism. This move from experienced particular to expected general at the organic level is our 'habit of life' (101/74). The contemplative soul as organic synthesis or habitual contraction can also be called a 'passive self' or 'larval subject' (107/78).

Now Deleuze cannot go directly to his key notion of the organic synthesis qua contemplative soul because he must first free a notion of habit from the illusions of psychology, which fetishizes activity. Psychology, by fear of introspection, misses the element of passive 'contemplation'. Indeed, psychology says the self cannot contemplate itself due to fear of an infinite regress of active constituting selves.[2] Deleuze's response is to pose the question of the ontological status of habit. Instead of asking how contemplation is an activity of a constituted subject, we can ask whether or not each self is a contemplation (100/73). How do we get to habit as what a subject is rather than what it does? First, we must determine what habit does. It draws (*soutire à*) something new from repetition: difference. Habit is essentially 'contraction' (101/73). Now we must distinguish two genres of contraction: (1) contraction as activity in series as opposed to relaxation or dilation, and (2) contraction as fusion of succession of elements. With the second form of contraction, we come upon the notion of a 'contemplative soul' which must be 'attributed to the heart, the muscles, nerves and cells' (101/74). Deleuze knows the notion of an organic 'contemplative soul' might strike his readers as a 'mystical or barbarous hypothesis' (101/74), but he pushes on; passive organic synthesis is our 'habit of life', our expectation that life will continue. So we must attribute a 'contemplative soul' to the heart, the muscles, the nerves, the cells, whose role is to contract habits. This is just extending to 'habit' its full generality: habit in the organic syntheses that we are (101/74).

We cannot follow all the marvelous detail of Deleuze's text in which he discusses 'claims and satisfactions' and even the question of pleasure, of the 'beatitude of passive synthesis' (102/74). We have to move to the question of rhythm.

In descriptions that will be echoed by the enactivists and by the contemporary biologists we will discuss, Deleuze claims that organic syntheses operate in series, and each series has a rhythm. Organisms are polyrhythmic: 'the duration of an organism's present, or of its various presents, will vary according to the natural contractile range of its contemplative souls' (105/77). There are thousands of rhythmic periods that compose the organic being of humans: from the long periods of childhood, puberty, adulthood and menopause to monthly hormonal cycles to daily cycles (circadian rhythms) to heart beats and breathing cycles, all the way down to neural firing patterns. Everything has a period of repetition, everything is a habit, and each one of these repetitions forms a living present that synthesizes the retention of the past and the anticipation of the future as need. Now 'need' can be 'lack' relative to active syntheses, but 'satiety' relative to organic passive syntheses. Deleuze writes: 'need marks the limits of the variable present. The present extends between two eruptions of need, and coincides with the duration of a contemplation' (105/77).

Organic Subjectivity

We now have to address a change in vocabulary, as Deleuze moves toward the notion of larval subject, which will be our link to the enactivists. First, the contemplative soul becomes the 'passive self', which is 'not defined simply by receptivity – that is, by means of the capacity to experience sensations – but by virtue of the contractile contemplation that constitutes the organism itself before it constitutes the sensations' (107/78). As we will see, we have to insist on the merely logical nature of this 'before'. But before that, one last vocabulary shift: the passive selves are 'larval subjects'. Of course, we cannot just replicate whole selves all the way down the organic scale. That would just be 'tracing', positing identities beneath identities. Deleuze insists: 'this self, therefore, is by no means simple: it is not enough to relativize or pluralize the self, all the while retaining for it a simple attenuated form' (107/78). The larval subject is itself 'dissolved', Deleuze will insist: 'Selves are larval subjects; the world of passive syntheses constitutes the system of the self, under conditions yet to be determined, but it is the system of a dissolved self' (107/78).

We might think that selves merely accompany contemplation: 'There is a self wherever a furtive contemplation has been established, whenever a contracting machine capable of drawing a difference from repetition functions somewhere' (107/78–9). But it is better to say that selves are, in fact, contemplations. Contracting contemplations or habits or organic syntheses draw a difference from repetition. That is exactly what a self is: 'The self does not undergo modifications, it is itself a modification – this term designating precisely the difference drawn [from repetition]' (107/79). Since organic processes are serial, there is a series of such larval subjects, 'Every contraction is a presumption, a claim – that is to say, it gives rise to an expectation or a right in regard to that which it contracts, and comes undone once its object escapes [*se défait dès que son objet lui échappe*]' (107/79). This undoing of the larval subject with the rhythm of fatigue and satisfaction is the key to the notion that the self is not simple, but dissolved: that is, serial and differential.

To grasp Deleuze's notion of the organism as larval subject, everything depends on how we interpret the 'priority' of organic synthesis to perceptual synthesis as different levels of passive synthesis; that is, we have to interpret the term 'primary vital sensibility'. What we will learn from the enactive school is that organic and perceptual syntheses are always linked in reality. The priority of organic syntheses is merely logical, for all organisms, even the most simple, have both metabolism and sensibility, or as the enactivists will put it in a phrase that will alert Deleuzeans, 'sense-making'. We will see a reinforcement of Deleuze's merely logical 'priority' of metabolism over sense-making in Ezequiel Di Paolo's distinction between autopoiesis and adaptivity. To adopt an Aristotelian vocabulary temporarily, the enactivists will show that, although we can logically distinguish between them, in reality all organisms have both a vegetative (metabolism/autopoiesis) and sensible (sense-making/adaptivity) psyche.[3]

The necessary combination of metabolic and perceptual capacities in an organic subject is a little difficult to see in *Difference and Repetition*, as Deleuze is working with the example of multicellular organisms, where metabolism and sensibility are subserved by physically distinct systems. Now, even though in multicellular organisms we can spatially distinguish metabolic from sensory processes, we have to acknowledge internal monitoring, a 'sensing' of the state of organism – or better, a synthesis (that is, a differentiation/integration) that establishes the trajectory of the system: where a process is going and with what acceleration. In any event, Deleuze wants to expose thousands of contemplative souls or 'little selves' as thousands of organic syntheses 'before' passive perceptual syntheses and active intellectual syntheses (which Kant unifies in a subject via the transcendental unity of apperception). Deleuze's strategy is thus reminiscent of Nietzsche seeing a multiplicity of drives beneath the illusory unified ego.

But does Deleuze's emphasis on multiplicity mean he treats the organism as an 'illusion'? It all depends on how we interpret the following phrase from the Preface to *Difference and Repetition*. Discussing the 'generalized anti-Hegelianism' that is 'in the air nowadays [*dans l'air du temps*]' (1/xix; translation modified), Deleuze writes: 'The modern world is one of simulacra . . . All identities are only simulated, produced as an optical "effect" by the more profound game [*jeu*] of difference and repetition' (1/xix). Is this Deleuze writing in his own name, setting out his thesis, or is it a report of what is in the air? Is an organism only an 'illusion'? Whatever we might finally say about the unity of the organism in *Difference and Repetition* – although I briefly return to the issue in the Conclusion, I will defer that full reading for now – we can at least say that our task is made more difficult by the lack of an explicit discourse on the membrane, which does not appear until the following year's *Logic of Sense*. None the less, by the time we reach the straightforwardly realist and materialist stance of *A Thousand Plateaus*, it is clear that organismic stratification is not an illusion. Strata are real ('a very important, inevitable phenomenon that is beneficial in many respects' (Deleuze 1987: 40)) and valuable ('staying stratified is not the worst thing that can happen' (161)). On the other hand, with a long enough time scale, we can see that, although organisms are not illusions, they are only temporary patterns, diachronically emergent patterns unifying multiple material processes for a time. This does not prevent us from articulating Deleuze and enaction; the emphasis on synchronic emergence – on the necessary systematic functioning of metabolism – in autopoiesis as the essential structure of living things could never deny the death of individuals (Protevi 2009a).

What is radical about Deleuze's strategy is that by following its logic, this underlying multiplicity is true for unicellular organisms as well. Deleuze pluralizes even unicellulars, both synchronically (metabolism and perception are separate processes) and diachronically. Every iteration of a process, each case in a series of organic syntheses, is a contemplative soul, each has its own rhythm, and it is the consistency of those rhythms that allows the cell to live. Death, we can speculate, occurs when the rhythms of the processes no longer mesh. Shifting musical terms, we can say that life is harmonious music; death is disharmony. On the supra-organismic scale, death as disharmony is the condition for creativity, for the production of new forms of life, new processes.[4] But on the organismic scale, while we can also affirm disharmony as the condition of creativity, a prudent experimentation is called for: 'Dismantling the organism never meant killing yourself' (Deleuze 1987: 160).

So even though we must be literal when we say the 'living present'

– it occurs on the organic level 'before' it occurs on the perceptual and intellectual levels – we have to remember that this priority is merely logical; in all real organisms, organic synthesis is always accompanied by perceptual syntheses. In each organism, multicellular or unicellular, the synchronic emergent unity of the organism is always an achievement, a unification of many 'little selves'. But there is diachrony here as well; for Deleuze, each little self is never fully present to itself, but is 'dissolved' in a series of repetitions of its process. The key is to describe this dissolved or multiple or differential biological psyche without falling into a needless projection of unified active or intellectualist synthesis on to it; that is, the key is to describe passive synthesis as a logically distinct but really linked series of multiple organic and perceptual syntheses. In doing so, we will have isolated the level of the organic 'larval subject' and will have thereby defined the multiple levels of Deleuze's 'biological panpsychism'.

To summarize, then, the passive self is never fully self-present because the passive organic and perceptual syntheses upon which active syntheses are built are differential in three aspects. Each passive synthesis is serial (there is never one synthesis by itself, but always a series of contractions, each with its own rhythmic period); each series is related to other series in the same body (at the most basic level, the series of organic contractions is linked to those of perceptual contractions as these are related to those of motion; echoing the enaction school, we can say that all perception is sensorimotor); and each series is related to other series in other bodies, which are themselves similarly differential (the series of syntheses of bodies can resonate or clash). Together the passive syntheses at all these levels form a differential transcendental field within which subject formation takes place as an integration or resolution of that field; in other words, even at this most basic level, larval subjects are the patterns of these multiple and serial syntheses which fold in on themselves (again, a full treatment of the issue would demand we articulate the role of the membrane), producing a site of lived and living experience, spatio-temporal dynamism and sentience or minimal awareness, a 'primary vital sensibility'.

Enaction

Although the emphasis on difference for Deleuze and on autonomy for the enactivists make them somewhat strange bedfellows, the notions of 'primary vital sensibility' and of the 'larval subject' that we have just traced in *Difference and Repetition* can let us see some significant resonances between the two discourses with regard to organic time and organic subjectivity. For the first aspect, organic time, we will concentrate on Jonas (2003); for the second, on Di Paolo (2005); both of these are woven into the argument of Thompson (2007).

Organic Time

The enactivists straightforwardly talk of the new transcendental aesthetic we found in Deleuze as 'biological time and space' (Thompson 2007: 155; citing Jonas 2003: 86). We find this expressed as a living present found in the simplest of organisms, a synthesis of retention and protention (Jonas 2003: 85–6) Furthermore, need is as rhythmic and affective for the enactivists as it is for Deleuze. Thompson writes: 'concern, want, need, appetition, desire – these are essentially affective and protentional or forward-looking' (Thompson 2007: 156).

Let us turn to Jonas's magnificent essay, 'Is God a Mathematician?: The Meaning of Metabolism' (Jonas 2003: 64–92) for more detail on these notions; we will see the same first steps of a dynamic genesis (from instantaneity to the living present) here as in *Difference and Repetition*.

Jonas proposes to test, against the case of the organism, the modern claim that God is a mathematician (65). First, Jonas reviews the history of that notion, from Plato's *Timaeus* through Leibniz. What distinguishes the ancient and modern treatments of nature is the algebraic treatment of motion on the part of the moderns (67). Thus with the moderns we find 'analysis of becoming' rather than 'contemplation of being'; for the moderns it is process as such, rather than its perfection in an end state, that is the object of knowledge (67). This mathematical change of method, when applied to physics, means that 'the functional generation of a mathematical curve becomes the mechanical generation of the path of a body' (68).

Here is the key for us, the connection with Deleuze's reaching the starting point of dynamic genesis in the '*mens momentanea*' (Deleuze 1968/1994: 96/70). For Jonas, modern mathematical physics gives us time as a series of instants, such that the physical states of a process are externalized, one to the other, 'each of them determined anew by the component factors operative at that very instant' (Jonas 2003: 68). Such fragmentation means that analysis meets no resistance. In other terms, there is no wholeness, only an aggregation of moments, and so ontological emergence is denied: 'rationality of order . . . must be explained by reference to the . . . most elementary types of event . . . their singleness alone is the basically real, and the "wholeness" of their conjoint result is an appearance with no genuine ontological status' (69).

We cannot treat all the riches of the historical sections of Jonas's text, as he moves from a reading of the *Timaeus*, where the Demiurge is needed to redeem the passivity of matter (70), to modern materialism and its dualistic counterpart, idealism, a shift that results in a stunning inversion to which we have become inured: '"Matter" in fact, in the sense of "body," becomes more rational than "spirit"' (73). This entails that 'not only the mindless but also the lifeless has become the intelligible as such,' a standard that means the moderns must understand life starting from 'dead matter' (74).

Passing now to his interrogation of the purely mathematical physical analysis of metabolism (in other words, testing the reduction of biology to physics), Jonas proposes the wave as the physicist's model of complex physical form, a form that is wholly reducible to an aggregate. The wave, as an 'integrated event-structure' has no ontologically emergent status; 'no special reality is accorded that is not contained in, and deducible from, the conjoint reality of the participating, more elementary events' (77). Furthermore, Jonas, adds, what is true of the wave must be true of the organism as object of divine intellection. Without need of the 'fusing summation of sense', for God, 'the life process will then present itself as a series, or a web of many series, of consecutive events concerning these single, persisting units of general substance' (77). Once again, we find physical time as a pure self-exteriority, as a series of instants.

For Jonas, however, such a reductive account misses the ontological emergence that makes of life an 'ontological surprise', and the organism a system, a 'unity of a manifold'. The organism is 'whole' as 'self-integrating in active performance', an 'active self-integration of life' (79). The 'functional identity' of organisms relative to the materials it metabolizes is constituted 'in a dialectical relation of *needful freedom* to matter' (80; emphasis in original).

Both elements, need and freedom, constitute the 'transcendence' of life, and this transcendence constitutes a living present, a metabolically founded transcendental aesthetic or a priori form of organic time: 'self-concern, actuated by want, throws open . . . a horizon of time . . . the imminence of that future into which organic continuity is each moment about to extend by the satisfaction of that moment's want' (85). For Jonas, in a way that highlights the partiality of Deleuze's treatment in *Difference and Repetition*, organic space is founded by organic time; an organism 'faces outward only because, by the necessity of its freedom, it faces forward: so that spatial presence is lighted up as it were by temporal imminence and both merge into past fulfillment (or its negative, disappointment)' (85).

Jonas then draws the consequences for the question of the adequacy of purely mathematical physics for the phenomenon of life. In other words, he shows the necessity of a dynamic genesis from instantaneity to the living present: 'with respect to the organic sphere, the external linear time-pattern of antecedent and sequent, involving the causal dominance of the past, is inadequate.' With life on the scene, 'the extensive order of past and future is intensively reversed,' so that the determination of 'mere externality' by the past has to be supplemented by the recognition that 'life is essentially also what is going to be and just becoming' (86).

Organic Subjectivity

Even with the notion of the 'primary vital sensibility' of the larval subject of organic syntheses as our guiding thread, pairing Deleuze and enaction still seems odd. Developing out of the autopoiesis school, founded by Humberto Maturana and Francisco Varela, the enactive position worked out by Evan Thompson in *Mind in Life* (2007) seems too focused on autonomy and identity to be usefully paired with Deleuze's philosophy of difference. Although autopoietic theory, developed in the 1970s at the height of the molecular revolution in biology, performed an admirable service in reasserting the need to think at the level of the organism, it is clear that autopoiesis is locked into a framework which posits an identity horizon (organizational conservation) for (structural) change. For autopoietic theory, living systems conserve their organization, which means their functioning always restores homeostasis; evolution is merely structural change against this identity horizon (Protevi 2009a). Now, even if Deleuze ultimately does not think the organism is an 'illusion', when it comes to 'life' he stresses the creativity of evolution over against the conserved identity of the organism; thus for Deleuze the organism is 'that which life sets against itself in order to limit itself' (Deleuze 1987: 503). None the less, strictly with regard to the 'primary vital sensibility' of the organism we have seen in *Difference and Repetition*, Deleuze and enaction can be brought together, when we follow how Thompson supplements the undoubted emphasis on identity preservation of autopoiesis with a more dynamic and differential concept of 'adaptivity' drawn from the work of Ezequiel Di Paolo. With this addition, we can see the possibility of a more fruitful interchange with Deleuze.

The key is to recognize that autopoiesis entailed not just organizational maintenance, but cognition or 'sense-making'. For Maturana and Varela, autonomous systems have sufficient internal complexity and feedback that 'coupling' with their environment 'triggers' internally directed action. This means that only those external environmental differences capable of being sensed and made sense of by an autonomous system can be said to exist for that system, can be said to make up the world of that system (Maturana and Varela 1980: 119). The positing of a causal relation between external and internal events is only possible from the perspective of an 'observer', a system that itself must be capable of sensing and making sense of such events in its environment (81). So with autopoiesis the autonomous system is always linked to its environment and organization provides an identity horizon for structural change. But autopoiesis is only sufficient for maintenance of identity. To account for sense-making, Thompson turns to Ezequiel Di Paolo. 'A distinct capacity for "adaptivity" needs to be added to the minimal autopoietic organization so that the system can actively regulate itself with respect to its conditions of viability and thereby modify its milieu according to the internal norms of its activity' (Thompson 2007: 148).

With this important connection in mind, we can move to consider sense-making. Witness the single-celled organism's ability to make sense. 'Sense' has, perhaps fittingly, a three-fold sense: sensibility, signification and direction.[5] A single-celled organism can sense food gradients (it possesses sensibility as openness to the environment), can make sense of this difference in terms of its own needs (it can establish the signification 'good' or 'bad'), and can turn itself in the right sense for addressing its needs (it orients itself in the right direction of movement). This fundamental biological property of affective cognition is one reason why the Cartesian distinction of mental and material has no purchase in discussions of sense-making. There is no 'mental' property (in the sense of full-blown reflective consciousness) attributable to the single-celled organism, but since there is spontaneous and autonomous sense-making, there is no purely 'material' realm in these organisms either. The enactive claim is that affective cognition in humans is simply a development of this basic biological capacity of sense-making.

Turning now to Di Paolo's essay, we see that he distinguishes within Maturana and Varela's work the all-or-nothing character of organizational maintenance from a more dynamic notion of homeostatic regulation:

Whereas homeostasis connotes the existence of active mechanisms capable of managing and controlling the network of processes that construct the organism, conservation is a set-theoretic condition that may or may not be realized in an active manner. It merely distinguishes between changes of state without loss of organization and disintegrative changes. (Di Paolo 2005: 435)

For Di Paolo, organizational conservation cannot explain organismic sense-making – directed action responding to environmental change relevant for the organism – precisely because it is all-or-nothing: 'But what makes bacteria *swim up* the gradient? What makes *them* distinguish and prefer higher sugar concentrations? As defined, structural coupling is a conservative, not an improving process; it admits no possible gradation' (437). Di Paolo insists that an organism's sense-making, its judgment as to the improvement of conditions relative to its need, is beyond the scope of autopoiesis:

Even if the current rate of nutrient intake is lower than the rate of consumption (leading to certain loss of autopoiesis in the near future), bacteria will not seek higher concentrations *just because* they are autopoietic since improving the conditions of self-production is not part of the definition of autopoiesis. (437)

The key for us is to see that adaptivity requires a dynamic emergent self unifying a multiplicity of serial processes. We might say that autopoiesis entails synchronic emergence, whereas adaptivity entails diachronic emergence. Notice the dynamic monitoring of multiple processes Di Paolo isolates here as necessary for generating singular norms of each organism:

Only if they are able to monitor and regulate their internal processes so that they can generate the necessary responses anticipating internal tendencies will they also be able to appreciate graded differences between otherwise equally viable states. Bacteria possessing this capability will be able to generate a normativity *within* their current set of viability conditions and *for themselves*. They will be capable of appreciating not just sugar as nutritive, but the direction where the concentration grows as useful, and swimming in that direction as the right thing to do in some circumstances. (437)

Adaptive mechanisms (the measurement of the trajectory of the system against a norm and the regulative means of bringing deviations back to that norm – or indeed of changing the norm itself) are serial and so the emergent self of the organism is, in Deleuze's terms, a 'system of a dissolved self' (Deleuze 1968/1994: 107/78). In general, we have to stress the 'systematic' nature here to see the connection of Deleuze with adaptivity, but the dissolution of serial selves is clear when Di Paolo writes:

> The operation of single adaptive mechanisms is in normal circumstances self-extinguishing but their interaction, the ongoing coupling with the environment, and the precariousness of metabolism, make their collective action also self-renewing, thus naturally resulting in *valenced rhythms of tension and satisfaction*. (444–5; emphasis in original)

So, we might want to relate the 'simple self' of Deleuze to the all-or-nothing character of autopoiesis, and the 'system of a dissolved self' to the dynamic character of adaptivity. That is, in adaptivity there is a measuring of the trajectory of the organism against norms ('anticipating internal tendencies'). In order for it to be the continual monitoring and regulation of an ongoing organism in its life span, that measurement has to be serial: that is, rhythmic, dynamic and constantly renewable ('self-extinguishing'). It cannot just be abstract 'structural change' over against 'organizational maintenance'. Deleuze is going to call each snapshot of a dynamic series of modifications, each 'drawing of a difference from repetition', the 'larval subject'. The seriality of such a subject is indicated by the fact that the self 'comes undone [*se défait*] once its object escapes' (Deleuze 1969/1994: 107/79); this is the 'self-extinguishing' of a 'single adaptive mechanism' for Di Paolo.

E. coli Chemotaxis

We have brought Deleuze and enaction together, at least from a certain perspective. But what if neither discourse relates to contemporary biology? To ground the discussion, we will look at the description of organic and perceptual syntheses in *E. coli* chemotaxis, a favorite example of sense-making for the enactivist school, in two recent biology works, Howard Berg's *E. Coli in Motion* (2004) and Dennis Bray's *Wetware* (2009). We will look at two aspects of their work to make the connection with Deleuze and with enaction: first, their account of synthesis as differentiation–integration, as 'drawing a difference from repetition' – that is, their establishment of a transcendental aesthetic for organic life, the living present as retention and protention, a constantly renewed 'here and now'; and second, their fear of organic subjectivity coupled with their inability to forego first-person evaluative language.

Organic Time

We will find here the Deleuzean notion of passive synthesis as constituting the living present. Our authors stress the temporality of perception for their objects of study. Bray stresses the retentive aspect of *E. coli*, who 'continually reassess their situation' by means of 'a sort of *short-term memory*' (Bray 2009: 7; emphasis in original). Such 'bacterial memory' can be tested by exposing them to a step change in the concentration of an attractant: 'Now it is clear that what the bugs respond to is not the concentration of aspartate per se but its rate of change' (94). Bray interprets these results in terms that cannot fail to delight any reader of Deleuze:

> But once aspartate has settled down to a steady concentration, the bug no longer responds. Biologists call this adaptation, but a mathematician examining the time course of response would call it differentiation. By measuring the rate of change in the signal, the receptor cluster has in effect performed calculus! (94)

In other words, the bacterium has repeated its measurement of aspartate and drawn a difference from that repetition; it has performed a differentiation.

But the living present is a synthesis of retention and protention. Berg's work on temporal synthesis reveals the protention aspect, as well as the insightful character of Deleuze's treatment of contractile habit as 'drawing a difference from a repetition'. Berg first clearly shows retention as one aspect of the passive synthesis of the living present: 'to correct its course, the cell must deal with the recent past, not the distant past' (Berg 2004: 57). But then we see that the living present is serial, that it draws a difference from a repetition; Berg writes that 'to determine whether the concentration is going up or down, the cell has to make two such measurements and take the difference' (57). Berg shows that this perceptual synthesis is temporal rather than spatial; describing the results of a key experiment, he writes: 'the response to the positive temporal gradient was large enough to account for the results obtained in spatial gradients' (36). So the cell repeats its sampling procedure (it analyzes the environment, breaking it down to identify the concentration of molecules of interest) and then synthesizes the two results. What we see here in this passive synthesis is differentiation (calculation of the instantaneous rate of change of a gradient) and integration (calculating the trajectory of the change by combining the results of previous differentiations). We thus have sense-making in the living present: retention (of past differentiations) and protention (the integrated trajectory as indicating the future course of the organism).

In further confirmation of the Deleuzean and enactivist treatments of the living present, these passive syntheses are rhythmic. Due to its being buffeted by the Brownian motion of water molecules, after about 10 seconds, an *E. coli* cell 'drifts off course by more than 90 degrees, and thus forgets where it is going' (49). The living present has limits to its retention; it has an essential 'forgetting'. Continuing with his analysis, Berg writes: 'This sets an upper limit on the time available for a cell to decide whether life is getting better or worse. If it cannot decide within about 10 seconds, it is too late' (49–50). Just as it has an upper limit to its living present, 'a lower limit is set by the time required for the cell to count enough molecules of attractant or repellent to determine their concentrations with adequate precision' (50). More precisely,

> diffusion of attractants or repellents sets a lower limit on the distance (and thus the time) that a cell must swim to outrun diffusion (to reach greener pastures), as well as on the precision with which the cell, in a given time, can determine concentrations. (56)

As Berg puts it: 'if it is to go far enough to find out whether life is getting better or worse, it must outrun diffusion' (56). This minimal time for perceptual synthesis is 1 second, 'approximately equal to the mean run length' (56). With Berg's analyses of *E. coli* chemotaxis, we see here a constantly renewed living present, the constitution of a singular 'here and now' for each bacterium.

Organic Subjectivity

In his Preface Bray writes that he received a rejection note from another publisher accusing him of writing a book about 'single-celled organisms possessing consciousness' (Bray 2009: ix). Bray reacts indignantly, but we will see that he protests too much in writing that

> single cells are not sentient or aware in the same way that we are. To me, consciousness implies intelligent awareness of self and the ability to experience introspectively accessible mental states. No single-celled organism or individual cell from a plant or animal has these properties. (ix)

No one, least of all Deleuze and the enactivists, would complain of this perfectly defensible high bar to meet for the ascription of 'consciousness'. But Bray has thrown 'sentience' and 'awareness' in too quickly with 'consciousness', as we can see when he calls *E. coli* 'robots'. Bray writes that 'An individual cell, in my view, is a system that possesses the

basic ingredients of life but lacks sentience. It is a robot made of biological materials' (Bray 2009: ix). The 'robot' as line of defense against
accusations of biological panpsychism is repeated by Howard Berg, who
also writes, regarding his 'top down, or outside in' treatment of cell
populations, that from this perspective, *E. coli* should be seen as 'robots
programmed to respond to external stimuli' (Berg 2004: 19).

To avoid the charge of a too easy ascription of micro-subjectivity,
Bray takes a strong computationalist and representationalist stance. 'It
is as though each organism builds an image of the world – a description
expressed . . . in the language of chemistry' (Bray 2009: x). The most
intense locus of this representation is found in the genome and protein
synthesis: 'From a time-compressed view, the sequences and structures
of RNA, DNA, and proteins can be thought of as continually morphing
in response to the fluctuating world around them' (x). Thus we come to
the 'central thesis of the book – that living cells perform computations'
(xi). So, to avoid any hint of biological panpsychism, for Bray, cells are
non-sentient robots.

Once we enter the book, however, we find Bray bothered about
mechanism missing something:

> Like manic pathologists at an autopsy competition, we have littered our
> workbenches with the diåssected viscera of cells . . . But where in this
> museum of parts do we find sensation, volition, or awareness? Which
> insensate substances come together, and in what sequence, to produce
> sentient behavior? (5)

However, Bray soon returns to his computationalist position: 'The
molecular mechanism of *E. coli* chemotaxis is a superb illustration of
cellular information processing' (6). But he cannot sustain the mechanistic position. Due to Brownian motion from buffeting by water molecules, 'to pursue any direction for more than a second or so, bacteria
have to constantly reassess their situation' (7). But, if it is *their* situation,
they must have a proper point of view. It is not just 'the' situation, but
'their' situation. We can see here the instability of this discourse, its
shifting from third- to first-person perspective.

In his discussion of the mechanism of that reassessment, Bray is
worried about subjectivity:

> Words like *memory, awareness,* and *information* are easy to use but require
> careful definition to avoid misunderstanding. I'm using *short-term memory*
> here in a colloquial, nonspecialist way, referring to how a swimming bac-
> terium carries with it an impression of selected features of its surroundings
> encountered in the past few seconds. (7; emphasis in original)

But despite these qualifications, he has to return to the first-person perspective. Adding aspartate to a solution will take the percentage of tumbling cells from 20% to near zero. This is because 'the cells have experienced an improvement in their environment (a taste of food) and consequently persist in their current direction of swimming' (7). 'Experienced' here shows the inevitability of some notion of minimal subjectivity.

We see the same instability of discursive stances in Howard Berg. He first seems to indicate the necessity of a first-person perspective in his distinction between 'aesthetics' and 'material gain'. He writes that the modern era of *E. coli* research begins in the 1960s when 'Julius Adler demonstrated that *E. coli* has a sense of taste, that is, that bacterial chemotaxis is a matter of aesthetics rather than material gain' (Berg 2004: 15). In discussing such sampling, though, Berg reverts to a third-person perspective: 'Adler was able to show that *E. coli* responds to chemicals that it can neither transport (take up from surrounding medium) nor metabolize (utilize as a source of energy or raw material)' (24). Another example is perhaps more telling. Berg writes of 'attractants' and 'repellants', which seemingly imply a first-person perspective, but he defines them in purely third-person behavioral terms: 'chemicals whose gradients strongly affect the motile behavior of wild-type *E. coli*' (25; Table 3.1).

Much as they try, however, in the long run the authors cannot avoid a blend of third-person mechanism and first-person evaluation. Bray writes of how *E. coli* possesses 'a sort of short-term memory that tells them whether conditions are better at this instant of time than a few seconds ago. By "better" I mean richer in food molecules, more suitable in acidity and salt concentration, closer to an optimum temperature' (Bray 2009: 7). The seemingly innocuous term 'food' is the give-away, for 'food' is a relational term. Sucrose is only food 'for' an organism; it is not food in itself (Thompson 2007: 158). And clearly, 'suitable' and 'optimum' are relative to the life process of organisms.

A final example from Bray, linking retention in the living present to subjective evaluation: 'Bacteria store a running record of the attractants they encounter. This tells them whether things are better or worse: whether the quantity of food molecules in their vicinity is higher or lower than it was a few seconds ago' (Bray 2009: 94). Here again we see the mixture of mechanistic (third-person) and evaluative (first-person) language. If a 'quantity' of (chemical) 'molecules' is being measured, we have a third-person description of a mechanism, but if it is 'food' being measured, we have a first-person perspective; the measurement of food is relative to the need of an organism. The inevitability of first-person evaluative terms is clear soon when Bray writes: 'It's a pragmatic strategy: if conditions are improving, continue swimming; if not, tumble and try another direction' (94).

Let us conclude this all-too-brief discussion of the treatment of organic subjectivity in contemporary biology by returning to Berg, who is somewhat more straightforward in his adoption of evaluative terms and a first-person perspective. In discussing the run versus tumble behavior of individual cells, Berg writes that

> *E. coli* extends runs that are favorable (that carry cells up the gradient of an attractant) but fails to shorten runs that are not (that carry cells down such a gradient . . .. Thus, if life gets better, *E. coli* swims farther on the current leg of its track and enjoys it more. If life gets worse, it just relaxes back to its normal mode of operation. *E. coli* is an optimist. (Berg 2004: 35)

Conclusion

We cannot exaggerate the fit of enaction and Deleuze. We have stressed the serial, dynamic, affective and differential character of enaction, but we have underplayed some of Deleuze's radicality.

To have a full picture of the notion of organism in *Difference and Repetition*, we would have to discuss it in terms of static genesis, for the organism is one of the prime examples of Ideas, first discussed in terms of Geoffrey Saint-Hilaire and anatomical elements and then updated in terms of genetics (Deleuze 1968/1994: 239–40/184–5). But Ideas are incarnated by spatio-temporal dynamisms, which are processes of individuation, so a confrontation with Deleuze's reading of Simondon will be necessary (317/246). The larval subject is the individual in the process of individuation and hence tied to a metastable field in an ongoing process of 'transduction'. The priority of individuation over differenciation must be respected (318/247) and this leads Deleuze to a prescient critique of genetic determinism: 'The nucleus and the genes designate only the differentiated matter – in other words, the differential relations which constitute the pre-individual field to be actualized; but their actualization is determined only by the cytoplasm, with its gradients and its fields of individuation' (323/251).[6]

Even on the basis of this brief sketch, it might appear, then, that the emphasis in enaction on the notion of autonomous system overemphasizes the individual as self-conserving product as opposed to individuation as always ongoing process. From this perspective, the embryo as paradigmatic 'larval subject' is merely a more intense site of individuation than the adult; however sclerotic and habitual, the adult is only the limit of the process of individuation. It is never actually reached; no more than the virtual does the actual exist, rather than insist. In terms of autopoietic synchronic emergence, then, we might say that enaction relegates the metastable field to coupled environment and limits transduction to metabolism, while in terms of adaptivity's diachronic emergence, it neglects ontogenesis in favor of adult function and restricts transduction to homeostatic regulation. I am under no illusions as to my capacity at the present time to prove these assertions; I merely wish to record them as speculations to be pursued in future work.

Finally, we should note that by radicalizing what we might call the Bergsonian and Whiteheadean threads, which intersect the Simondonian thread, we can see a total panpsychism in *Difference and Repetition* that surpasses the biological. Deleuze notes that the mathematical and biological notions of differentiation and differenciation employed in the book are only a 'technical model' (285/220). Now if 'the entire world is an egg' (279/216), then every individuation is 'embryonic', we might say, even 'rocks' (282/219) and 'islands' (283/219). Now if rocks and islands as individuation processes are embryonic, then they too have a psyche: 'every spatio-temporal dynamism is accompanied by the emergence of an elementary consciousness' (284/220). We will not pursue this line of thought, but will note that by the time of *Anti-Oedipus* (Welchman 2009) and *A Thousand Plateaus* (Bonta and Protevi 2004; Protevi 2009b) Deleuze and Guattari explicitly thematize that the syntheses are no longer bound to 'experience', however widespread, but are fully material syntheses, syntheses of nature in geological as well as biological, social, and psychological registers. With this full naturalization of syntheses, the question of panpsychism is brought into full relief, as syntheses of things simply are syntheses of experience.

References

Ansell-Pearson, K. (1999), *Germinal Life: The Difference and Repetition of Deleuze*, New York: Routledge.
Beistegui, M. de (2004), *Truth and Genesis: Philosophy as Differential Ontology*, Bloomington: Indiana University Press.
Berg, H. (2004), *E. Coli in Motion*, New York: Springer.
Bonta, M. and J. Protevi (2004), *Deleuze and Geophilosophy: A Guide and Glossary*, Edinburgh: Edinburgh University Press.
Bray, D. (2009), *Wetware: A Computer in Every Living Cell*, New Haven, CT: Yale University Press.
Bryant, L. (2008), *Difference and Givenness: Deleuze's Transcendental Empiricism and the Ontology of Immanence*, Evanston, IL: Northwestern University Press.

DeLanda, M. (2002), *Intensive Science and Virtual Philosophy*, London: Continuum.

Deleuze, G. (1968), *Différence et Répétition*, Paris: PUF.

Deleuze, G. (1987), *A Thousand Plateaus*, trans. B. Massumi, Minneapolis: University of Minnesota Press.

Deleuze, G. (1990), *The Logic of Sense*, trans. M. Lester with C. Stivale, New York: Columbia University Press.

Deleuze, G. (1994), *Difference and Repetition*, trans. P. Patton, New York: Columbia University Press.

Di Paolo, E. (2005), 'Autopoiesis, Adaptivity, Teleology, Agency', *Phenomenology and the Cognitive Sciences* 4, pp. 429–52.

Hughes, J. (2009), *Deleuze's Difference and Repetition*, New York: Continuum.

Jonas, H. (2003), *The Phenomenon of Life: Toward a Philosophical Biology*, Evanston, IL: Northwestern University Press.

Maturana, H. and F. J. Varela (1980), *Autopoiesis and Cognition: The Realization of the Living*, Boston, MA: Riedel.

Oyama, S. (2000), *The Ontogeny of Information: Developmental Systems and Evolution*, 2nd edn, Durham, NC: Duke University Press.

Oyama, S., P. Griffiths, and R. Gray (2001), *Cycles of Contingency*, Cambridge, MA: MIT Press.

Protevi, J. (1990), 'The *Sinnsfrage* and the *Seinsfrage*', *Philosophy Today* 34:4, pp. 321–33.

Protevi, J. (1998), 'The "Sense" of "Sight": Heidegger and Merleau-Ponty on the Meaning of Bodily and Existential Sight', *Research in Phenomenology* 28, pp. 211–23.

Protevi, J. (2009a), 'Beyond Autopoiesis: Inflections of Emergence and Politics in the Work of Francisco Varela', in *Emergence and Embodiment: Essays in Neocybernetics*, ed. B. Clarke and M. Hansen, Durham, NC: Duke University Press.

Protevi, J. (2009b), *Political Affect: Connecting the Social and the Somatic*, Minneapolis: University of Minnesota Press.

Simondon, G. (1995) *L'Individu et sa genèse physico-biologique*, Grenoble: Millon.

Thompson, E. (2007), *Mind in Life: Biology, Phenomenology, and the Sciences of Mind*, Cambridge, MA: Harvard University Press.

Varela, F. J., H. Maturana, and R. Uribe (1974), 'Autopoiesis: The Organization of the Living, its Characterization and a Model', *BioSystems* 5, pp. 187–96.

Welchman, A. (2009), 'Deleuze's Post-Critical Metaphysics', *Symposium* 13:2, pp. 25–54.

Wheeler, M. (1997), 'Cognition's Coming Home: the Reunion of Mind and Life', in *Proceedings of the Fourth European Conference on Artificial Life*, ed. P. Husbands and I. Harvey, Cambridge, MA: MIT Press, pp. 10–19.

Williams, J. (2003), *Gilles Deleuze's Difference and Repetition: A Critical Introduction and Guide*, Edinburgh: Edinburgh University Press.

Zahavi, D. (2005), *Subjectivity and Selfhood: Investigating the First-Person Perspective*, Cambridge, MA: MIT Press.

Notes

1. The major commentators on *Difference and Repetition* – Hughes 2009; Bryant 2008; Beistegui 2004; Williams 2003 – do not isolate the level of organic synthesis. The exceptions are Ansell-Pearson 1999 and DeLanda 2002.
2. For a treatment of the infinite regress problem in philosophical psychology, see Zahavi 2005.

3. Of course, Aristotle himself thought that plants possessed only the nutritive or vegetative psyche and that only animals had a sensible psyche. For an interesting take on the Aristotelian resonances here in the context of contemporary philosophy of mind and cognitive science, see Wheeler 1997.

4. We cannot treat the very rich discussion of the double aspect of death in *Difference and Repetition*, but we are here alluding to the way Deleuze reads the 'death instinct' as 'an internal power which frees the individuating elements from the form of the I or the matter of the self in which they are imprisoned . . . .. the liberation and swarming of little differences in intensity' (Deleuze 1968/1994: 333/259).

5. There is an archaic sense of the English word 'sense' meaning 'direction', as in 'the sense of the river'. This sense is still present in French, as in, among other uses, the expression *sens unique* for 'one-way street'. I have treated the three-fold 'sense of sense' in Protevi 1990 and 1998.

6. For contemporary critiques of genetic determinism, see the 'Developmental Systems Theory' school of thought, whose founding document is Oyama 2000; see also Oyama, Griffiths, and Gray 2001.

Chapter 3
Bodies of Learning

Anna Cutler and Iain MacKenzie

Swimming: in an interesting passage in *Difference and Repetition* (1994) Deleuze considers what is involved in learning to swim. The general point of this passage is that learning to swim should not be understood as simply the passive reception of knowledge from an expert. None of us, after all, would expect to be able to swim after taking some classes by the side of the pool. Rather, learning to swim is a process that requires the engagement of one's own body with a body of water. From the outset, we can say that there are at least two bodies involved. But in what sense do these bodies interact with each other in the process of learning? To understand this interaction we must first grasp that a person's body and a body of water, according to Deleuze, are composed of both universal and singular aspects. Each body has a universal aspect to the extent that it is constituted by a system of differential relations – relations of height, depth, limits and turbulences, for example – such that we can talk of how a human body embodies these relations as opposed to the manner in which these relations are embodied within a body of water. Deleuze refers to the system of differential relations that constitute bodies as the objective Idea of the body. None the less, every body (be it of a person or of water) is composed of particular variations within the system of relations that constitute the objective idea (as when we say, for example, that the shallow end stops here, for me, but not someone else). To learn how to swim is to bring the singularities of one's own body into contact with the particular depths, waves and eddies of the body of water that one enters. It is only when this happens that the problem of learning how to swim can be properly formed. As Deleuze puts it: '[t]o learn to swim is to conjugate the distinctive points of our bodies with the singular points of the objective Idea in order to form a problematic field' (1994: 165). Already we can see that Deleuze understands learning as a very bodily activity.

The bodily nature of learning how to swim, however, highlights that learning is not just an interaction of two different bodies: human and water. After all, while we learn through engagement, we do none the less come to know how to swim. We must consider, therefore, how this view of learning as bodily engagement impacts upon what we think of as knowledge. In the example of swimming, knowledge is expressed through the person of the swimming instructor and it is certainly the case that this knowledge can be very useful. (It helps to know that one is swimming in water rather than wet cement, which would have rather different qualities and, therefore, the problem of learning how to swim in it would be differently constituted.) We can now say, indeed, that there are always at least three bodies involved – the body of the learner, the body of water and the body of knowledge. Moreover, the swimming instructor embodies knowledge to the extent that she or he has an approach to the problem of learning how to swim. In other words, the body of knowledge is made manifest in the body of the instructor by way of the method of instruction. Method presumes that knowledge of swimming can be transmitted through the regulation of the learning process and it is premised upon the idea that every learner learns the same way.

In modern societies (and, in an important sense, this is a criterion for the modernity or not of a society), the body of knowledge as expressed through regulative method determines the relationship between the three bodies involved in learning. In all manner of modern learning environments, one learns the correct method in order to know what the instructor knows (to be the same as the instructor). If learners do not adopt the appropriate method, then they will be disciplined by the instructor on the grounds that they are not really learning (but merely doing the doggy-paddle, for instance). This understanding of the dominant place of knowledge culminates in the claim that one stops learning when one knows (how to swim). Learning, it is assumed, is a process which culminates in an end we call knowledge. Deleuze argues that this assumption constitutes one of the eight 'postulates' that underpin the dogmatic image of thought, albeit a privileged one in that it 'incorporates and recapitulates all the others': 'the postulate of knowledge' (1994: 167). Simply put, this postulate assumes that knowledge is superior to learning. In other words, it is presumed that the process is subordinate to the result and that what Deleuze calls a culture of learning is subordinate to a method for the attainment of knowledge. This dual subordination constitutes a form of dogmatism in the sense that it 'profoundly betrays what it means to think' (1994: 167). Clearly, without learning there would be no knowledge and, more importantly, learning is not the same as knowing. One of the tasks, therefore, of taking thought beyond this dogmatic image, according to Deleuze, is to think about learning as distinct from its modern subordination to knowledge.

Is it really legitimate, however, to discuss learning as a process of bodily engagement and to elide this with claims about the postulate of knowledge underpinning the dogmatic image of thought? In other words, in what sense is the third body – the body of knowledge – related to the other bodies? Perhaps we have strayed away from very literal renderings of the human body and the body of water to the metaphorical notion of a body of knowledge? Two Deleuzian responses can be made to these concerns. The first is that by body we mean an extended and relatively closed system of differential relations where 'relatively' denotes a degree of distance from the chaos of pure difference but also that bodies are never fully closed off from that chaos. With this definition in hand, there is not a category mistake involved in treating human bodies, bodies of water and bodies of knowledge as all forms of body. As Deleuze puts it: 'a body can be anything; it can be an animal, a body of sounds, a mind or an idea; it can be a linguistic corpus, a social body, a collectivity' (1988: 127). As Deleuze and Guattari succinctly express the same point: '[t]he "body"... is not ... the special field of biology' (1994: 123). Of course, it is equally clear that these three bodies are different. The difference, for Deleuze and Guattari, is to be found in the ways in which each body is individuated as an extended and relatively closed system; or, to invoke one of their most famous borrowings (from Antonin Artaud), the difference resides in the way each body is organised (1988: 149–66). The second response, therefore, speaks to one of the ways we commonly express the difference in organisation between a physical body (of a person or of water) and an ideational body (of knowledge); namely, it is usually assumed that the latter is organised by way of conscious conceptual construction whereas the former are the result of unconscious, physical processes. Moreover, this difference is thought to establish a qualitative and unbreachable distinction between knowledge of the body and knowledge as a body. It is a distinction that Deleuze does not accept. Indeed, it is a principal feature of the dogmatic image of thought that knowledge is conceptualised as the product of 'a "premeditated decision" by the thinker' (1994: 165). Installing learning, rather than knowledge, as a transcendental condition of thought requires that we treat learning, first and foremost, as 'an involuntary adventure' (1994: 165). Learning is an operation on the preconscious activity of the learner by way of a process of bodily engagement. Williams captures this well as he sums up the same discussion:

[w]e do not learn consciously since learning must go beyond our conscious faculties (*If I knew how to swim, I'd do it!*). Instead, we have to experiment in ways that connect to the unconscious processes that relate us to water or any other thing that we must enter into a new relation to. (2003: 137)

Learning is the formation of bodily habits and in the activity of learning we form knowledge in our bodies. This subsequently becomes conscious to us as a body of knowledge.

This account works well when thinking of animal learning, or even the learning that takes place on the organic plane more generally; the rat learns its way around the maze and the flower learns to lean into the sun. Considering human learning, though, it seems counter-intuitive to describe it as merely the acquisition of bodily habits when we typically think of learning as an activity that goes on in the mind of the learner. Of course, and as noted above, it is precisely this image of the knower consciously acquiring knowledge and then passing on knowledge to one that does not know that Deleuze is seeking to undermine with his critique of the postulate of knowledge. Yet, there is still a sense that an important aspect of human learning is missing if we overemphasise the unconscious, bodily acquisition of habits against the conscious activity of learning. But what could we possibly mean by the conscious activity of learning if not that there is a subject actively synthesising its world?

In one sense, this concern is easily resolved by simply extending the notion of acquired bodily habits to include 'habits of mind'. Indeed, this is one way of expressing the relationship between Deleuze's (1991) early work on Hume and the main concerns of *Difference and Repetition*. In what ways are we able to move away from the dogmatic (Kantian) image that the world is synthesised actively by a human subject that transcends this world? How can repetition be for itself and not just for a subject? How can we conceive of Ideas 'objectively' rather than subjectively? In what ways are we able to sense 'objective Ideas' if it is merely a case of bodies acting upon bodies? Deleuze's guiding intuition in response to these, and related, questions is that human subjects synthesise the world that they inhabit *passively*. Deleuze argues that in order to avoid the dogmatic image of thought we must not conceptualise human learning as the *activity* of a subject but the subject as the result of a process of learning that is in itself characterised by *passivity*: the passive synthesis of the sensible. This provides a compelling counterweight to the subjectivism lurking within most accounts of learning. There is, none the less, a danger in overemphasising passivity. To acknowledge and address this danger is to follow two lines of inquiry within Deleuze (and Guattari's) philosophical labours. One leads us to a further specification of their philosophical understanding of the organic body (though we will discuss this with particular reference to the human body); the other takes us into their remarks on the brain in the conclusion to *What is Philosophy?* After noting the former, it is the latter trajectory that gives direction to the rest of our discussion.

First, if we simply stop at the claim that humans learn by way of non-consciously acquired bodily habits it is not clear that the organisational specificity of human bodies is addressed. This specificity arises from the fact that as bodies we are defined by 'what affects us', but what affects us, as living bodies, is not just our ability to extend our body (raise our arm in response to water's extension as a wave of a certain height). Rather, human bodies are able to intensify affects and thereby intensify the system of relations that constitute our body. This process of intensification is not a subjective one in that it does not presuppose a subject that intends to intensify a bodily affect; rather, as Deleuze and Guattari put it, our capacity for intensification as living bodies is that we are able to 'proceed by differentiation' (1994: 123). Becoming a swimmer is not primarily about adding extension to our bodies, even though we may come to stretch our arms and legs a little further in the process; it is to differentiate a set of relations within our bodies that come into play when one interacts with the body of water. That is, there is the creation of *new* relations 'internal' to our biological bodies that condition the 'external' interaction with the physical body of water (though we use 'internal' and 'external' here only provisionally as this is a binary opposition that much of the literature on the body, rightly in our view, has called into question). It is this process of internal differentiation that conditions our sense of having learnt something new. This experience is subjectively rendered when we say, 'I can swim now (when before I could not),' though it is not necessary to conceive of this as the conscious acquisition of knowledge by an already formed subject. It is, as Deleuze (1991) found in Hume, simply the habit we have acquired of saying 'I' when in fact the 'I' in question is itself the result of bodily acquired habits; 'I, the swimmer'. As such, from this perspective, the acquisition of new bodily habits that we call learning also marks a change in one's internal sense of oneself. In this way, we can account for the sensation we have of being conscious and active learners, without undermining the transcendental priority of 'passive' learning.

Although this provides a way of accounting for the sensation of an active consciousness at work within the learning process, it does so retrospectively: that is, still at a distance from the sense that we have as regards the subject's active role in the learning process. The experience of being a body that is capable of actively learning new things still seems under-theorised. Is it possible to address this experience of active learning without compromising the requirement for passive learning as a transcendental condition of thought? Is it possible to articulate a non-subjective account of what we call active learning without reinstating the postulate of knowledge? These questions lead us to trace a line of inquiry within the work of Deleuze and Guattari that none the less takes us beyond their own tracings of this line. It is to follow the second trajectory towards acknowledging and addressing the experience of activity that seems to be a hallmark of human learning. The challenge is to conjugate the passive and the active registers of learning without compromising Deleuze and Guattari's critique of subjectivism.

That this does not mark a radical departure or break from Deleuze and Guattari, is evident from their last collaborative work together, *What is Philosophy?* In 'Conclusion: From Chaos to the Brain' we find the claim that guides the rest of our discussion:

> If the mental objects of philosophy, art and science (that is to say, vital ideas) have a place, it will be in the deepest of the synaptic fissures, in the hiatuses, intervals and the meantimes of a nonobjectifiable brain, in a place where to go in search of them will be to create. (1994: 209)

But in order to unpack what is at stake in this claim we must look to develop it in regard to the three bodies that we have so far discussed: the (organic, human, lived) body, the (physical) bodies in the world, and the bodies of knowledge that emerge from the engagement of the first two. As we have already argued, though, this requires that we maintain the priority of learning as a condition of thought if we are to avoid postulating the end of knowledge as that which binds the human to the world. At this point we can generalise everything we have already established about learning to swim and apply it to the three forms of knowledge about the world that we call philosophy, art and science. Each discipline, while tending towards specialised knowledge based on regulative method, establishes bodies of knowledge that themselves presuppose prior relationships that we can call bodies of learning. Learning to philosophise is not the process of simply acquiring philosophical knowledge; learning to be an artist is not simply a matter of absorbing the canon of previous artistic creations; learning to think scientifically is not simply a matter of employing the correct method. Rather it is an engagement with 'forms of thought or creation' (Deleuze and Guattari 1988: 208). As such, they are not bodies of expert knowledge, already established or progressing on the basis of what is already known. Rather, philosophy, art and science are creative disciplines, themselves bodies of learning, defined as processes of engagement with what Deleuze and Guattari call 'vital ideas'. The vitality of these ideas derives from the fact that they are 'those that must be created' to become known (1994: 207) and, as we will discuss below, the 'place' of learning (the place where the vital ideas of philosophy, art and science are created) is the nonobjectifiable brain. The primary aspect of Deleuze and Guattari's claim, in our view, is that we will not find this place of learning simply by 'looking at', by coming to know through simple observation or modelling, this nonobjectifiable brain. Rather, the place of learning will only be 'found' if we go in search of the nonobjectifiable brain by creating new relationships between the three bodies involved in the learning process: organic bodies, physical bodies and bodies of knowledge. We will argue that embedded within this claim is the link between the active and the passive sides of learning in Deleuze and Guattari; the body that learns to engage actively with the world is that which creates new bodies of learning in the world through this engagement. It is only this sense of 'active learning' that maintains learning as a transcendental condition of what it means to think.

The remainder of our discussion will unpack these claims. In the next section we provide an overview of some of the problems that persist in contemporary conceptualisations of the body and the brain; these conceptualisations are problematic, we will argue, to the extent that they retain the dominance of knowledge over the bodily processes of learning. We go on to argue that aspects of contemporary neuroscience provide a route out of these problems consonant with Deleuze's understanding of the transcendental priority of learning over knowledge. With this established, the concluding section will return to the problem of what is meant by an active, yet non-subjective, approach to the learning process.

The Body and the Nonobjectifiable Brain

There are many ways to map the literary/historical/economic/social construction of the body, but apparently few discernible contours. In our view, Grosz (1994) provides an exemplary overview of these contours, particularly with regard to what she calls 'the persistence of dualism' in modern forms of thinking about the body. It is not our intention, therefore, to retread this well-worn path. Rather, we accept with Grosz that the Cartesian dualism of soul/nature has become such a dominant configuration within the literature that attempts to surpass it often amount either to an over-emphasis upon relatively discrete contours that traverse one or another aspect of the lived body (usually discipline-specific or ideological imperatives such as the examination of gender, social relations, medicine, etc.) or to attempts at the reconciliation of the dualism that, none the less, remain problematic because still trapped within the purview of soul and nature as two discrete substances. We accept, therefore, that the Cartesian configuration is still present in many attempted post-Cartesian philosophies of the body as the *pre*figured point of reference.

With the example of swimming, we have already pointed towards a route beyond persistent dualism in our claim that there are always at least three bodies involved in learning. It remains to be seen to what extent this meets the challenge of Grosz's analysis, however, as it is necessary to articulate more fully how our three-body perspective circumvents Cartesianism. We will do this in two ways in this section (although it is not until the concluding section that this claim can be comprehensively addressed). First, we will use the perspective we have developed to make a critical assessment of two of the, in our view, most fruitful yet flawed attempts at overcoming dualist accounts of the body: those of Merleau-Ponty (2002) and Butler (1993).[1] Second, we will explore some of the ways in which recent trajectories in neuroscience give substance to a three-body perspective on the nature of learning. Although we will also express some reservations with regard to the Cartesian dualism that persists in this domain of enquiry, we turn to neuroscience with a more positive outlook than Grosz, who has claimed that 'attempts to correlate ideas or mental processes with neurological functions have thus far failed, and the project itself seems doomed' (1994: 7).

It is in the respective theorisations of the body by Merleau-Ponty and Butler that the prefiguration of Cartesian dualism meets some of its sternest challenges. Both present the body as a problem for traditional conceptions of knowledge: how is the body known 'for a subject', in Merleau-Ponty, and how is the body constructed as 'the known' of the subject, in Butler? In both cases, to problematise the body is to situate it at the porous boundary of soul and nature (as well as many other dualisms that map on to this primary Cartesian one). For Merleau-Ponty, the lived body is unknowable as an object like other objects in nature because it is the condition upon which our knowledge of those other objects is based (2002: 104–5). Correlatively, the lived body is even unknowable subjectively, as our own body, because it is impossible to objectify it while it acts as the condition for knowledge of objects. In this way, Merleau-Ponty rightly introduces some scepticism into Descartes' claims that we can know the nature of the body (*res naturans*) as that which thinking being (*res cogitans*) is not. Moreover, in place of these two discrete natures, he argues that the body is 'our means of communication' with the world, where the world is 'the horizon latent in all our experience and itself ever-present and anterior to every determining thought' (2002: 106). Thinking and being, split by Descartes, are united within this pre-reflective horizon; the body is the horizon of knowledge about the world on condition that the world itself functions as the horizon of our knowledge about our body.

In Butler's work, the critique of Cartesian dogmatism operates in a similar manner. Nature, as either the substance that is not thinking substance (sex not gender, for example) or the substance that is innately inscribed upon thought (sexual difference as the basis of gendered inscriptions upon the female body), must be replaced with a dynamic account of how nature 'materialises' in and through repeated attempts to know the nature of (sexed) nature. It is 'the materializing effects of regulatory power in the Foucaultian sense' (1993: 9–10) that give nature its internal dynamic trajectory. We come to know this dynamism by virtue of the way that it is halted in the regulative mechanisms themselves, such that they produce 'the stylised repetition of acts', albeit never halted completely or eternally. Butler's analysis can be affirmed as a critique of the Cartesian dualism of an inert nature as distinct from an active soul because what we know and how we know are locked into the same process of materialization. Indeed, both these challenges to Descartes criticise the alleged certainty of his deduction of ontological dualism by maintaining that the nature of the body is an on-going epistemic problem. Knowledge of the body, therefore, becomes one of the privileged sites of post-Cartesian philosophy.

The insightful nature of these approaches is beyond doubt. It is our claim, however, that they remain flawed by virtue of being constrained within a perspective that privileges what we have called the body of knowledge over the lived, organic body and the physical bodies with which it interacts. In Merleau-Ponty (2002), this is evident in his construction of the pre-reflective horizon as the de-subjectified and de-objectified condition of intelligibility of subjects and objects. This may indeed undermine Cartesian dualism by situating subject and object on the same terrain. None the less, the latency of the horizon prefigures what can be known of the body by overdetermining the process of interaction between bodies in and of the world as an intelligible process with knowledge of the horizon itself as its end. The case of Butler is similar in that she also postulates the priority of knowledge over learning but she does this through privileging the regulative mechanisms through which bodies emerge as knowable. In situating these regulative mechanisms at the centre of knowledge she foregrounds the methodological materi- alisation of what is known as nature. Although she discusses the ways in which non-regulated bodies emerge as a challenge to body norms, there is no fundamental challenge to the priority of the epistemological problematic. As such, any account of the real interaction of bodies con- stitutive of learning must always remain 'relative to a linguistic domain' (1993: 207). Both Merleau-Ponty and Butler, therefore, reinstate the postulate of knowledge that Deleuze argues is one of the struts under- pinning the dogmatic image of thought. To know the body as embodied within a horizon of intelligibility and to know the body as it emerges in our regulated knowledge of it are two strategies that still privilege knowledge itself over the bodily process of learning that condition the emergence of such knowledge. As such, there is still a lurking dogmatism in these attempts to complicate our knowledge of the body because the known, however complicated, is still said to condition the emergence of learning (not the other way around). That 'what is known' is constituted as a problem – as lived on the horizon of the intelligible or as enacted through regulatory frameworks – marks an advance on Descartes in that it dispenses with the dualism of an active soul that conditions the inert nature of nature itself. Yet, as long as the body is situated as a problem of knowledge, that which is said to be known about the body will tend to be imposed upon the lived and physical bodies in much the same way that Descartes' deduction of the necessity of a soul imposed itself upon the existence of nature by conditioning it as inert. In this we follow Deleuze and Guattari's claim that, 'in the cerebral domain par excellence of apprenticeship or the formation of habits' that we call learning, 'the occurrences, must, as Hume showed, be contracted in a contemplating "imagination" while remaining distinct in relation . . . to knowledge' (1994: 213).[2] In the concluding section, we will return to this critique of the privileged role of knowledge vis-à-vis learning by way of Alliez's account of 'the concept as a real being, a fold of the brain folding in on itself, micro-brain' (2004: 82). But first, we will discuss what current trends in neuroscience reveal about both the persistence of dualism and the bodily nature of learning.

The task as we see it is this: is it possible to articulate the three bodies that interact in learning (including the body of knowledge) in a way that establishes these in a relationship of co-emergence rather than in rela- tionships that privilege one of the three (typically, after Descartes, the body of knowledge) as the condition for the emergence of the other two? It is our view that this task requires us to challenge Grosz's claim about the necessarily 'doomed' nature of neuroscientific accounts of the brain. We will argue that it is in a non-Cartesian, non-reductive account of the brain that we find the means to articulate the relationships that support the co-emergent nature of the three-fold bodily interaction that, with Deleuze, we call learning. In this sense, the persistence of Cartesianism may not simply or even primarily reside in the persistent reiteration of substance-dualism but in the privileged place of knowledge within Descartes' philosophy that led him to deduce these two discrete substances in the first instance. Perhaps the real challenge to Cartesianism lies not in reconfiguring how we know what we know but in dethroning the epistemological project itself by considering the body of knowledge on the same material plane of existence as the lived and the physical bodies? Perhaps the challenge is to treat learning as an ontological rather than an epistemological problem?

It is clear that there are research trajectories in contemporary neuroscience that are moving beyond reductive accounts of the brain in their own attempts to overcome the legacy of Cartesian dualism in their disciplinary presumptions. Modell sums up the current state of the discipline well when he says: '[n]o philosopher or scientist today is a substance dualist; no one believes in an immaterial mind. However, Descartes' influence has been so profound that traces of this Cartesian duality persist even among eminent scientists' (2003: 195). Without necessarily endorsing the sweeping nature of this claim, we would agree and have argued above that the legacy of Cartesianism is so profound that even some of the most challenging philosophical attempts to overcome it have not succeeded. Just as many philosophers, Grosz included, are looking to overcome dualism within philosophy, so it is that some neuroscientists are not as fatalistic as Grosz about their own discipline despite its dualist tendencies. It is our view that Grosz rather pre-empts what the neuroscientific project is capable of achieving by dismissing it as inherently 'doomed' because reductive. Rather, we would argue, neuroscience and philosophy find themselves in a similar place. As we will show, both neuroscience and philosophy are looking to push the boundaries of their disciplinary languages to encompass non-reductive accounts of the brain's role in what we have called the three bodies: the lived, the world and knowledge. In our view, therefore, it is clear that the possibility exists for a productively porous boundary between neuroscientific discourses and those of philosophy.

Approaching a critique of Cartesianism from the perspective of neuroscience, therefore, can create new possibilities for thinking about the relationship between lived bodies, physical bodies and bodies of knowledge. The first claim that guides the neuroscientific move in this direction is summed up neatly by O'Shea; the brain is not 'an independent agent, residing in splendid and lofty superiority in our skulls . . . the word "brain" is a shorthand for all of the interdependent, interactive processes of a complex dynamical system consisting of the brain, the body, and the outside world' (2005: 3). From our point of view, this marks a significant advance because it opens up the problem of their interdependency rather than viewing this as the problem of how two incompossible substances can interact. As Rose expresses it, '[t]he point about brains is that they are open, not closed, systems in continued interaction with their environments' (1998: 14–15). Rose extrapolates what he means by 'environment' as follows: 'for humans, that environment is both the immediate present constituted by the society in which we are embedded, and the past, expressed in our individual and social histories' (15). He goes on: '[c]onsciousness is fundamentally a social phenomenon, not the property of an individual brain or mind. Of course, Marx said something similar back in the nineteenth century and so, as I was recently reminded, did Nietzsche' (15). Is it not the case, however, that Rose's appeal to the social nature of the 'environment' constitutes a surreptitious reinstitution of dualism?

The concern that leads us to ask this question is that the argumentative strategy employed by Rose is by no means self-evident. To conclude that conscious awareness is 'social' because it is not 'the product of an individual brain or mind' only follows if we presuppose that the necessary conceptual opposite of the individual is the social. From the perspective of contemporary sociological and philosophical thinking this necessity is not without its problems. More to the point, perhaps, it may also be the case that these are not even the right concepts to use when talking of 'the environment' (must we presume that the environment *is* social as opposed to individual?). In our view, these presumptions compromise his understanding of the interconnected nature of the brain and the world. The source of this compromise is that, in using a philosophical 'system of description' within, or as an adjunct to, a neurobiological one, he risks reinstituting dualism by embracing too rapidly some of the contested concepts of these philosophical perspectives. As we have already argued, with regard to Merleau-Ponty and Butler, even some of the most sensitive and challenging philosophical theories about the body's relationship to the world, theories that explicitly challenge notions of the individual and the social, are overcoded with a latent Cartesianism by virtue of privileging the constitutive nature of knowledge in the founding of this interaction.

Despite this critique, treating the brain as an extended bodily system interacting with its environment may be productive if we specify further aspects of this interaction and interdependency. Singer (1998) provides one interesting way of developing what is meant by interdependency, particularly with regard to how our sense of ourselves as conscious beings is conditioned by these interactions. He argues that

> one does not have to take a dualistic stance to account for the seemingly immaterial attributes of the self. The reason why I think these attributes transcend the reach of purely neurobiological reductionism is that they come into existence only through communication among different brains. (1998: 241)

It is Singer's view, therefore, that the human experience of subjective awareness is the product of a prior 'communication'. It is important to stress, however, that Singer views this 'communication' as occurring 'among *different* brains'. This is not, therefore, a return to Merleau-Ponty's invocation of a pre-subjective horizon of intelligibility, as communication among different brains does not, in our view, presuppose knowledge of our subjective experience. Rather, in proposing the differentiated nature of each 'brain' that communicates with others, Singer is arguing that any knowledge of ourselves – no matter how intertwined with the world as horizon (or regulatory framework) – is conditioned by the prior emergence of differentiated brains that have the capacity for communicating with each other. Communication occurs, we can say, before the horizon of the self and the world is formed. To reiterate our response to Rose, the neurobiological meaning of 'environment' is not necessarily analogous to the individual/social dichotomy. In our view, this claim resonates with Deleuze and Guattari's dispute with phenomenology: it is 'the brain that thinks and not man' (1994: 210).

We make these connections despite Singer's own retreat to the language of 'the social' in his attempt to rethink the 'emergent properties of brains'. As with Rose, care is needed when invoking 'the social' as this description itself may reinstitute the Cartesian dualisms that neuroscientists like Singer are looking to overcome in their own discipline. More productively, however, Singer's account of communication among differentiated brains provides the resources with which to substantiate the priority of learning over knowledge as it provides one way of understanding what Deleuze and Guattari meant by the 'nonobjectified brain'. The argument has these steps. Recalling O'Shea's claim that 'the word "brain" is a shorthand for all of the interdependent, interactive processes of a complex dynamical system consisting of the brain, the body, and the outside world' (2005: 3), it would be more accurate to state that the brain's role in the emergence of subjectivity is dependent upon the prior differentiation of the brain in other bodies. Singer makes the point well when he says that without pre-subjective communication, self-awareness 'would simply not exist' (1998: 242). However, in our view, and given Singer's account of 'communication', there is no need to privilege the communicative capacities of human bodies with each other over the communication between lived (organic but non-human) bodies more generally; witness Singer's own discussion of precognitive awareness in non-humans (1998: 230–3). By extension, it seems to us unnecessary to privilege communication (in Singer's sense) at the organic level over that which occurs between physical bodies understood in the Deleuzian sense of organised systems of differential relations. In which case, it makes sense to talk of the brain of the body of water communicating with the brain of the human learning to swim. Indeed, it is telling that Singer describes the capacity for communication between differentiated brains as 'a dynamic selection process' (1998: 231): a process that occurs for all systems of differential relations. That is, all bodies (though not in the same way, as it is important to recall Deleuze's specification of the organic body as capable of intensifying that which affects it) contain this capacity for communication. At which point, we can specify Deleuze and Guattari's understanding of the 'nonobjectifiable brain'; it is 'non-objectifiable' precisely because it emerges through a process of pre-subjective communication understood as a process of selection. As we have already characterised this process of selection as the learning that occurs through bodily interaction – the selection of dynamic relations between the lived body and the body of water in swimming, for example – we can now conclude that learning 'amongst differentiated brains' has a transcendental priority to any knowledge we have of that learning process. We have already acknowledged the importance of differentiation in our discussion of Deleuze and Guattari in the double sense that each of the three bodies involved in learning is differentiated from the other and each lived body is differentiated from other lived bodies by virtue of being a particular expression of the organisation of the lived, the human. What we have gained by considering Singer's account is that the communication he highlights between differentiated brains is both pre-subjective yet expressed through the emergence of the brain as a system of differential relations: that is, as a body. Where we differ from Singer is that we prefer, with Deleuze, to call this communication learning.

At which point it would seem that we have simply 'found' the place of 'vital ideas' in the nonobjectifiable brain. Yet, we have said all along that we wish to follow the trajectory of Deleuze and Guattari's claim that to locate these vital ideas in the brain one has 'to go in search of them' by creating. To pursue this trajectory we have to focus on the body of knowledge. Can we understand the body of knowledge as the product of bodily processes of learning and can we understand this production as an active, yet pre-subjective, process? Is it possible to trace the body's emergence as a brain as we have just traced the brain's emergence as a body? In the next section we will see that the answer to these questions requires that we consider the body of knowledge as a brain communicating with other brains, in the sense that we have now elaborated.

Bodies of Learning as the Condition of True Critique

We have argued, with regard to both philosophy and neuroscience, that attempts to overcome dualism have created a set of ideas that usefully complicate our grasp of the body in the world: one from the perspective of the worldliness of the body, the other from the perspective of worldliness of the brain (such that both dethrone the mind as the otherworldliness of the subject that knows). However, both trajectories still contain traces of Cartesianism to the extent that they presuppose that knowledge of the body in the world is constitutive of our sense of subjectivity (thereby reinstating the knowing subject upon the throne of the world). In this sense, the postulate of knowledge is re-inscribed on to this newly complicated terrain. The result is that the bodily acquisition of habit that we call learning remains subordinate to the end of knowledge; the body of knowledge is conceptualised as that which conditions the learning that brings bodily being into the world. That said, we have also traced a trajectory within neuroscience, as mapped by Singer, which established a neuroscientific rendering of Deleuze and Guattari's invocation of a 'nonobjectifiable brain'. What remains to be done is to connect bodies of learning to the philosophical construction of knowledge in a manner that does not return to a privileged subjectivity and that does not, therefore, reinstate the priority of knowledge over learning. Deleuze's example of learning how to swim, as we have discussed above, suggests that overcoming the philosophical roots of Cartesian dualism will not be achieved by privileging the body of knowledge over how we learn but by learning, creatively, how knowledge emerges as a body.

What does this mean? We will give two answers to this question. The first is ontological in that it presents bodies of learning as the real condition for the emergence of knowledge. The second is critical in that it activates this ontological claim as a mode of creative experimentation in the world. In the end we will see that these are not so different. As Deleuze puts it in *Difference and Repetition*,

> The conditions of a true critique and a true creation are the same: the destruction of an image of thought which presupposes itself and the genesis of the act of thinking in thought itself. Something in the world forces us to think. This something is an object not of recognition but of a fundamental encounter. (1994: 139)

The 'fundamental encounter' is learning, but the first task in order to reach this claim is to establish the role of bodies of learning in 'the genesis of the act of thinking'.

In our view, Alliez provides the best account to date of how this can be understood within Deleuze and Guattari's ontological system when he elaborates the 'pedagogy of the concept' that animates *What is Philosophy?* (2004: 6). The task of a 'pedagogy of the concept' is the production of 'the concept of the concept'. On Alliez's account of this pedagogy there is a two-fold movement of the concept that signals its production as concept. On the one hand, there is the self-positing of the concept. As Deleuze and Guattari (1994) make clear in their discussion of philosophy, every conceptual creation is also the simultaneous production of the plane of immanence that the concept surveys and a conceptual persona that establishes the perspective of the concept to the plane. As we have shown above, the concept 'learning' can be said to institute a plane of immanence that is populated by a form of pre-subjective communication amongst differentiated brains instantiated in lived and physical bodies. Moreover, we can now add that what we have called the body of knowledge is a perspective that emerges within the interaction of bodies we call learning. Knowledge is not the end of learning; rather, it is a perspective upon the learning that takes place. Knowledge emerges 'as one learns'; it is not that which learning must presuppose as end. Maintaining the perspectival nature of the body of knowledge vis-à-vis learning is not an easy task: for example, the tendency within philosophy and neuroscience to treat the body of knowledge as that which determines the nature of the learning that occurs between bodies. However, this understanding of the concept of learning as that which resists determination as knowledge does not in itself address the conceptuality of learning as that which occurs beyond its presentation in a form of philosophical idealism.[3] The pedagogy of the concept of learning has yet to reach to 'the pedagogy of the concept of the concept'. As Alliez makes clear, the self-positing of the concept can only be understood if there is also a materiality to the concept itself. We must address, he says, 'a pedagogy of the concept that is also its material ontology' (2004: 23). This is the second movement of the self-positing concept.

It is a movement that Alliez traces initially to the body and then to the brain (though perhaps too quickly, as we will come to argue). The movement he traces is from the conceptualisation of bodies and brains to the materialisation of the body and brain of the concept. Recalling the Spinozist critique of Cartesian dualism at the heart of Deleuze and Guattari's discussion of philosophy, Alliez situates the real emergence of concepts in the 'affections of the body' (2004: 27). Once conceived in this way, as he demonstrates, there is no disagreement to be had between the 'order and connection' between lived and physical bodies and the 'order and connection' between concepts that establish a body of knowledge.[4] In the lexicon that we have deployed, this amounts to the claim that the body is the material site of the production of learning *and* the perspective that knowledge brings to this productive process; or, better still (and with the help of Singer), the communication between bodies is the process of learning that simultaneously gives rise to the body of the concept (that knows). It follows then that learning is not just a concept of the real of knowledge but it is primarily the real of the pedagogy of the concept; learning *is* the concept of the concept. Learning both conditions the production of the known and is the real genesis of conceptuality itself. What we have referred to above as the co-emergence of the three bodies in learning can now be specified: learning occurs as the communication between bodies that produces knowledge as a perspective upon that communication, where communication itself is now understood as the real production of concepts as bodies.

In a move we agree is decisive in reading Deleuze and Guattari, Alliez refers to the real production of concepts as 'an operation of being' called 'brain'. The brain 'is ontology delivered over to the pragmatics of being' (2004: 62). In what sense does the brain deliver ontology to pragmatics? Alliez refers to this process as 'the creation of self-determining concepts' (2004: 64). As we have expressed it, though, this process must occur between bodies in order to ward off any latent idealism of the self-positing concept; that is, it is a process of bodily communication. As such, the brain can be understood as that which expresses that communication. The brain inhabits a body but only to the extent that it is the result of communication between bodies that creates the brain: ontology delivered to pragmatics, in Alliez's incisive phrase. In this sense, we can avoid the latent Cartesianism of some neuroscientific accounts by conceiving of the brain as the process of interaction between bodies that we call learning. Even Singer's account of 'communication amongst differentiated brains' can be further specified: the communication is between differentiated bodies and it is this communication that *is* the brain among these bodies. Therefore knowledge, to the extent that it is found in brains, is not located in a brain that belongs to an individual (human being); rather, knowledge is embodied in the brain that is produced by the interaction of bodies in the world. Knowledge, that is, can never be possessed by an individual subject; rather it is produced in the communication between bodies that conditions how we learn to become subjects.

In this sense, we can specify Alliez's account of the brain as 'an operation of being' when we say that the brain is that process of communication that enables bodies to learn how to become, to be, and to keep becoming, a body. In which case, the becoming-brain of learning is always inscribed within a becoming-body of learning and there is a mutual and irreducible conditioning of the one by the other. This is the transcendental condition of a post-Cartesian philosophy of the body and a post-Cartesian neuroscience of the brain. Moreover, maintaining this condition as the real of the pedagogy of the concept will not occur unless the body and the brain are conceptualised in the same movement of thought. Where that movement is maintained, learning is the 'genesis of the act of thinking in thought itself' now understood as the becoming-brain of bodies and the becoming-body of brains.

While this ontological account establishes both the necessity of bodies and the necessity of communication between bodies that constitute brains as conditions for the real emergence of learning as the transcendental condition of thought, we must return to Deleuze and Guattari's enigmatic claim that to go in search of the place of vital ideas in the nonobjectifiable brain is to create. It is this claim that gives their ontological subversion of epistemology a critical dimension, in the sense that Deleuze refers to a 'true critique' as an act of creation. We return, therefore, to the question that emerged from our consideration of learning how to swim: can the creative dimension of learning be expressed in a form that does not subvert Deleuze's account of the passive synthesis of the sensible? This question can now be recast as follows: how does learning function as the real condition for the emergence of a true critique?

On the one hand, this real conditionality is provided by the destruction of knowledge claims that do not acknowledge the learning that constitutes them. It is one of the fundamental elements of a true critique that it must hold all knowledge claims, including those that emerge within the critique itself, as perspectival to the concept and the plane it institutes. On the other hand, such destruction is only possible where learning is able to flourish within the critique itself. For learning to flourish, the real conditions for the emergence of concepts must be maintained; namely, the communication that occurs between bodies, their instantiation as brains, must remain open to new forms of becoming (where this means new forms of the individuation of bodies and brains). This does not simply mean new ideas, at least not if these are understood as the product of a subject's synthesis of the world. Rather, it means that there must be a creative experimentation between bodies in the world, where bodies are understood as systems of differential relations, as objective ideas. Deleuze was fond of Spinoza's claim that 'we do not yet know what a body can do' (1992: 217–34); learning becomes active to the extent that it becomes an expression of what our bodies are capable of doing. But what they are capable of, above all (so to speak), is the creation of a vital idea as the brain of bodily interaction (not the creation of ideas located in the brain of a human body). To find the vital ideas of the nonobjectifiable brain is to create because it is to make new brains. Equally, we can now say that to go in search of the vital ideas in the brain is to create because it is to create new bodies of learning within the real.

References

Alliez, E. (2004), *The Signature of the World: What is Deleuze and Guattari's Philosophy?*, London: Continuum.

Butler, J. (1993), *Bodies That Matter: On the Discursive Limits of Sex*, London: Routledge.

Deleuze, G. (1988), *Spinoza: Practical Philosophy*, San Francisco: City Lights.

Deleuze, G. (1991), *Empiricism and Subjectivity: An Essay on Hume's Theory of Human Nature*, New York: Columbia University Press.

Deleuze, G. (1992), *Expressionism in Philosophy: Spinoza*, New York: Zone.

Deleuze, G. (1994), *Difference and Repetition*, New York: Columbia University Press.

Deleuze, G. and F. Guattari (1988), *A Thousand Plateaus: Capitalism and Schizophrenia, vol. 2*, London: Athlone.

Deleuze, G. and F. Guattari (1994), *What is Philosophy?*, London: Verso.

Grosz, E. (1994), *Volatile Bodies: Toward a Corporeal Feminism*, Bloomington: Indiana University Press.

MacKenzie, I. (1997), 'Creativity as Criticism: The Philosophical Constructivism of Deleuze and Guattari', *Radical Philosophy* 86, pp. 7–18.

Merleau-Ponty, M. (2002), *Phenomenology of Perception*, London: Routledge.

Modell, A. H. (2003), *Imagination and the Meaningful Brain*, Cambridge, MA: MIT Press.

O'Shea, M. (2005), *The Brain: A Very Short Introduction*, Oxford: Oxford University Press.

Rose, S. (1998), 'Brains, Minds and the World' in *From Brains to Consciousness? Essays on the New Sciences of the Mind*, ed. S. Rose, London: Penguin, pp. 1–17.

Singer, W. (1998), 'Consciousness from a Neurobiological Perspective' in *From Brains to Consciousness? Essays on the New Sciences of the Mind*, ed. S. Rose, London: Penguin, pp. 228–45.

Williams, J. (2003), *Gilles Deleuze's* Difference and Repetition: *A Critical Introduction and Guide*, Edinburgh: Edinburgh University Press.

Notes

1. Our primary points of reference will be *Phenomenology of Perception* and *Bodies That Matter*. We recognise that the thought of each thinker has trajectories within it that include refinements and self-critiques to the positions elaborated within these texts. It is not the aim of this discussion to map these trajectories within their respective œuvres.

2. The ellipsis removes a reference to 'action', where action is defined as that which is intended by the subject, not the interaction of bodies that constitute subjectivity.

3. See MacKenzie (1997) for an account of how Deleuze and Guattari's constructivist presentation of philosophy can be read as a challenge to philosophical idealism.

4. He quotes Spinoza: 'the order and connection of ideas is the same as the order and connection of things and, vice versa, the order and connection of things is the same as the order and connection of ideas' (Alliez 2004: 28).

Chapter 4

Believing in the World: Toward an Ethics of Form

Joe Hughes

We need an ethics or a faith.[1]

(Deleuze 1989: 173)

Cinema 1 could, without too much distortion, be read as an extended theory of the body. Adapting some of Bergson's theses from *Matter and Memory* to his own ends, Deleuze outlines the body's immersion in matter; he describes the ways in which it subtracts itself from this matter by selecting, reorganizing, and reacting to it; and, through the theory of the cliché, he begins to account for the ways in which the body can be co-opted and covered over by codes, concepts, institutions, and rituals. Ultimately it is the body that 'explains' cinema. Cinema's images 'express' perception, affection, and action, and its narrative would be unrecognizable were it not for the natural causality of the action-image.

Cinema 2, however, begins with the crisis of action. Characters no longer know how to respond to situations, and, like Karin on the side of Stromboli's volcano, they freeze in moments of helplessness. In this crisis of action, the body vanishes from the horizon of Deleuze's inquiry. Cinema becomes defined as thought and thought becomes defined as a set of alogical connections and irrational cuts aligned along an infinite series of anamorphoses. What is more, this state of non-action, in which cinema comes into contact not with perception, feeling, or action, but with a disembodied, 'immaterial' thought, does not simply represent the inactivity of cinema; it represents cinema's essence.

We could therefore characterize Deleuze's conception of cinema as one which celebrates its essence as disembodied inactivity. In Deleuze we move from Eisenstein to Ozu, from affirming the dissolution of the individual in a revolutionary élan to staring at a vase waiting for time to show itself in its purity. Peter Hallward has argued that this escape from the world and from action is the trajectory of Deleuze's thought in general, and the cinema books would seem to confirm this better than many of the others.[2] But is this where Deleuze leaves us? Paralyzed in optical and sound situations whose only redeeming quality is a transcendental experience of empty time? In fact, the final chapters of *Cinema 2* return to a conception of the body – a body that is no longer sensory-motor, or passive, but active.[3] It is this movement that I want to begin to trace here, and in particular I want to try to make sense of Deleuze's claim that this return depends on a faith – or an ethics.

The Body-Hyphen

To do so, it is worth briefly reviewing Deleuze's 'deduction' of the body in *Cinema 1*. Deleuze asks us to grant him two concepts: a plane of immanence and an interval on that plane.

The plane of immanence is the apparently unregulated interaction of matter. It is a tumultuous world in which material elements, 'images', act and react on one another in all their parts and facets to infinity.

> Let us call the set of what appears 'Image'. We cannot even say that one image acts on another or reacts to another. There is no moving body (*mobile*) which is distinct from executed movement. There is nothing moved which is distinct from the received movement. Every thing, that is to say every image, is indistinguishable from its actions and reactions: this is universal variation. Every image is 'merely a road by which pass, in every direction, the modifications propagated throughout the immensity of the universe'. *Every image acts on others and reacts to others, on 'all their facets at once' and 'by all their elements'*.[4]

The plane of immanence, or the 'set of what appears', is indeed a field of matter in flux, but the fact that these elements – images – are material is hardly what is most important for Deleuze, and asserting a simple materialism is not at the fore of his agenda. The plane of immanence is not so much as a field of pure material bodies, but the 'universal *variation*' of bodies. Whatever appears in this set is entirely dissolved in its affections and reactions, and to be a body, as he put it in *Expressionism and Philosophy*, is to be 'affected in a very great number of ways'.[5] It is this uninterrupted and universal rhythm of action and reaction that defines the plane of immanence.

The importance of this definition becomes clear in the second given of the deduction: the interval. The interval interrupts the immediate transformation of action into reaction by introducing a space of delay between two movements. 'By virtue of the interval' there are now 'delayed reactions which have time to *select* their elements, to *organize* them or to *integrate* them into a new movement' (1986: 62; my emphases). In the interval, reaction no longer follows immediately from action. Movements are selected, organized, and then reintegrated back into the plane of immanence.

Bergson calls this originary delay the body. The body is 'a *place of passage* of the movements received and thrown back, a hyphen, a connecting link between the things which act upon me and the things upon which I act – the seat, in a word, of the sensory-motor phenomena' (Bergson 1991: 152). Both Deleuze and Bergson will emphasize that the body is part of the world – it is, 'in this material world, that part of which we directly feel the flux' (Bergson 1991: 139) – but the overwhelming emphasis at this early stage seems to fall on its function as a hyphen. It is a 'connecting link' between action and reaction – a link that is also a pause which gives the body time to select, organize, and reintegrate its (re)actions.

This changes the nature of the relation between action and reaction. Whereas images on the plane of immanence acted on and reacted to one another in all of their parts in an infinite communication,[6] now, by virtue of the interval, the body mediates action and reaction, and in doing so, it changes the character of action and reaction. The actions of other bodies on mine become 'excitations' which my body perceives. Reactions become 'my actions'. The mediating gap, a space of retention and organization, is called 'affection'. Thus the deduction shows the formal possibility of differentiating subjectivity into three basic forms: perception, affection, and action; selection, organization, integration. From this point of view we could say that the entire assemblage of sensory-motor subjectivity that animates *Cinema 1* never steps outside a theory of the body.

However, Deleuze rarely speaks of 'the body' in his deduction. He seems to prefer the expression 'interval'. I think it is here that we first encounter a significant difference between the Bergson of *Matter and Memory* and Deleuze. In Deleuze's commentary on Bergson, he does take up the word 'body', but he increasingly qualifies it to the point that we have to wonder whether there is anything there at all:

My body is an image, hence a set of actions and reactions. My eye, my brain, are images, parts of my body. [. . .] External images act on me, transmit movement to me, and I return movement: how could images be in my consciousness since I am myself image, that is, movement? And can I even, at this level, speak of 'ego', of eye, of brain and of body? Only for simple convenience; for nothing can yet be identified in this way. It is rather a gaseous state. Me, my body, are rather a set of molecules

and atoms which are constantly renewed. Can I even speak of atoms?
(1986: 58)

Here we have the central components of the Bergsonian body. The body
is an image; it participates directly in the flux of matter; it is a center
of indetermination which allows me to select, organize, and transmit
received movements. But it is just as clear that the body is not yet the
fully constituted body. It is an unconstituted, 'gaseous' body. Depending
on our taste for imagery we could follow Deleuze in *The Logic of Sense*
and say either that our body is dissolved in matter like a drop of wine
in the ocean or that it is uncontrollably tossed about in a universal cesspool.[7] In either case, ocean or cesspool, it seems that Deleuze is saying
simultaneously that our body is a part of this flux and that it is not
yet our body; we can only call it 'a body' for the sake of convenience
because it not yet anything more than a hyphen which is 'constantly
renewed'. Our body is not yet constituted as a body. It is dissolved in
the sea of universal variation, in the 'primeval soup' of consciousness or
of life (1986: 63).

The deduction of the body, then, is not a simple conceptual deduction. It is rather something like the post-Kantian's genetic deduction,
one which does not simply show, conceptually, the possibility of
the body but attempts to capture it in its process of production.[8] (In
Expressionism and Philosophy, Deleuze will claim that 'this process is
that of all generation or formation, that is of all coming into existence'
and not just that of living bodies as the context of Bergsonism might
suggest (1992: 210).) As we move from the gaseous body to the acting
body, the interval itself becomes increasingly more determined, its
passive memory accumulating more and more potential configurations
of the body, until the body itself takes on its 'characteristic relation'.

The first half of the story of this process of production is as follows.
The body begins its life dissolved in a very great number of affections,
subject to the 'laws of communication of movement' (Deleuze 1992:
210). But, by means of the interval, it is able to 'select' or 'perceive'
only a small number of these affections (perception-image). By means
of a passive memory it is able to 'organize' and 'record' these selected
affections (affection-image). And, finally, it is able to 'reintegrate' these
recorded affections as it needs them (action-image). By means of this
process of selection, organization, and reintegration, the gaseous body
begins to take on its 'characteristic relations' or the 'structure' which
defines it.[9]

Cinema's role in this is complicated. On the one hand, Deleuze will constantly claim that it is this theory of images and their combinations that 'explains' cinema. This is a well-grounded table of images which lets us classify what we see in actual films in the same way that Linnaeus's table allowed him to classify what he saw in his plants.[10] On the other hand, however, cinema has a revelatory function, and it can explain, in turn, these various stages in the progressive development of the body. As Paola Marrati puts it, cinema transforms here into an 'instrument in service of revelation' (Marrati 2008: 41). For Deleuze, Beckett can bring us all the way back to the 'plane of matter and its cosmic eddying of movement-images' (1986: 68). Deleuze will find somebody else for each subsequent moment. Vertov shows us 'the *genetic element* of all possible perception' (83; original emphasis). Duras and Michael Snow reveal the genetic element of the affection-image (122). Kazan shows us the genetic element of the action-image (155).

But this is only the first half of the story. The body that is produced here is almost entirely passive, or sensory-motor. The kind of action we see in the action-image in *Cinema 1* is an involuntary, almost reflexive, action.

Crises in Recognition

The action-image is the third moment of the passive – or sensory-motor – subject, the moment of reintegration into the plane of immanence. It is one of the most complex of all the images, but in its most general structure it is relatively straightforward: 'we enter into the realm of the action-image' when 'qualities and powers are apprehended as actualized in states of things' (1989: 123). The action-image is the synthesis of two things: 'qualities and powers' and 'states of things'. 'Qualities and powers' are the components of the affection-image. In the action-image these powers and qualities are 'apprehended as actualized in states of things'. In other words, affections are folded back on to states of things, or perceptions. The affection-image is combined with the perception-image. This is exactly the genetic definition of the action-image: 'The pair of *object* and *emotion* thus appears in the action-image as its genetic sign' (158; my emphasis). From a genetic point of view the action-image is the synthesis of perception (object) and affection (emotion). This unity constitutes a preliminary link between 'man' and 'world'.

In Bergson this unity of a perception with a memory is called 'recognition'.[11] Recognition is 'the concrete process by which we grasp the past in the present' or the way we utilize a 'past experience for a present action' (Bergson 1991: 90, 78). From this point of view Deleuze remains thoroughly Bergsonian; the action-image is a synthesis of recognition.

For Bergson there are two types of recognition, involuntary and voluntary, and it is important to emphasize that the kind with which we are concerned in the action-image and its eventual crisis is only the first kind of recognition: sensory-motor or involuntary recognition. Involuntary recognition has several important characteristics. First, it is entirely pre-representational. It is an 'instantaneous recognition, of which the body is capable by itself, without the help of any explicit memory-image. It consists in action and not in representation' (1991: 93). Bergson will often say that in motor recognition the past is not represented, but acted. Second, and closely related, involuntary recognition, as the name suggests, is habitual, passive, and does not require the intervention of an active, conscious mind. It is composed of 'motor mechanisms created by repetition'. 'Our whole life is passed among a limited number of objects,' Bergson tells us.

> Each of them, as it is perceived, provokes on our part movements, at least nascent, whereby we adapt ourselves to it. These movements, as they recur, contrive a mechanism for themselves, grow into habit, and determine in us *attitudes* which automatically follow our perception of things. (1991: 84; my emphasis)

Sensory-motor recognition thus remains on the plane of immanence, in the world of action and reaction. It never passes through representation or conscious activity. The cosmic eddies on the plane of immanence throw trillions of excitations our way, and our body passively adapts itself to them. It 'contrives a mechanism' for coping with various excitations, and our responses, or reactions, are not expressed in representations, but in bodily *attitudes* or *postures* (81–2).

There are, however, important systematic differences between Deleuze and Bergson that emerge at this point. Both Deleuze and Bergson – unlike Kant – make the failure of recognition an integral part of their philosophy, but Deleuze will take this considerably further than Bergson. In *Matter and Memory*, there is indeed something like a crisis in the action-image; recognition fails repeatedly. In an unfamiliar situation, for example, I might not be able to find a habitual response in my affective memory. In such a situation, Bergson says, I have to pay attention and penetrate more deeply into the object. And, further, I have to mobilize memory-images which will allow me to respond actively to received movements. I have to become active and figure out the nature of my new world. The whole dialectic between body and world moves from the pre-representational world of motor memory to the representational world of attentive perception and memory-images. But this hardly constitutes a crisis. It is simply a fact of life. In fact, it seems that memory rather likes it. Cut off from the real, and powerless to realize itself by itself, memory exerts a constant pressure on the body, waiting for a chance to slip back into the real (1991: 152–3).

> Always inhibited by the practical and useful consciousness of the present moment, that is to say, by the sensori-motor equilibrium of a nervous system connecting perception with action, this memory merely awaits the occurrence of a rift between the actual impression and its corresponding movement to slip in its images. (95)

Memory cannot realize itself of its own accord; it merely waits. And when a rift – a crisis in the action-image – occurs, memory 'slips in' to the body. (Bergson uses this verb consistently.) What I want to emphasize here is that this active or voluntary recognition appears as a backup plan. In the event that sensory-motor recognition fails, intellectual recognition slips in and fills the gap. It not only gives the body what it needs to determine an action, but, in exchange, 'memory borrows' from the body 'the warmth which gives it life' (153). In other words, in Bergson the man–world link is immediately restored. The only cases when the link is not restored are those in which it is quite literally severed: 'cerebral lesions' or 'diseases of the faculty of recognition' (107–8).

Deleuze, however, makes this crisis of recognition an integral part of non-diseased subjectivity in general. At the end of *Cinema 1* we remain entirely within the context of the failure of involuntary recognition, and this is where *Cinema 2* begins: 'This is the first aspect of the new cinema: the break in the sensory-motor link (action-image), and more profoundly in the link between man and the world (great organic composition)' (1989: 173). In the early chapters of *Cinema 2*, however, Deleuze progressively takes away the prospects of a voluntary recognition slipping into this gap. In German expressionism and certain surrealist films, a 'character finds himself prey to visual and sound sensations', just as the characters of Antonioni and Rossellini had when their involuntary recognition failed. With the expressionists and surrealists, however, 'these actual sensations and perceptions are as cut off from memory-based recognition as they are from motor recognition' (55). What we finally reach in the early Welles is something beyond all recognition: 'as soon as we reach the sheets of past it is as if we were carried away by the undulations of a great wave, time gets out of joint, and we enter into temporality as a state of *permanent crisis*' (112; original emphasis). The crisis in recognition thus throws us into time itself, but it gives us time as a permanent crisis.

In Deleuze, then, the failure of recognition does not lead to a new opportunity for memory. The opposite is the case. The turn to voluntary recognition in a representational memory becomes not only 'pointless', but 'impossible'. By the end of his career,

> Welles is no longer content to show the pointlessness of an evocation of the past, in a permanent state of crisis of time; he shows the impossibility of any evocation, the becoming-impossible of evocation in a still more fundamental state of time. (1989: 114)

And not even Welles goes far enough for Deleuze, because in Welles, 'a fixed point persists' (116). What cinema, in the hands of Resnais and Artaud, finally shows us is 'time as perpetual crisis', as a pure 'sheet of transformation' or a 'network of non-localizable relations' which subtends all sheets of past and which holds them together (123). We come face to face with the 'aleatory point' (175) or the impossibility of thinking that is thought. Thought loses its character as a 'regime of localizable relations, actual linkages, legal causal and logical connections' (127), and becomes instead an infinite overlapping of perspectives defined by relationships which make no immediate sense and by connections which have no apparent relation to the demands of action or life (129–30). It is because thought is radically cut off from the world that we will need something like a concept of faith to restore the world to man.

This systematic difference between Bergson and Deleuze has deep roots in Deleuze's earlier philosophy. In the *Logic of Sense* he even invented a principle for it: 'counter-actualization'. In this text the virtual – or 'sense' – does not simply break from sensory-motor subjectivity.[12] It actively maintains its hard-won distance from the universal cesspool of corporeal depths through counter-actualization. If 'actualization' is the name for the process by which thought (and its Ideas) returns to matter and individuates it, counter-actualization is the process by which thought holds the ocean of *un*-individuated materiality – like that matter vibrating across the plane of immanence – at a distance (1990: 168). The aleatory point, or the 'non-actualizable part of the event', counter-actualizes corporeal depths and allows thought to go about its work of forming Ideas with minimal distraction.

Just as the virtual thus actively maintains its autonomy from corporeality, the time-image has to remain radically independent of the plane of immanence. Beyond sonsigns and opsigns, crystal images and dream images, cinema reveals time as the 'permanent crisis' of recognition. And in this crisis it discovers both thought's essence – the aleatory point – and its own essence (1989: 168). This is perhaps the central difference between Deleuze and Bergson: in Bergson the subject becomes active too quickly.

To theorize such a radical break from corporeality presents a real problem, however. Not only is the essence of both subjectivity and cinema now revealed as disembodied inactivity, but also, if individuation is at all possible, thought is going to have to return to matter – and not only is it going to have to return, it is also going to have to remain compatible with the world it had just escaped. Thus, at the foundation of actualization, as its first principle, Deleuze needs a concept which will relink man and the world.

If Deleuze's thought were only the pursuit of an unbounded creativity, and if the sole end of its method were to leave us face to face with Ozu's vase in semi-mystical experience of time, it would be enough to stop here. But, obviously, Deleuze does not stop here in any of his works. Once the virtual is discovered, the task is to show how its Ideas are actualized. In other words, the task is to show how Ideas individuate and thereby shape the world.

Becoming-active

In Deleuze's earlier work, this return of thought to matter is figured in different ways. In every case, however, to discover the essence of thought is not to luxuriate in disembodied transcendence. To find one's essence is to find one's vocation. Take, for example, *Expressionism in Philosophy*. In this work, the body begins as a composition of 'extensive parts' which '"affect one another" *ad infinitum*' (1992: 217). In this situation the body is completely passive. It is subject to a 'very great number of affections' over which it has little to no control. The properly ethical question asks how this body can become active or 'attain to active affections' (219). To do so, it is not enough to multiply joyful affections or give in to an all-out hedonism. Nor is there a memory waiting in reserve ready to slip into a potential gap in recognition. In order for the body to become active, it must discover its power of action – and we know 'by reasoning that the power of action is the sole expression of our *essence*' (226; my emphasis). The body discovers this essence over a long empirical genesis in which, aided by the civil state, the body increases its joyful affections so that reason becomes less and less distracted by the sad affections and can begin forming common notions. It is not necessary to follow this genesis in detail here. We can see already that our essence, even in a rationalist philosophy, is a power of action. The name for this essence in Spinoza is reason: 'reason is the soul's power of action' (274).

If reason is a power of action and not a faculty for the disinterested contemplation of the divine, it is because 'Reason in its initial development is the effort to *organize encounters* on the basis of perceived agreements and disagreements' (280; my emphasis). In other words, to become active is to return to the order of fortuitous encounters and passive affections in order to organize our encounters rationally. When we tap into our power of action we "*have the power of ordering and connecting the affections of the body according to the order of the understanding*" (285; my emphasis).[13] To become active, then, is to become capable of ordering the affections of the body according to our essence.[14] This is why the pursuit of God is ethical and not strictly philosophical or theological; in becoming active we acquire the power to organize our bodies according to our essence rather than the order of fortuitous encounters. This means we enter not only into the third kind of knowledge when we become active but also into a third way of living. As Deleuze puts it, 'the different kinds of knowledge are also different ways of living, different modes of existing' (289). This is because they are different organizations of the body. When we discover our essence, then, we do not just open up a conversation with God. We return to our bodies and shape them.

Difference and Repetition also unfolds along a dialectic which moves from passivity to essence to a reclaimed passivity. Here, too, everything begins with a passive sensibility immersed in a field of intensity (1994: 144). A series of passive or sensory-motor syntheses bind these intensities (96). But the third passive synthesis enters into a crisis. In this crisis – which I have argued elsewhere is also a crisis of recognition (Hughes 2009: 115) – thought raises itself to a new level. It finds its essence in an aleatory point which carries out an 'ideal synthesis of difference' (1994: 198). But again, the Ideas produced in this new faculty do not remain cut off from the world. They return to it. And just as reason co-opted, for its own ends, the imagination's organizing powers in *Expressionism and Philosophy* (1992: 296), the Ideas of *Difference and Repetition* take over the passive syntheses, making them active syntheses capable of cancelling and individuating intensity. This process is aptly named 'dramatization'. The faculties which once passively selected, organized, and reintegrated intensity now play the role given to them by Ideas. In doing so, they become active.

We have every reason to expect, then, that the simultaneous discovery of thought's essence and cinema's essence in *Cinema 2* is going to lead to a becoming-active of the subject. And it does. The only problem is that, in *Cinema 2*, the concept that names this link between man and the world is faith.

> Man is in the world as if in a pure optical and sound situation. The reaction of which man has been dispossessed can be replaced only by belief. Only belief in the world can reconnect man to what he sees and hears. (1989: 172)

Faith or Ethics: The Fosbury Flop

This concept is odd for several reasons. First, Deleuze regularly claims that thinking can only begin in a radical atheism and that the condition of philosophy is a tranquil atheism.[15] But, at a pivotal moment in *Cinema 2*, Deleuze is not only calling on the concept of faith, he is calling on an explicitly Catholic conception of faith: 'It is clear from the outset that cinema had a special relationship with belief. There is a Catholic quality to cinema' (1989: 173). We can explain this away with relative ease if we note the context in which he makes these claims. Not only are the film-makers under discussion here either are forthrightly Catholic or deal with specifically Catholic themes – Bresson, Rossellini, Rohmer, Dreyer – but he is also drawing on Élie Faure's comments on the cult of Catholicism in *Fonction du cinéma*.[16] We could thus say Deleuze's claims regarding cinema's Catholic quality are an effect of his free-indirect philosophizing and the Catholicism at work here is at the level of the films themselves – that is to say, at the level of historical fact – but not at the level of Deleuze's theory.

This still does not explain the concept of faith itself, Catholic or not. Deleuze himself returns here to the Pascal–Kierkegaard motif that resurfaces across his œuvre (1989: 177).[17] Belief here bears on the way of life of the believer; belief determines a certain mode of existence. In *Nietzsche and Philosophy*, for example, Deleuze explains that Pascal's wager is not a theological principle, but an anthropological one. It 'merely concerns two modes of existence of man, the existence of the man who says that God exists and the existence of the man who says that God does not exist' (2006: 37). To believe or not to believe says nothing about the existence or non-existence of God, then (1989: 177). It does not imply a hidden, secret, or (un)known relation with the divine or a channel to transcendence. It is strictly anthropological. The idea of God's existence results in one possibility of life; the idea of his non-existence results in another. As Deleuze and Guattari put it in *What is Philosophy?*, even if the writings of Pascal and Kierkegaard embody a constant striving for the divine, they remain immured in immanence. Pascal and Kierkegaard

> are men of a transcendence or a faith. But they constantly recharge imma-
> nence: they are philosophers [. . .] who are concerned no longer with the
> transcendent existence of God but only with the infinite immanent possi-
> bilities brought by one who believes that God exists. (Deleuze and Guattari
> 1994: 74)

The concept of faith, then, seems to signify the way in which an Idea – in this case, that of God – determines a mode of existence and might even open up 'infinite immanent possibilities' of life. To give the concept of faith its broadest possible extension, we could say that it describes our 'relationship to truth' (Deleuze and Guattari 1994: 53).

If we follow this structural definition of faith, two questions then arise: (1) can we only use the word 'faith' to designate our relationship to the idea of God (God = truth), or does belief express our relation to ideas in general? (2) What does Deleuze mean by 'mode of existence'?

Deleuze insists in all of these discussions that Kierkegaard and Pascal do not go far enough. As he puts it in *What is Philosophy?*, the concept of faith needs to undergo an 'empiricist conversion' (Deleuze and Guattari 1994: 75). This was Hume's 'accomplishment', and through this empiricist conversion the notion of belief begins to express our relationship not only to God but also to ideas in general.

> When I see the sun rise, I say that it will rise tomorrow; having seen water
> boil at 100 degrees, I say that it necessarily boils at 100 degrees. Yet
> expressions such as 'tomorrow', 'always', 'necessarily', convey something
> that cannot be give in experience: tomorrow isn't given without becoming
> today, without ceasing to be tomorrow, and all experience is experience of
> a contingent particular. (2001: 40)

To know that the sun will rise or to know that water will boil at 100 degrees, is to believe or infer that these things will happen. In *Empiricism and Subjectivity*, Deleuze explains that in Hume belief 'posits the past as a *rule* for the future' (1991b: 94; original emphasis). This is exactly the empiricist conversion in the concept of faith that Deleuze and Guattari were looking for in *What is Philosophy?*: in Hume belief 'is no longer a matter of turning toward [truth] but rather of following tracks, of infer- ring rather than grasping or being grasped' (Deleuze and Guattari 1994: 53). While this clearly picks up the terms of the faith/knowledge debate as it played out in post-Kantianism, Deleuze is shifting the opposition. It is not a question here of whether some things can be known, while others (e.g. the absolute) can only become the object of faith as in Jacobi and Hegel. For Deleuze's Hume, knowledge *is* belief. Hume 'puts belief at the basis and the origin of knowledge' (2001: 40). Hume has shifted the problem: it is not whether belief can function as knowledge. At its foundation all knowledge is belief. The problem is knowing whether or not belief is legitimate or illegitimate.

We can therefore free up the notion of faith from its ties to transcendence in general and to the idea of God in particular. In Pascal and Kierkegaard faith expressed the way in which an idea determined a mode of existence. The idea in this case was always God. With Hume the idea can be water boiling or the sun rising or knowledge in general. What, then, about the second question? If, by means of faith, our mode of existence is determined or formed in some way or another, we need to have some clarity about this expression.

I want to suggest, following Deleuze (1995: 100), that this concept is explicitly Spinozist. We saw above that in Deleuze's reading of Spinoza 'the different kinds of knowledge are also different ways of living, different modes of existing' (1992: 289). This is because a mode of existence in *Expressionism in Philosophy* is defined as a certain relation among the parts of the body (212). The body's configuration at any given time is its mode of existence. If the different kinds of knowledge are also different ways of living or different modes of existing, it is because in each kind of knowledge I become capable of organizing the parts of my body in different ways (285).

In the context of an empiricist and immanent conception of faith, then, the concept begins to mean something like: the ideas I have directly determine the configuration of my body. After the 'empiricist conversion', faith expresses the unity of thought and the body. Speaking of technical innovations in sports, Deleuze gives several clear examples of what this might mean:

> Sports do of course have their quantitative scale of records that depend on improvement in equipment, shoes, vaulting-poles . . . But there are also qualitative transformations, *ideas*, which are to do with style: how we went from the scissors jump to the belly roll and the Fosbury flop, how hurdles stopped being obstacles, coming to correspond simply to a longer stride. [. . .] Each new style amounts not so much to a new 'trick' as to a linked sequence of *postures* [. . .]. (1995: 131; my emphases)

Here the idea to which the body relates is no longer God or boiling water, but the Fosbury flop. In so far as this Idea determines a linked series of postures, it determines a mode of existence. Each new idea is actualized in a linked sequence of postures. The concept of faith thus takes on an extraordinarily broad extension, and perhaps it is better to call what we are talking about here 'style' or 'syntax', as Deleuze does in this interview. Whatever we call it, we are dealing with the ethical question: to what extent is the body determined by an idea?

I think it is possible on the basis of these comments scattered across Deleuze's texts to rethink the concept of faith in a way that makes sense within the context of *Cinema 2*. First, we can see that faith does not appear here as a conduit to another world nor is it allied to a specific doctrine (e.g. Catholicism). What is at issue, as Deleuze says in *What is Philosophy?*, is the possibility of a 'secular belief' (Deleuze and Guattari 1994: 53). Second, thanks to Pascal and Kierkegaard, despite all of the theological baggage the term carries it does have one virtue; like the concept 'power of action' in Spinoza, it creates a link between 'truth' and the 'mode of existence' of the one who believes in that truth. To secularize belief fully, however, we need to submit this link between 'truth' and 'mode of existence' to an empiricist conversion. God is no longer the truth. Truth is knowledge understood as the production of a rule for the future. This rule can govern whether we are in church on Sunday mornings or how we jump over hurdles.

Believing in the Body

In Deleuze the concept of faith expresses the way in which ideas determine the configuration of the body. If the concept of faith arises at this moment in the cinema books, it is not because he suddenly found himself dealing with a series of post-war Catholic film-makers or because he had to account for Francesco's impassioned lines in *Rome Open City*.[18] While this may have been an occasional cause, the real cause is at the level of the theory itself. When we followed the deduction of subjectivity from the plane of immanence and its intervals up to the time-image we ended up with a subjectivity radically cut off from the world. If the crisis in recognition is not the consequence of a lesion or a disease, if it is an essential moment in the development of subjectivity as such, Deleuze needs to explain how we get from a state of permanent crisis back to the sphere of action.

In so far as it expresses the way in which ideas determine a certain organization of the body, supplying a 'linked sequence of postures', faith seems to be moving toward an answer to this problem. But it only names the relation. It only says that we must think and that we must apply those thoughts to the body. The question that remains is how

Deleuze works this application out. If we stay with *Cinema 2*, however, this question is bound to go unanswered. Deleuze does not work this process out in any detail. He only alludes to it and counts on us to trace these allusions back to his earlier work.

Even so, there are three stages in this process which we can abstract from *Cinema 2*:

1. Faith in the world, we find out, can only be restored by a 'problematic, aleatory, and yet non-arbitrary point: grace or chance' (1989: 175; translation modified).[19] This is 'an always extrinsic point of thought' (175), a 'point of the outside' (176). This point 'alone is capable of restoring the world and the ego to us' (177, cf. 181).

2. While this aleatory point, by definition, establishes unpredictable and alogical links between images, it is still possible for us to determine these links and to do so methodically. This is what Godard supposedly does when he discovers a 'new synthesis' (184). Godard makes two innovations. First, he replaces montage with 'mixing' (179). Mixing is the progressive determination of 'differential relations' in the image (179). He then creates a table of categories or genres – 'categories of problems' (186) – which regulate the mixing of images, arranging them in ordered series (184).

3. Categories are then applied to the body. Although Deleuze likens these categories to the Aristotelian categories, it is clear from the start that they are not at all general concepts. They are 'categories of life' (189). And in so far as the attitudes of the body are organized (this is the theory of gesture (192–3)) in the right way, these categories 'put time into the body, as well as thought into life' (192). We are then able to 'restore images to the attitudes and postures of the body' (193).

In its most abstract, then, when we follow the movement from thought back to the body, we find: (1) an aleatory point which (2) produces categories that regulate the connection between images, but which can only do so by (3) becoming integrated in the mechanisms of the body.

I want to say two things about this itinerary. First, this has very little to do with the history of cinema as such. The general movement by which thought returns to the body was already laid out in *Difference and Repetition* in just these terms. There, too, thought enters into a crisis in which it discovers its higher power in an aleatory point. This aleatory point forms Ideas, 'animat[ing] ideal problems [and] determining their relations and singularities' (1994: 283). Once these Ideas are completely determined, they function – to allude simultaneously to the

Humean concept of belief and to the Kantian concept of the category – as rules for the future.[20] Through the process of dramatization, Ideas are incorporated into the body. They regulate its passive or sensory motor syntheses, directing them to produce determinate objects which are individuated with regard to their extensity, quality, and duration. Syntheses that are rule-governed are called active syntheses. The concept of faith, then, appears at this moment in *Cinema 2* because it is integral to Deleuze's conception of subjectivity from the start, and if we want a fuller picture of it, Deleuze's allusions seem to say, we can find it in the theory of actualization in *Difference and Repetition*.

Second, this crucial term – actualization – seems to be missing here. In the absence of a fifth commentary on Bergson, however, it is worth emphasizing that its attendant concepts are not. To 'put time into the body, as well as thought into life' (1989: 192) is already a good way of describing actualization, but the second passage I quoted above – which states that by virtue of faith we are able to 'restore images to the attitudes and postures of the body' – is a direct allusion to *Matter and Memory*. In order for recollections and memory-images to pass into movements and thus become actual, the body must first take on 'a certain attitude into which recollections will come to insert themselves' (Bergson 1991: 99). Not only can certain postures 'call back [their] memory-image', but also, conversely, if the body does not adopt the proper attitude, memories stand no chance of becoming 'actual' (99, cf. 130). Deleuze systematized Bergson's comments in his own account of actualization in *Bergsonism*. There are four aspects of actualization, Deleuze explains: translation, rotation, dynamic movement, and mechanical movement:

> translation and rotation, which form the properly psychic moments; dynamic movement, the attitude of the body that is necessary to the stable equilibrium of the preceding two determinations; and finally, mechanical movement, the motor scheme that represents the final stage of actualization. (1991a: 70)

It is these last two stages that are at issue here: the dynamic attitude of the body and its mechanical movement. To actualize a memory-image the body must assume the correct posture or attitude, and once that posture is assumed, memory will be able to re-enter the plane of immanence in the form of a reaction or a mechanical movement.

While the theory of the believing body is not developed in the kind of detail with which Deleuze had developed the theory of the passive or sensory-motor subject, by outlining what Deleuze means by a secular faith and following out the allusions to Bergson and the structure of the discussion, it becomes clear that Deleuze is drawing heavily on his earlier work in *Difference and Repetition* and *Bergsonism*.

The theory of the body in the final chapters of *Cinema 2* thus completes the deduction of subjectivity. After a detour through the virtual, the believing subject re-enters the plane of immanence and restores images to the attitudes and postures of the body, and ultimately to mechanical movement. This is why believing in the world is ultimately believing in the body: 'What is certain is that believing is no longer believing in another world, or in a transformed world. It is only, it is simply believing in the body' (1989: 172).

Cinema's Vocation

I want to raise two final questions: first, what do we get by radically cutting thought off from the body?; and second, why bring cinema into this drama?

Both of these questions have the same answer: what we get by radically separating thought from the world is thought's essence. But for Deleuze to discover one's essence is to discover one's vocation. This faith in the concept of a vocation or of an internal end comes from Deleuze's theory of the faculties developed through a reading of Kant. In §28 of the *Critique of Judgment*, Kant claims that when the imagination discovers its limit in the sublime, the mind also discovers its vocation (Kant 2000). In *Difference and Repetition* Deleuze brings this formula to bear on all four of the faculties Deleuze will mobilize in his own philosophy: sensibility, imagination, memory, and thought (1994: 144; 2000: 99). Each encounters its own limit, and this limit raises it to its unique operation, its transcendent exercise (1994: 141).

Christian Kerslake has put these comments at the center of his recent reading of Deleuze. Whereas the end of reason in Kant was the pursuit of systematic unity, Deleuze sets up the end or vocation of thought as a boundless creativity. Thought discovers its creative essence when it enters into a transcendental 'apocalypse' (2009: 255) – an apocalypse which cinema reveals in the time-image in the form of a permanent crisis of recognition. But, according to Kerslake, this apocalypse also gives thought its vocation, 're-grounding [. . .] the subject in a properly ontological and creative "life"' (255). Deleuze is able to 'transform Kantianism from within' and 'produce a self-grounding post-Kantian system of complete self-differentiation [. . .] in which spiritual creativity and "becoming" take over as the true "ends" of thought' (26).

This is what I have not yet stressed: the creativity of thought. In the same way that Nietzsche overtakes Spinoza as the thinker of immanence in *Difference and Repetition* (1994: 40–1) we need to transcend Spinoza's conception of essence here. For Spinoza our essence or power of action was reason and to become active meant being able to organize the affections of the body rationally. In Deleuze, our essence is no longer reason, but thought – and 'to think is to create' (1994: 147; 2000: 97).

Deleuze had already drawn this distinction between creative thought and legislating reason from the point of view of their relation to life in *Nietzsche and Philosophy*.

> Rational knowledge sets the same limits to life as reasonable life sets to thought; life is subject to knowledge and at the same time thought is subject to life. Reason sometimes dissuades and sometimes forbids us to cross certain limits: because it is useless (knowledge is there to predict), because it would be evil (life is there to be virtuous), because it is impossible (there is nothing to see or think behind the truth). (2006: 101)

This characterization of reason depends on the close relation between thought and life. When thought is rational, so is life, and when life is rational, so is thought.[21] The alliance of both with reason, however, sets limits to each. Thought as reason predicts outcomes, determines the good, and thinks the true. Life acts accordingly and becomes rational life.

But Nietzsche gives thought a new determination, according to Deleuze. He frees it from its subjection 'to reason and all that reason expresses' (101). Deleuze asks, does this not give thought 'another sense', making it a 'thought that would go to the limit of what life can do'?

> Life would be the active force of thought, but thought would be the affirmative power of life. Both would go in the same direction, carrying each other along, smashing restrictions, matching each other step for step, in a burst of unparalleled creativity. Thinking would then mean *discovering, inventing, new possibilities of life*. (101)

The faculty of thought indeed takes on an entirely new sense here. It is no longer constrained by reason or by rational life, and life is no longer bound by the ideals of the good, the true, and the useful. In other words, the Spinozan ideal of a rational organization of life no longer holds and our power of action is not reason. But neither does the Bergsonian insistence on the utility of thought – that all thoughts, even the most general, are ultimately subject to the 'fundamental law of life which is a law of action' (1991: 150). Thought, in Deleuze's Nietzsche, breaks from the category of utility as well as that of rationality. In smashing all restrictions, it represents the permanent crisis recognition and its rule-bound unity. Thought becomes creative and life opens on to new possibilities. 'There is creation, properly speaking, only insofar as we make use of excess in order to invent new forms of life' (101).

The close connection between thinking and life remains constant in this new formulation of the faculty of thought. The Spinozan view according to which the 'different kinds of knowledge are also different ways of living, different modes of existing' because they are different configurations of life still seems to structure Deleuze's thinking. Indeed, Deleuze's typology in *Nietzsche and Philosophy* – the guilty man, the ascetic man, the man who cannot have done with anything, and so on – is based on different configurations of life; each type is discovered by inquiring into 'the real forces that *form* thought' (103; original emphasis). What has changed between Spinoza and Nietzsche is not the close connection between thought and life but the definition of 'thought' itself. It is no longer a *ratio* reinforcing reactive, sensory-motor forces, but an unbounded creativity from which active affections flow. When the subject reaches this essence or vocation and becomes active, it no longer organizes its affections rationally. It takes advantage of its excess to create new possibilities for life or new configurations of the body. The name for the type of thinker who affirms life, carrying thought and life toward new possibilities, is 'the artist'.

In *Cinema 2*, when thought passes through its transcendental apocalypse it discovers its highest power: the power of the false. The artist who takes advantage of thought's creativity is Welles. He embodies the 'artistic will' (1989: 141; 2006: 103). 'What the artist is, is *creator of truth*, because truth is not to be achieved, found, or reproduced; it has to be created. There is no other truth than the creation of the New' (1989: 146–7).[22] Concretely, this means that in Welles, 'Description stops presupposing a reality and narration stops referring to a form of the true' (1989: 135). Instead, description creates its reality and narrative produces the true. And for this reason, Welles is 'always increasing the power to live, always opening new possibilities' (1989: 141).

If faith is the word for our relationship to truth, it is this produced truth that we relate to in *Cinema 2*. And if the properly ethical question is how the body can attain to active affections, the answer here seems to be: by taking advantage of the crisis in recognition to create new forms. However, Deleuze makes a subtle but important distinction here. The vocation of thought is to 'take control of the New from its birth' (1989: 147). Welles accomplishes this, as do Godard, Astruc, and Dreyer, when they invent new, formal connections between images or give old techniques new meanings. The vocation of cinema, however, is not simply to create these new forms, but to bring those forms to bear on the body and thus to change its 'characteristic relation'. The 'less human the world is, the more it is the artist's duty to believe and produce belief in a relation between man and the world' (171).[23] In this, 'cinema seems to have a real vocation' (161).

Far from celebrating cinema as essentially disembodied inactivity, then, Deleuze's cinema project, when taken as a whole, develops a new pedagogy of the image (1989: 247–50). Deleuze develops a new kind of ethical formalism in which the senses are no longer trained in relation to cultural, rational, or useful ends but according to the possibilities of life created by the artistic will.

References

Beiser, F. C. (2002), *German Idealism: The Struggle against Subjectivism 1781–1801*, London: Harvard University Press.

Bensmaïa, R. (2004), 'Cinéplastique: Gilles Deleuze lecteur d'Élie Faure', *in Cinéma, Art(s) Plastique(s)*, ed. P. Taminiaux and C. Murcia, Paris: L'Harmattan.

Bergson, H. (1991), *Matter and Memory*, trans. N. M. Paul and W. S. Palmer, New York: Zone.

Deleuze, G. (1985), *Cinéma 2: L'Image-temps*, Paris: Minuit.

Deleuze, G. (1986), *Cinema 1: The Movement-Image*, trans. H. Tomlinson and R. Galeta, Minneapolis: University of Minnesota Press.

Deleuze, G. (1988), *Spinoza: Practical Philosophy*, trans. R. Hurley, San Francisco: City Lights.

Deleuze, G. (1989), *Cinema 2: The Time-Image*, trans. H. Tomlinson and R. Galeta, Minneapolis: University of Minnesota Press.

Deleuze, G. (1990), *The Logic of Sense*, trans. M. Lester and C. Stivale, ed. C. Boundas, New York: Columbia University Press.

Deleuze, G. (1991a), *Bergsonism*, trans. H. Tomlinson and B. Habberjam, New York: Zone.

Deleuze, G. (1991b), *Empiricism and Subjectivity: An Essay on Hume's Theory of Human Nature*, trans. C. Boundas, New York: Columbia University Press.

Deleuze, G. (1992), *Expressionism in Philosophy: Spinoza*, trans. M. Joughin, New York: Zone.

Deleuze, G. (1994), *Difference and Repetition*, trans. P. Patton, New York: Columbia University Press.

Deleuze, G. (1995), *Negotiations 1972–1990*, trans. M. Joughin, New York: Columbia University Press.

Deleuze, G. (2000), *Proust and Signs*, trans. R. Howard, Minneapolis: University of Minnesota Press.

Deleuze, G. (2001), *Pure Immanence: Essays on a Life*, trans. A. Boyman, New York: Zone.

Deleuze, G. (2006), *Nietzsche and Philosophy*, trans. H. Tomlinson, New York: Columbia University Press.

Deleuze, G. (2007), 'Pericles and Verdi', in *Dialogues II*, trans. J. Hughes and V. Robinson, New York: Columbia University Press, pp. 153–65.

Deleuze, G. and F. Guattari (1994), *What is Philosophy?*, trans. H. Tomlinson and G. Burchell, New York: Columbia University Press.

Foucault, M. (2002), *The Order of Things*, London: Routledge.

Guéroult, M. (1930), *L'Evolution et structure de la doctrine de la science chez Fichte*, 2 vols, Paris: Belles Lettres.

Hallward, P. (2006), *Out of this World: Deleuze and the Philosophy of Creation*, New York: Verso.

Hughes, J. (2009), *Deleuze's Difference and Repetition: A Reader's Guide*, New York: Continuum.

Hyppolite, J. (1974), *Genesis and Structure of Hegel's* Phenomenology of Spirit, trans. S. Cherniak and J. Heckman, Evanston, IL: Northwestern University Press.

Kant, I. (2000), *Critique of the Power of Judgment*, trans. P. Guyer and E. Matthews, New York: Cambridge University Press.

Kerslake, C. (2009), *Immanence and the Vertigo of Philosophy: From Kant to Deleuze*, Edinburgh: Edinburgh University Press.

Marrati, P. (2001), 'The Catholicism of Cinema: Gilles Deleuze on Image and Belief', in *Religion and Media*, ed. H. de Vries and S. Weber, Stanford, CA: Stanford University Press.

Marrati, P. (2008), *Gilles Deleuze: Cinema and Philosophy*, trans. A. Hartz, Baltimore, MD: Johns Hopkins University Press.

Peterson, K. R. (2004), 'Translator's Introduction', in F. W. J. Schelling's *First Outline of a System of the Philosophy of Nature*, trans. K. R. Peterson, Albany, NY: SUNY Press.

Pisters, P. (2003), *The Matrix of Visual Culture: Working With Deleuze in Film Theory*, Stanford, CA: Stanford University Press.

Rodowick, D. N. (1997), *Gilles Deleuze's Time Machine*, Durham, NC: Duke University Press.

Rossellini, R. (1985), *The War Trilogy: Open City, Paisan, Germany – Year Zero*, trans. J. Green, New York: Garland.

Spinoza, B. (1992), *Ethics*, trans. S. Shirley, ed. S. Feldman, Indianapolis: Hackett.

Zabunyan D. (2006), *Gilles Deleuze: Voir, parler, penser au risque du cinéma*, Paris: Sorbonne Nouvelle.

Notes

1. Deleuze 1989: 173, translation modified; see 1985: 225.
2. See, in particular, Hallward 2006: 113–17.
3. Deleuze's comments on the body at the end of *Cinema 2* have already been well covered in the secondary literature (Pisters 2003; Rodowick 1997). In this essay I want to add two things to this discussion: an insistence on the systematic need for this return to the body and a strong connection with the narratives structuring Deleuze's other texts.
4. Deleuze 1986: 58, original emphasis. Deleuze downplays Bergson's claim that images on the plane of immanence are regulated by the laws of nature. Bergson: 'Here I am in the presence of images, in the vaguest sense of the word, images perceived when my senses are open to them, unperceived when they are closed. All these images act and react upon one another in all their elementary parts according to constant laws which I call laws of nature' (1991: 17).
5. Deleuze 1992: 217. Modal existence is defined in *Expressionism in Philosophy* in the same way the plane of immanence is here: 'the nature of extensive parts is such that they "affect one another" *ad infinitum*' (1992: 217; cf. 201–2).
6. See Deleuze 1992: 191–9.

7. For the drop of wine in the ocean, see Deleuze 1990: 6; for the discussion of universal cesspools, see 1990: 187.
8. Dork Zabunyan reads the deduction in the cinema books in relation to Deleuze's frequent claims that Kant discovered the conditions of possible experience, but not those of real experience (Zabunyan 2006: 60–7). On the concept of a genetic or synthetic deduction, see Deleuze 1988: 113–14. Deleuze is drawing on Guéroult here (Guéroult 1930: 174). For a good overview in English of the issues involved, see Beiser 2002: 506–28; Peterson 2004: xviii–xxvii; or Hyppolite 1974: 5–11.
9. Cf. Deleuze 1992: 218, 250.
10. Deleuze himself made this analogy (1986: xiv; 1995: 46–9). For a lucid description of Linnaean classification, see Foucault 2002: 136–77.
11. In Kant recognition was also the synthesis of perception (apprehension) and a passive memory (reproduction). In Bergson the rule for this synthesis is provided by affection or memory. In Kant it is supplied by the understanding. My argument below is that in Deleuze, as a result of the permanent crisis in recognition, this rule has to be created. Deleuze assigns this role to Godard, the creator of categories.
12. In *Cinema 2* Deleuze frequently links 'virtuality', 'sense', and the time-image. See, for example, 1989: 99.
13. Deleuze is quoting Spinoza here (Spinoza 1992: V.10.d).
14. It is interesting to note that this only works, on Deleuze's reading, in so far as there is a hidden relationship between the imagination – which directly organizes the affections of the body – and reason. Once we come into our power of activity, reason takes control of the imagination through a kind of schematism. Reason does not directly organize affections. It directs the imagination (1992: 295–6).
15. See, for example, his short memorial essay on François Châtelet, *Pericles and Verdi*: 'The non-existence or death of God are not problems but the conditions one must have already acquired' in order to think (2007: 153).
16. On Deleuze's Catholicism see Marrati (2001) and Bensmaïa (2004). In this fascinating essay Bensmaïa expresses initial surprise at Deleuze's 'ecumenical optimism' but goes on to argue that this is hardly the most interesting concept Deleuze took from Faure (and that it would thus be too hasty to discount Faure as merely one more thinker for Deleuze to ventriloquize). Deleuze found in Faure an early account of the plasticity of cinema – an account of cinema as a sort of 'architecture in movement' in which relations of movement and rest can create determinate effects in the viewer.
17. See, for example, Deleuze's 1956 lecture *What is Grounding?*, *Nietzsche and Philosophy*, and *Difference and Repetition*.
18. Francesco: 'It'll end, Pina, it'll end, and spring will come back and it'll be more beautiful than ever, because we'll be free. We have to believe it, we have to want it! See, I know these things, I feel them, but I can't explain it [. . .] But I think that's the way it is, that we shouldn't be afraid now or in the future. Because we're in the right, the right's on our side' (Rossellini 1985: 69–70).
19. The French reads, 'ce point problématique, aléatoire, et pourtant non-arbitraire' (1985: 228). In the current English edition, 'aléatoire' has been translated as 'uncertain', thus obscuring an important connection between *Cinema 2* and Deleuze's earlier texts.
20. For an extended discussion of this, see Hughes 2009: 143–9.
21. It is this close relation between life and thought that unites many of the thinkers in Deleuze's 'aberrant' history of philosophy. It is the doctrine of parallelism in Spinoza that animates the ethical, rather than moral, vision of the world and

inspires the *cri*, 'What can a body do?' (Deleuze 1992: 256–7). Bergson will insist that for any thought we think, even the most general, our bodies will also be able to act it (Bergson 1991: 161).

22. Translation modified: 'trouvée' (1985: 191) has been translated as 'formed' rather than 'found'.

23. See Marrati 2008: 86–9.

Chapter 5

Matter as Simulacrum; Thought as Phantasm; Body as Event

Nathan Widder

Perhaps Deleuze's first and most fundamental ontological claim is that being is expressive, that it expresses sense. This claim is evident in his early review of Hyppolite's *Logic and Existence*, where Deleuze maintains the lesson of Hegel's thought to be that '*Philosophy must be ontology, it cannot be anything else; but there is no ontology of essence, there is only an ontology of sense*' (Deleuze 1997: 191); it is central to his turn to Spinoza, with whom 'univocal being ceases to be neutralised and becomes expressive' (Deleuze 1994: 40); and it appears in his turn to Nietzsche, whose eternal return goes beyond abstract expression so that 'univocal being is not only thought and even affirmed, but effectively realised' (41–2).[1] Being expresses sense, but it is not necessarily clear what 'sense' means. For Deleuze, as for Hegel (Hyppolite 1997: 24), sense is a hybrid concept, the term referring to the physical (the sense of smell), the mental and meaningful (the sense of a statement or thought), and, in the case of the French *sens* but not its English counterpart, the notion of direction. The word's polysemy leads both thinkers to see a philosophy of sense as being not a philosophy of the superficial – the implication being that beneath the appearance of sense lies some essence – but a philosophy able to theorize these divergent domains as a single assemblage. It is therefore a philosophy in which the idea of synthesis is crucial – a synthesis that is dialectical in the case of Hegel and in Deleuze's case one that is 'disjunctive'. In this respect, Deleuze argues that being must be conceived as difference, rather than the contradiction that characterizes Hegel's dialectical thought (Deleuze 1997). If being is expressive, what it expresses is the difference that constitutes it as a synthetic multiplicity.

As this project proposes to encompass a series of traditionally irreconcilable oppositions, including the material and conceptual, the particular and the universal – in short, the binary categories related to the classical philosophical problem of body–mind dualism – it faces significant hurdles related to the genesis and reciprocal conditioning of these different domains. In relation to this quandary, Hegel argues in the *Phenomenology* that 'Spirit' must not be conceived as a bone or another dead thing, but as the dialectical negation of a thing's thinghood into something higher (Hegel 1977: §§343–6), while Marx, inverting Hegel's idealism, declares that 'It is not the consciousness of men that determines their being, but, on the contrary, their social being that determines their consciousness' (Marx 1978: 4). Both Hegel and Marx insist on an internal ontological connection between thought and matter, and each faces a comparable difficulty: Hegel's prioritization of consciousness leaves him unable to connect it fully to its material conditions, and his dialectic remains sunk in abstractions[2]; Marx's privileging of 'concrete' modes of production opens well-known questions about how the superstructure can react back upon and influence the economic base and whether the economy can remain the determinant 'in the last instance'. What Deleuze, Hegel, and Marx share – and this follows from their common focus on synthesis – is a commitment to philosophical immanence; being is not only expressive, but the incorporeal side of its sense must not issue from some second world transcending this one. The material and the mental must relate to each other without a reduction of their divergence. For Deleuze, this indicates that sense and meaning must arise from within this world, even if they remain irreducible to the world's corporeality; they must delineate and organize this corporeal world, even though they do not change the latter's materiality. He puts the resulting paradox in the following terms: 'How can we maintain both that sense produces even the states of affairs in which it is embodied, and that it is itself produced by these states of affairs or the actions and passions of bodies (an immaculate conception)?' (Deleuze 1990: 124).

There is probably no firm and final answer to this problem, but Deleuze's solution is distinctive. He proposes to conceive both matter and thought outside the strictures of identity and representation – outside the terms of universality, particularity, and an impoverished notion of singularity. Classical philosophy and idealist dialectics treat matter as instantiating and thus particularizing universal concepts, and to the extent that matter itself is seen to be extra-conceptual or singular, outside the identity of the concept that gives it form, it is held to be unknowable, unconscious, and empty.[3] Psychoanalysis, although it considers its approach to be scientific rather than philosophically idealist, similarly conceives matter as brute and inanimate, as evidenced in Freud's idea of the death instinct as a return to an inorganic state

(Deleuze 1994: 103–4). And materialist dialectics treats matter as active, but conceives its dynamism dialectically and therefore in terms of identity. In the case of thought, Deleuze maintains that classical and contemporary philosophy's commitment to identity and representation restrict it to a certain image in which its right and privilege is to grasp 'truth' and in which its sense is restricted to what is 'common' and 'good'.[4] Thought is thereby tied to essences or identities rather than 'the evaluation of what is important and what is not, to the distribution of singular and regular, distinctive and ordinary points, which take place entirely within the inessential' (189). Against these views, Deleuze holds that matter and thought must be conceived as multiplicities that differ from the One and the Many – multiplicities, that is, that cannot be resolved into unity, dialectical or otherwise, but whose unrepresentable excess cannot be understood in negative terms as a lack or absence. Deleuze gives the name simulacrum to his material multiplicity[5] and phantasm to thought's multiplicity. His ontology ultimately concerns how these two multiplicities relate to and co-determine each other, their relationship too exceeding the terms of identity and resemblance or contradiction and opposition.

The following will examine Deleuze's ontology of sense, particularly as it is developed in *The Logic of Sense* and to an extent in *Difference and Repetition*, in terms of three key engagements: his reversal of the Platonist hierarchy of Ideas over physical copies, which reveals a simulacrum that characterizes the material and the sensible; his adaptation of the Stoic theory of incorporeals embedded in the interstices of bodies and within language, from which he draws a concept of the phantasm; and his turn to Melanie Klein's story of pre-Oedipal and Oedipal development, which foregrounds a relationship between the infant's phantasies and the material world of part-objects, and which Deleuze uses and reworks to account for the development that takes sense from its material, sensible beginnings to the domain of thought, and ultimately to the thought of eternal return. In each of these moves, ontological difference is the key to unpacking and resolving the paradox of sense, which ultimately, for Deleuze, concerns a resonance that defines the body as an event. Through this difference, as will be seen, thought and body, language and thing interact and 'make sense'.

Platonism and the Simulacrum

Deleuze identifies a Platonic dualism that differs from the dualism between Ideas and physical beings:

It is a more profound and secret dualism hidden in sensible and material bodies themselves. It is a subterranean dualism between that which receives the action of the Idea and that which eludes this action. It is not the distinction between the Model and the copy, but rather between copies and simulacra. (Deleuze 1990: 2)

A fundamental ambiguity pervades Plato's treatment of simulacra – of art, illusion, simulation, and the human figures who embody these, such as the artist, actor, and sophist. On the one hand, simulacra are treated merely as copies of copies; in the example given in *Republic*, Book X, there is the Idea of the couch, a physical couch manufactured by a craftsman, and a painting of a couch, each with a different degree of reality and truth (Plato 1961: *Republic*, 596b–9).[6] In this respect, simulacra are merely weak imitations inhabiting the lowest portions of Plato's divided line. On the other hand, Plato worries that simulacra have a deceptiveness that allows them to masquerade as representations of truth. Hence, despite proclaiming that, following the principle that each individual has a single skill he or she does best, no actor can play different roles such as comedy and tragedy equally well (396a–b), Socrates declares that the ideal city will ban any actor 'who was capable by his cunning of assuming every kind of shape and imitating all things' (398a). Deleuze contends that Plato's hierarchy of Idea and copy aims fundamentally to establish the difference between copies and simulacra – the distinction between Beauty and the beautiful thing ultimately serves to distinguish what genuinely partakes of beauty and what feigns participation. Plato therefore splits the material world in two, holding copies to have an internal resemblance to their Ideas, while the deceptive simulacrum simply 'produces an *effect* of resemblance' (Deleuze 1990: 258). Only in this way can copies raise themselves above simulacra and claim legitimate participation in their Ideas. This requires, Deleuze, argues, 'subordinating difference to instances of the Same, the Similar, the Analogous and the Opposed' (Deleuze 1994: 265). This condemnation of difference, however, 'has no motivation apart from the moral' (ibid.), and so lacks any ontological basis. Moreover, the reduction of simulacra to being copies twice removed is wholly inadequate to this task; copies of copies are necessarily degraded, which precludes their having any capacity to appear to be more than they are. The likeness to legitimate copies that this capacity gives them must therefore be 'completely external and produced by a totally different means than those at work within the model' (Deleuze 1990: 258).

If simulacra elude the power of Ideas, Deleuze maintains, it is because they exceed the order of identity and resemblance. They are therefore characterized by a 'pure becoming', one that moves not in a single direction, as is the case with legitimate copies guided by their partici- pation in Ideas, but in two directions (senses) at once. Plato holds that things of this world partake in opposing qualities due to their relations to one another (*Phaedo* 102b) and due to their transience (*Republic* 479a–b). This duality creates a series of paradoxes that are outlined in *Parmenides*. Where one thing is older than another, for example, as they continue through time the older will become relatively younger without ever being younger than the other, and vice versa, while at the same time no such change will occur, since their age difference remains constant throughout (*Parmenides* 154a–155c). And, in relation to itself, 'Whatever occupies time must always be becoming older than itself, and "older" always means older than something younger. Consequently, whatever is becoming older than itself . . . must also be at the same time becoming younger than itself' (141a–b). Plato remains largely uninter- ested in the implications of this pure becoming – indeed, if he pursued them, Parmenides's claim in the dialogue that the worlds of being and becoming cannot relate (133d–134a) would be insurmountable.[7] Hence in *Philebus*, for example, Socrates dismisses a formulation of this dual becoming by calling it 'childish, obvious, and a great nuisance to argu- ment' (14d). However, Deleuze holds this duality to be the positive trait the simulacrum displays when it is no longer denigrated as a copy of a copy. Seen affirmatively, simulacra are multiplicities.

> The simulacrum is built upon a disparity or upon a difference. It inter- nalizes a dissimilarity. This is why we can no longer define it in relation to a model imposed on the copies, a model of the Same from which the copies' resemblance derives. If the simulacrum still has a model, it is another model, a model of the Other (*l'Autre*) from which there flows an internalized dissemblance. (Deleuze 1990: 258)

Deleuze thus defines simulacra as 'systems in which different relates to different through difference itself' (Deleuze 1994: 277). They are structured by a 'disjunctive synthesis' in which divergence is affirmed. When differences are conceived in negative terms under the principles of identity, they communicate only to the degree to which an overarching similarity relates them. In contrast, the challenge, Deleuze holds, is to make 'divergence . . . no longer a principle of exclusion and disjunction no longer a means of separation. Incompossibility is now a means of communication . . . the whole question, and rightly so, is to know under what conditions the disjunction is a veritable synthesis' (Deleuze 1990: 174). This synthesis requires that 'everything happens through the resonance of disparates, point of view on a point of view, displacement of perspective, differentiation of difference, and not through the identity of contraries' (ibid.). The bivalence of simulacra achieves this resonance, by which they elude identity and representation, but it must also engender the effects that allow them to deceive. In this way, simulacra would be multiplicities that present the appearance of stability, as patterns on the surface of flowing water might appear fixed from a great distance: 'an identity would be found to be necessarily projected, or rather retrojected, on to the originary difference and a resemblance interiorised within the divergent series. We should say of this identity and this resemblance that they are "simulated"' (Deleuze 1994: 126). It is off this semblance of stability that Plato is able to posit transcendent Ideas that give the world of appearances its direction and sense. The irony, as Deleuze describes it, is that the identity, similarity, and stability that allow Plato to denigrate simulacra are actually generated by simulacra themselves.

'"To reverse Platonism"', writes Deleuze, 'means to make the simulacra rise and affirm their rights among icons and copies. The problem . . . has to do with undertaking the subversion of this world [of representation] – the "twilight of the idols"' (Deleuze 1990: 262). This does not mean the destruction of Ideas as such – indeed, in *Difference and Repetition* Deleuze presents a theory of Ideas as virtual multiplicities[8] – but rather the elimination of their transcendent status. It is 'the poisoned gift of Platonism . . . to have introduced transcendence into philosophy, to have given transcendence a plausible philosophical meaning' (Deleuze 1998: 137). Against this, it is necessary to show that the categories of representation, which allow transcendence to gain a foothold, are 'the site of transcendental illusion' (Deleuze 1994: 265). The first step in this process, for Deleuze, is to locate a multiplicity within the material and sensible that already shows that matter is neither inanimate substance nor a passive formlessness that merely awaits organization.

Stoic Incorporeals

Deleuze contends that 'the Stoics are the first to reverse Platonism and to bring about a radical inversion' (Deleuze 1990: 7). They do this primarily through an immanent dualism and a new understanding of causality. Concerning the former, the Stoics conceive being as fundamentally corporeal. Its primary genus is material substrate, but all qualifications and dispositions of substrate, which are given in substantial terms and directly affect or modify substance, are corporeal as well. Hence the qualities 'rational' and 'animal', which delineate substrate and together define human essence (following Aristotle, man is a rational animal), are corporeal, as is virtue – an internal disposition of the corporeal soul – and fatherhood – a disposition of one body relative to another.[9] However, being is part of a larger category of 'something', which includes four incorporeals (*asōmatos*): place, void, time, and 'sayables' (*lekta*). The Stoics refuse to associate incorporeality with Platonic Ideas, holding the latter to be 'neither somethings nor qualified, but figments of the soul which are quasi-somethings and quasi-qualified' (Stoebius in Long and Sedley 1987: 176). Although they are distinct from corporeal bodies, which are mixtures of heterogeneous matters that include a corporeal breath or *pneuma* that completely infuses bodies to give them cohesion and continuity, incorporeals are nevertheless indispensable for determining the full sense and significance of these bodies. Drawing on this tradition, Deleuze holds incorporeals to be an immanent excess residing on the surface of bodies and denoting a simulacral multiplicity that characterizes an immanent kind of Idea: 'What was eluding the Idea climbed up to the surface, that is, the incorporeal limit, and represents now all possible *ideality*' (Deleuze 1990: 7).

The role of incorporeals appears chiefly in the Stoic accounts of causality and language. Causation, they maintain, is corporeal and refers specifically and solely to the interaction of bodies, but in a special way. Bodies are causes *to* one another, but the effects they produce are entirely incorporeal:

> The Stoics say that every cause is a body which becomes the cause to a body of something incorporeal. For instance the scalpel, a body, becomes the cause to the flesh, a body, of the incorporeal predicate "being cut." And again, the fire, a body, becomes the cause to the wood, a body, of the incorporeal predicate "being burnt." (Sextus Empiricus in Long and Sedley 1987: 333)

These incorporeal effects are impassive, 'not of a nature either to act or be acted upon' (ibid.: 272), and thereby differ from the new corporeal qualities or properties that causes also induce in bodies. Fire's action in relation to wood engenders a new corporeal mixture with the corporeal quality of heat, but it also produces a meaningful surface effect – an impassive being or becoming burnt. A correspondence thus exists between corporeal qualities and incorporeal attributes and effects, but they cannot be reduced to a single order. They designate distinct but interconnected levels of forceful bodies and surface effects that arise in the interstices of these bodies.

The actions of external bodies affect or impress themselves on the corporeal soul, creating thoughts, conceptions, and cognitions, which are corporeal dispositions of the mind.[10] Thought, in turn, has a power of corporeal utterance, within which subsist incorporeal 'sayables' that signify corporeal states of affairs. 'Sayables' have nominative and appellative elements, which denote substances and common qualities, but these cannot form propositions without verbs, which correspond to the incorporeal effects generated by bodies.[11] The propositions constituted by 'sayables' are, like other incorporeal effects, impassive, and even though they are affirmed of bodies, they belong to a different order. Together, 'sayables' mediate the relations between utterances and the external objects and events to which their meanings refer, between corporeal thought and things.

Deleuze's reading of the Stoics is principally indebted to Émile Bréhier's seminal work, *La Théorie des incorporels dans l'ancien stoïcisme*, and specifically two of Bréhier's main claims. First, Bréhier maintains that incorporeal effects have the character of facts, happenings, or, in the term that has so much currency in contemporary thought, events.[12] For Deleuze, this character is found in both the Stoic emphasis on verbs – 'For it is not true that the verb represents an action: it expresses an event, which is totally different' (Deleuze 1990: 184) – and the impassive becomings of incorporeal effects (4–5). Deleuze goes on to say that the duality of sense is best expressed in the infinitive form of verbs, which, being indifferent to the different directions or senses that the verb may take, is impassive; put simply, 'God is' and 'God is not' have the same sense ('to be'), as does 'the tree greens' and 'the tree does not green' ('to green') (31–2). There is thus a pure becoming at the foundation of Stoic language, just as there is one in the incorporeal effects arising from the interactions of bodies. Second, Bréhier argues that while incorporeals may seem to have a secondary status in so far as they are effects of the interactions of bodies, their subsistence in the intersection of corporeal substances gives them a constitutive role. On the one hand, the essence of 'sayables' is the verb that corresponds to the surface effects of bodies. On the other hand, bodies themselves can only interact because of the incorporeals of place and time. Holding that the extremities of bodies are neither wholes nor parts but rather incorporeals, so that it is impossible for two bodies to touch,[13] the Stoics maintain that bodies must interpenetrate, which allows them to maintain that different bodies can occupy the same place at the same time and to posit the mixtures and immanent tensions that bring about surface effects (Bréhier 1997: 40). Bréhier maintains that the Stoics redefine place as the site of this interpenetration, making it a product of bodies but also a presupposition for corporeal activity (52–3). With respect to time, Bréhier argues that the Stoics treat it as the structure, rather than the measure, of movement and change (55). This structure too is characterized by interpenetration, with the present being a mixture of past and future rather than an indivisible instant. It is the temporal structure that Deleuze links to pure becoming, which has the 'capacity to elude the present' (Deleuze 1990: 2).[14] Time, Bréhier continues, is not a cause and does not determine bodies or events; it is rather an empty form ('une forme vide' (Bréhier 1997: 59)) that contours beings and surface events, giving them their sense. In these ways, the Stoics, through Bréhier's interpretation, provide an answer to Deleuze's paradox of how sense produces and is produced by the states of affairs in which it arises.

Deleuze's claim that the Stoics reverse Platonism, however, is rather overstated. There is no pure becoming in two directions at once, as described in *Parmenides*, and the Stoics' commitments simply would not allow it. Their blended mixtures comprise heterogeneous materials, but they hardly resemble simulacra, as any dissonance within them is subordinated to unity. Thus in the case of the most important mixture, 'the whole of substance is unified by a breath which pervades it all, and by which the universe is sustained and stabilized and made interactive with itself' (Alexander in Long and Sedley 1987: 290). Furthermore, the Stoics' universe remains ordered, following a pattern of birth, destruction, and rebirth that realizes an eternal return of the same, in which 'there will be nothing strange in comparison to what occurred previously, but everything will be just the same and indiscernible down to the smallest details' (Nemesius in Long and Sedley 1987: 309). Finally, their entire philosophy of language and events is governed by a will to truth, the Stoics never doubting the possibility of the wise man's infallible knowledge, based on a correspondence of external bodies and events to mental dispositions and 'sayables'. Since rational concepts arise from the traces of real bodies impressed on the mind, the two sides can correspond; because the surface events of corporeal bodies and the logical incorporeals embedded in language and thought are neither bodies nor qualities, they can also completely coincide (Bréhier 1997: 18–19, 21–2). While the Stoics introduce multiplicity into both matter and thought, with the incorporeal side of their sense irreducible to their material conditions of emergence, these multiplicities remain tempered by commitments to identity and representation.

What is required is that the incorporeals residing on the surfaces of corporeal bodies, qualities, and dispositions take on the character of 'differenciators' – a term Deleuze uses for the conduit that, within the disjunctive synthesis, relates differences through their difference rather than through identity.[15] With this, the resonance that marks the simulacrum can be achieved. By affirming divergence, the differenciator obliterates any correspondence between thought and bodies, and between incorporeal 'sayables' and events, but the challenge this poses to knowledge differs from the traditional problems that the Stoics address. They hold the wise man to have the ability to distinguish true impressions – or *phantasia* – from false figments – *phantasma* – giving as an example of this power the ability to distinguish two objects that appear entirely the same, such as identical twins. Hence they maintain that 'no hair or grain of sand is in all respects of the same character as another hair or grain' (Cicero in Long and Sedley 1987: 246), thereby asserting ultimate conceptual differences between otherwise identical things. The differenciator, however, is an unrepresentable and nonconceptual excess that cannot be reduced to a lack or absence, and that exceeds the metaphysical order of truth and falsity. It is a surface multiplicity and its effects in thought, Deleuze holds, 'might be called "phantasms," independently of the Stoic terminology' (Deleuze 1990: 7–8). Simulacra, Deleuze says, produce phantasms that never correspond to them because simulacra are not models that can be copied well or badly. But phantasms nevertheless express sense, as they too, like simulacra, are multiplicities.

Melanie Klein and the Oedipal Phantasm

While the Stoics merely assert the existence of incorporeal 'sayables' that raise vocal utterances and corporeal thoughts to the status of language and signification, Deleuze contends that it is necessary to account for 'what liberates sounds and makes them independent of bodies . . . how speaking is effectively disengaged from eating, how the surface itself is produced, or how the incorporeal event results from bodily states' (Deleuze 1990: 186–7). To do this, he turns to child psychoanalyst Melanie Klein.[16] Klein is known for contesting the centrality of the Oedipus and castration complexes by tracing infant psychic development through two pre-Oedipal positions, and also for being almost alone among post-Freudians in taking the death instinct seriously as a fundamental component of the psyche, holding it to operate from birth. These aspects of Klein's thought are important to Deleuze's reading, but her initial importance to him comes from her portrayal of the early infant's world being comprised of part-objects that it seeks to organize and from which it constructs its inner world of phantasy. In Klein's story of development, the infant is gradually able to integrate part-objects into complete objects with stable boundaries and identities, overcoming the multiplicity of the two worlds of phantasy and reality, and bringing them into correspondence. Deleuze, in contrast, re-reads this story through his ontology of difference, establishing a disjunctive synthesis in which the thought that arises from its material conditions, rather than seeking or achieving identity and truth, culminates in the thought of difference.

The Kleinian infant's world is initially one of chaotic part-objects from which

> 'springs . . . the phantastic and unrealistic nature of the child's relation to all objects . . .. The object-world of the child in the first two or three months of its life could be described as consisting of hostile and persecuting, or else gratifying parts and portions of the real world. (Klein 1998: 285)

Lacking firm distinctions, these part-objects easily blend into one another, so that, for example, 'according to the child's earliest phantasies (or "sexual theories") of parental coitus, the father's penis (or his whole body) becomes incorporated in the mother during the act' (219). The child forms its inner world by introjecting these part-objects, but it also projects its loving and aggressive instincts on to them, establishing object-relationships and defining the components of its inner and outer worlds in a dialectical fashion. The most important part-object is the breast, which, containing all nourishment but never guaranteeing its presence or generosity, is the prototype for good and bad part-objects alike. However, through the processes of introjection and projection, all internal and external part-objects attain a comparable bivalence, and so for Deleuze they may rightly be called simulacra: 'We call this world of introjected and projected, alimentary and excremental partial internal objects the world of *simulacra*' (1990: 187). The infant's ego being weak and undeveloped, it is left at the mercy of its own sadistic instincts and the part-objects it encounters, with each world mirroring the other: 'for all children in the beginning external reality is mainly mirror of the child's own instinctual life . . . from the beginning of psychic development there is a constant correlation of real objects with those installed within the ego' (Klein 1998: 233, 266). But this mirroring also magnifies and distorts each side, resulting in both internal and external objects tending towards the extremes of good and evil.

In this initial situation, the infant strives to separate good and bad. It uses both phantasies and real actions because it cannot fully tell the difference, and thus takes its own sadistic phantasies to be acts it has really carried out on its parents. Its aggressive instincts being ascendant, the infant aims to divide part-objects, expelling and destroying what is bad and introjecting and possessing the good. But as its world lacks any firm boundaries, these separations cannot be sustained. When the infant seeks to introject the good, for example, it inevitably feels that it absorbs the bad as well, making its own inner world a dangerous place; as it seeks to attack the bad, it is overwhelmed by persecutory anxieties and phantasies of bad objects retaliating; and in projecting its aggression on to external part-objects, the infant cannot help but identify with them so that it re-internalizes the bad. Good part-objects easily transform into bad and vice versa. This entire dynamic defines the 'paranoid-schizoid' position that marks early life.

As the child's ego develops, however, it is less susceptible to paranoid anxiety and the extremes that projection and introjection create. As sexual development approaches the genital stage and sexual instincts attain independence from vital and aggressive instincts, the child's capacity to love grows and early sadism subsides. The child becomes able to synthesize part-objects into complete objects, but in achieving this synthesis, which unites good and bad part-objects, the result is a complete but damaged love object. This marks the beginning of a new 'manic-depressive' position, which is characterized by the loss of the loved object – 'Not until the object is loved *as a whole* can its loss be felt as a whole' (Klein 1998: 264) – and from which the child tries to repair the parent it believes it has damaged and gain approval from the good. Here the infant vacillates between depressive anxiety from the harm it believes it has committed and a sense of omnipotence, which allows it to combat anxiety and feel confident that it can repair the loved object, but which is also wrapped up in unconscious sadistic impulses, so that 'the child feels again and again that his attempts at reparation have not succeeded, or will not succeed' (350). The penis – visible in the boy's case and introjected from the father in the girl's – becomes the representative of power (244) and is thus the tool of reparation.

All this prepares the way for the Oedipal complex, which, contra Freud, begins early in the second year of life. The passage through the pre-Oedipal positions results in a more developed demarcation between consciousness and the unconscious, allowing the ego to use repression as its primary means to secure itself. Repression is also a pre-requisite for symbol formation, which functions primarily to direct the sublimation of libido energies towards non-sexual interests.[17] The next several years are filled with vacillations and regressions, but conclude with the resolution of the Oedipus complex and the establishment of the final form of the superego.

For Klein, normal psychic development sees the splitting between good and bad 'carried out on planes which gradually become increasingly nearer and nearer to reality' (Klein 1998: 288), so that eventually 'the internalized imagos will approximate more closely to reality and the ego will identify itself more fully with "good" objects' (Klein 1989: 180). For Deleuze, however, this resolution is impossible; the child cannot outgrow the world of part-objects because reality is a simulacrum, which the infant's internal world cannot copy well or badly. Consequently, even if psychic development and the dynamic between inner and outer worlds see the emergence of language and thought through repression, this emergence of sense must take place through difference rather than identity. The result, for Deleuze, is that 'There is a disjunction between speaking and seeing, between the visible and the articulable: "what we see never lies in what we say" and vice versa' (Deleuze 1988: 64).[18]

For Deleuze, the infant still seeks to separate good and bad, but as all corporeal part-objects are incomplete, none can signify the principle of goodness and purity needed to inspire this endeavor. Consequently, the processes of introjection and projection cannot isolate the good object necessary to move the infant from the first pre-Oedipal position to the second:

> introjection, to be precise, does not allow what is wholesome to subsist . . . the equilibrium proper to the schizoid position and its relation to the subsequent depressive position do not seem capable of coming about from the introjection of the good object as such, and they must be revised. (Deleuze 1990: 188)

Instead, Deleuze maintains that the principle of purity must come from the simulacrum's differenciator, which he here calls the 'body without organs' and which he links to the urethral attacks associated with the infant's anal-sadistic phase (188–9), noting that Klein makes no such distinction between urine and faeces (351–2 n3).[19] This fluid body without organs circulates through the dispersed part-objects, establishing a never fully graspable reference point for the child to organize itself and its surroundings. However, its resistance to introjection puts it on another level. The simulacrum in this way generates the simulation of transcendence, with the good object taking the form of an 'idol on-high' (192). This idol is not the body without organs as such, but it emerges from the corporeal dynamic that it establishes. It moves the infant to the manic-depressive position, setting the conditions for the subsequent castration threat and the Oedipus complex.

Consigned to the heights, 'the good object is by nature a lost object. It shows itself and appears from the start as already lost, as *having been lost*' (Deleuze 1990: 191). Its ambivalence, for Deleuze, is thus fundamentally different from the ambivalence of part-objects in the paranoid-schizoid position; it is both loving and threatening because it is pure, mysterious, and good (ibid.). Although it consolidates the division between good and bad, initiating processes of identification,[20] the good object in fact operates as a differenciator, relating differences through their difference. In the first instance, the good object organizes the erotogenic zones of the body's physical surface, a process culminating in the genital stage and the independence of libido energies, which become 'a veritable *superficial* energy' (199). The phallus thus becomes the privileged signifier of the lost object – or, rather, it is an image donated by the good object and serving 'the direct and global function of integration, or of general coordination' (200). Following Klein's view of the penis, the phallus is 'an instrument of the surface, meant to *mend* the wounds that the destructive drives . . . have inflicted on the maternal body, and to reassure the good object, to convince it not to turn its face away' (201). However, in positioning the boy in place of the father and thereby instituting castration anxiety and the Oedipus complex, a new and more profound differentiation occurs. Destructive impulses that were repressed in the depressive position return in a new form, as the Oedipal drama establishes 'intention as an ethical category' (206), which raises the agency of aggressive instincts to a new level of thought. Death and castration carry out a desexualization of libido energies, which are sublimated to form 'the second screen, the cerebral or metaphysical surface' (218). Oedipus thereby institutes not only a trace of castration on the physical surface of the body, but enacts a process of symbolization on a surface of thought (208).

Death, castration, and murder now become the never fully identifiable components of a third differenciator, the Oedipal phantasm, which circulates between the sexualized surface of the physical body and the metaphysical surface of thought.[21] Through the phantasm, sexuality is brought into thought, as the trace of castration remains even after sexual energies have been sublimated, while thought, via symbolization, reinvests its desexualized energies on to the body's surface (Deleuze 1990: 242–3). The domains of body, sexuality, and thought thereby fold into each other, yet remain irreducible; the sexual organization of thought prefigures language (230–3, 241–2), but language only arises in so far as sexuality is sublimated into something different; symbolization, in turn, never fully collapses the symbol into what is symbolized. The Oedipal phantasm resonates between these sexualized and desexualized surfaces, but it also refers to pre-genital and genital organizations of the sexualized body, since the Oedipus complex signifies a traumatic event that separates these two orders and constitutes them through this separation (226). Through the phantasm, pre-genital and genital sexualities continue to resonate in the unconscious (240). Ultimately, by way of this series of disjunctions upon disjunctions – from the body without organs to the lost object to the Oedipal phantasm – a resonance is established between body and thought that 'makes sense'.

Sense and the Eternal Return

Although the body without organs and the good object are also differenciators, it is the phantasm that brings together and thereby constitutes all the dimensions of sense. Because of this, 'throughout all of that which language will designate, manifest, or signify, there will be a sexual history that will never be designated, manifested, or signified in itself, but which will coexist with all the operations of language, recalling the sexual appurtenance of the formative linguistic elements' (Deleuze 1990: 243).[22] Ultimately, however, 'the phantasm develops to the extent that the resonance induces a *forced movement* that goes beyond and sweeps away the basic [sexual] series . . . the forced movement of an amplitude greater than the initial movement' (239). Thought must develop beyond its corporeal and sexual origins in order to execute a creative break with the compulsions and necessities of both the instincts and the past. For Deleuze, this occurs when thought realizes the Nietzschean eternal return – when sexuality gives rise to the thought of difference.

In *Difference and Repetition*, Deleuze serially links his three syntheses of time to the components of Freud's second model of the psyche, the eternal return being associated with the formation of the superego through a trauma that ungrounds and dissolves the ego.[23] In explaining the temporal structure of the eternal return, he argues that 'the present is no more than an actor, an author, an agent destined to be effaced, while the past is no more than a condition operating by default' (94). While the past delineates the conditions for action in the present, and present action requires not only past conditions but a consolidation of the ego in relation to an ego-ideal that makes the self equal to its task (110–11), the act brings about the new by demolishing this unity:

> the event and the act possess a secret coherence which excludes that of the self; . . . they turn back against the self which has become their equal and

smash it to pieces, as though the bearer of the new world were carried away and dispersed by the shock of the multiplicity to which it gives birth: what the self has become equal to is the unequal in itself. (89–90)

The eternal return is thus realized when a moment of unification – around an ideal that is only a simulation of something higher – is used to disperse unity into difference. *The Logic of Sense* links this same development to the disjunctive movement of the phantasm; although the phantasm 'finds its point of departure (or its author) in the phallic ego of secondary narcissism', seeming to depend on the pre-Oedipal consolidation of the ego through identification with the lost good object, within the phantasm the ego 'is neither active nor passive and does not allow itself at any moment to be fixed in a place, even if this place were reversible' (Deleuze 1990: 212). Through this dissolution of the ego, the Oedipal phantasm becomes 'the site of the eternal return' (220). It must not be confused, however, with a similar dissolution carried out by dialectics: 'if the ego is dissipated in it [the phantasm], it is perhaps not because of an identity of contraries, or a reversal whereby the active would become passive' (213). Arising from disjunction, it transforms the ego into an event: 'the individuality of the ego merges with the event of the phantasm itself, even if that which the event represents in the phantasm is understood as another individual, or rather a series of individuals through which the dissolved ego passes' (213–14).

Freud holds that 'A person's own body, and above all its surface, is a place from which both external and internal perceptions may spring,' and for this reason, 'The ego is first and foremost a bodily ego; it is not merely a surface entity, but is itself the projection of the surface' (Freud 1961: 25, 26). In this way the body, just like its dispersed ego, becomes an event. It is not merely a factual or real 'thing', but the site of a communication between the real and the phantastic, the corporeal and the incorporeal. The body as an event is Deleuze's answer to the problem of traditional dualisms that his ontology of sense invites. It is neither one side of an insurmountable binary opposition nor a moment within a dialectical passage. It connects two multiplicities through a disjunctive synthesis and, as such, includes a difference that exceeds identity and representation. The body is the expression of this sense of difference, of the being of sense itself.

References

Bréhier, É. (1997), *La Théorie des incorporels dans l'ancien stoïcisme*, 9th edn, Paris: Librairie Philosophique J. Vrin.

Deleuze, G. (1988), *Foucault*, trans. S. Hand, London: Athlone.
Deleuze, G. (1990), *The Logic of Sense*, trans. M. Lester and C. Stivale, New York: Columbia University Press.
Deleuze, G. (1994), *Difference and Repetition*, trans. Paul Patton, London: Athlone.
Deleuze, G. (1997), 'Review of Jean Hyppolite', in J. Hyppolite, *Logic and Existence*, trans. L. Lawlor and A. Sen, Albany, NY: SUNY Press, pp. 191–5.
Deleuze, G. (1998), *Essays Critical and Clinical*, trans. D. W. Smith and M. A. Greco, London: Verso.
Deleuze, G. (2006), *Two Regimes of Madness: Texts and Interviews, 1975–1995*, ed. D. Lapoujade, trans. A. Hodges and M. Taormina, New York: Semiotext(e).
Freud, S. (1961), 'The Ego and the Id', in *The Standard Edition of the Complete Psychological Works of Sigmund Freud*, ed. and trans. James Strachey, 24 vols, 19:3–66, London: Hogarth and Institute for Psycho-Analysis.
Hegel, G. W. F. (1977), *Phenomenology of Spirit*, trans. A. V. Miller, introduced by J. N. Findlay, Oxford: Oxford University Press.
Hyppolite, J. (1997), *Logic and Existence*, trans. L. Lawlor and A. Sen, Albany, NY: SUNY Press.
Kerslake, C. (2007), *Deleuze and the Unconscious*, London: Continuum.
Klein, M. (1975), *Envy and Gratitude and Other Works: 1946–1963*, New York: Delacorte/Seymour Lawrence.
Klein, M. (1989), *The Psycho-Analysis of Children*, trans. A. Strachey, revised by H. A. Thorner and A. Strachey, London: Virago.
Klein, M. (1998), *Love, Guilt and Reparation and Other Works: 1921–1945*, introduced by H. Segal, London: Vintage.
Long, A. A. and D. N. Sedley (1987), *The Hellenistic Philosophers, Vol. 1: Translations and Principle Sources with Philosophical Commentary*, Cambridge: Cambridge University Press.
Marx, K. (1978), *The Marx–Engels Reader*, 2nd edn, ed. R. C. Tucker, New York: W. W. Norton.
Nietzsche, F. (1974), *The Gay Science, with a Prelude in Rhymes and an Appendix of Songs*, trans. Walter Kaufmann, New York: Vintage.
Plato (1961), *The Collected Dialogues of Plato, Including the Letters*, ed. E. Hamilton and H. Cairnes, Princeton: Princeton University Press.
Widder, N. (2009), 'From Negation to Disjunction in a World of Simulacra: Deleuze and Melanie Klein', *Deleuze Studies*, 3:2, pp. 207–30.
Žižek, S. (2004), *Organs Without Bodies: On Deleuze and Consequences*, New York: Routledge.

Notes

1. With respect to the expressive character of being, Nietzsche writes: 'How far the perspective character of existence extends or indeed whether existence has any other character than this; whether existence without interpretation, without "sense," does not become "nonsense"; whether, on the other hand, all existence is not essentially actively engaged in *interpretation* – that cannot be decided even by the most industrious and scrupulously conscientious analysis and self-examination of the intellect. . . . But I should think that today we are at least far from the ridiculous immodesty that would be involved in decreeing from our corner that perspectives are permitted only from this corner' (Nietzsche 1974: §374).
2. This is the basis of Marx's critique of Hegel's *Phenomenology*: 'Hegel having posited man as equivalent to self-consciousness, the estranged object – the

estranged essential reality of man – is nothing but *consciousness*, the thought of estrangement merely – estrangement's *abstract* and therefore empty and unreal expression, *negation*. The annulment of the alienation is therefore likewise nothing but an abstract, empty annulment of that empty abstraction – the *negation of the negation*. The rich, living, sensuous, concrete activity of self-objectification is therefore reduced to its mere abstraction, *absolute negativity* – an abstraction which is again fixed as such and thought of as an independent activity – as sheer activity. Because this so-called negativity is nothing but the *abstract, empty* form of that real living act, its content can in consequence be merely a *formal* content begotten by abstraction from all content. As a result there are general, abstract *forms of abstraction* pertaining to every content and on that account indifferent to, and, consequently, valid for, all content – the thought-forms or logical categories torn from *real* mind and from *real* nature' (Marx 1978: 122).

3. 'Matter unites the following two characteristics: it allows a concept which is absolutely identical in as many exemplars as there are 'times' or 'cases'; and it prevents this concept from being further specified by virtue of its natural poverty, or its natural state of unconsciousness or alienation. Matter, therefore, is the identity of spirit – in other words, of the concept, but in the form of an alienated concept, without self-consciousness and outside itself' (Deleuze 1990: 285–6).

4. This image of thought is worked out most extensively in Deleuze 1990 (ch. 3).

5. Deleuze leaves behind the language of simulacra in later writings, declaring it to be 'all but worthless' (2006: 362). None the less, he certainly retains the positive multiplicity that was designated by the term.

6. All further references to Plato's dialogues are taken from Plato (1961) and cite the dialogue, where appropriate, and the Stephanus pagination.

7. Some hold Plato to have become disenchanted with the theory of Ideas in the *Parmenides* and later dialogues, but they can also be interpreted as an exploration of the theory's necessary conditions. These conditions require rejecting a strict separation between being and becoming – hence when it is upheld in *Theaetetus*, knowledge is impossible, but when it is denied in the *Sophist*, the false philosopher can be defined – and, as seen in *Philebus* (15b–18b), an ordered and denumerable plurality that mediates between the One and the Many.

8. See Deleuze 1994: ch. 4.

9. See Seneca, Simplicius, and Galen in Long and Sedley 1987: 176–7.

10. See Cicero and Aetius in Long and Sedley 1987: 237–8.

11. See Diogenes Laertius in Long and Sedley 1987: 198.

12. 'Ces résultats de l'action des êtres, que les Stoïciens ont été peut-être les premiers à remarquer sous cette forme, c'est ce que nous appellerions aujourd'hui des faits ou des événements: concept bâtard qui n'est ni celui d'un être, ni d'une de ses propriétés, mais ce qui est dit ou affirmé de l'être' (Bréhier 1997: 12).

13. See Plutarch in Long and Sedley 1987: 299.

14. In contrast to the chronological time of bodies, incorporeal events 'are not living presents, but infinites: the unlimited Aion, the becoming which divides itself infinitely in past and future and always eludes the present' (Deleuze 1990: 5).

15. 'In accordance with Heidegger's ontological intuition, difference must be articulation and connection in itself; it must relate different to different without any mediation whatsoever by the identical, the similar, the analogous or the opposed. There must be a differenciation of difference, an in-itself which is like a *differenciator* . . . by virtue of which the different is gathered all at once rather than represented on condition of a prior resemblance, identity, analogy or opposition' (Deleuze 1994: 117).

16. Deleuze's relationship to Klein has been left virtually unexamined, despite the fact that his engagement with her work takes up some fifty pages of *The Logic of Sense*. It is completely ignored by Žižek (2004), who treats the book as a Lacanian work when the engagement with Klein is the most obvious piece of evidence that it is not. It is also ignored by Kerslake's (2007) book-length study of Deleuze and the unconscious. Against this trend, see Widder (2009).

17. See Klein 1998: 86, 211; also Klein 1975: 83, 115, 137–8.

18. Deleuze makes this statement in an analysis of Foucault, but it equally applicable to his reading of Klein.

19. For Klein, urine and faeces serve as poisonous weapons for the child to attack and destroy the bad in the paranoid-schizoid position.

20. 'It is no longer a matter of the mechanisms of introjection and projection, but of identification. . . . The depressive split is between the two poles of identification, that is, the identification of the ego with the internal objects and its identification with the object of heights' (Deleuze 1990: 192).

21. Deleuze here rejects the Kleinian ascription of phantasms to the pre-Oedipal positions, holding the phantasm to arise only with desexualization and symbolization, not prior to them (Deleuze 1990: 215–16).

22. Deleuze maintains that propositions relate directly to things by denoting states of affairs, which may be true or false, possible or impossible; they relate to subjects by manifesting the intentions of a speaking 'I'; and they relate to concepts by signifying universal concepts. Sense, however, cannot be subsumed under these relations, since a proposition has sense even if it cannot be linked to a speaking subject and even if it signifies an incoherent concept (i.e. square circle), and since propositions denoting opposing states of affairs ('God is' and 'God is not') can have the same sense. For these reasons, Deleuze calls sense, as a disjunctive synthesis that operates outside these orders of identity, the fourth dimension of propositions and the dimension that allows the others to function (see Deleuze 1990: 12–22).

23. See Deleuze 1994: 96–121.

PRACTICAL DELEUZISM

Chapter 6

The 'Virtual' Body and the Strange Persistence of the Flesh: Deleuze, Cyberspace and the Posthuman

Ella Brians

There is no doubt that Deleuze's work, particularly his joint work with Guattari, has inspired certain theorists of cyber culture. Wherever one looks in contemporary cyber discourse, one encounters Deleuze and Guattarian concepts, especially those of the rhizome, the minoritarian, the molecular, assemblages, and of course, becoming-machine. Neil Spiller has even hailed *A Thousand Plateaus* as 'the philosophical bible of the cyber-evangelists', and suggested that 'this book is possibly one of the most quoted philosophical texts in connection with the technological "spacescape" that computers have created and augmented' (Spiller 2002: 96). Via cyber theory, Deleuze and Guattarian concepts have entered the realm of popular techno-culture, as evidenced by the New Museum's adoption of 'www.rhizome.org' as the name for its program dedicated to supporting and preserving 'emerging artistic practices that engage technology'.[1]

While the link between Deleuze and Guattarian concepts, cyber theory and internet-related technologies may seem self-evident to some, it is not without its tensions. As John Marks has noted, Deleuze himself was not a 'cybertheorist' (Marks 1998: 48). Indeed, Deleuze's few comments on 'information technologies' and their relation to emerging 'control societies' are primarily negative (Deleuze 1995: 175, 177–82). As Marks wisely suggests, while Deleuze's work with Guattari offers many ideas that speak to cyber theory, it also contains others that make it potentially critical of cyber theories (Marks 2006: 195). This is particularly the case, I would argue, when we consider Deleuze's work as a whole, especially his rejection of transcendent thinking and his ontological critique of representation.

There is one area in particular where I believe Deleuze's work can be critically and productively employed to challenge certain tendencies in cyber theory: namely, on the central question of the body, its materiality, and its relation to identity. Historically, cyber discourses have been characterized by a desire to transcend the perceived limits of materiality, which inevitably means transcending the body. Whether utopian or dystopian, cyber fantasies, often couched as predictions of an imminent future, share the idea that 'cyber' technologies will finally allow human beings to become 'pure' intelligence, no longer hindered by the needs and demands of the body. While versions of cyber discourse that argue for taking embodiment seriously have emerged, the fantasy of escaping the flesh persists. This fantasy has recently migrated from cyber-specific discourses to a certain strain of posthumanism, which looks to a variety of 'emerging sciences' (genetics, molecular biology, neuroscience) as well as the 'cybernetic' sciences (artificial intelligence and information/network technologies) for a future free of the flesh.

The argument of this paper is inspired by and directed against the subtle, and therefore insidious, temptation for cyber and posthuman discourses to adopt Deleuze and Guattarian terms while arguing for a transcendence of the material world that is decidedly un-Deleuzian. There is, of course, something indelicate about suggesting that there is a 'proper' way to read Deleuze. He would, perhaps, be the first to suggest that we 'take him from behind' and use him for our own purposes. That said, I believe there are very good reasons for maintaining fidelity to Deleuze's materialism and his repeated rejection of any transcendent worldview. Not least among these is that it is in this context that the entire Deleuzian project hangs together and gains its critical edge. In the specific realm of cyber theory, a rigorous application of a Deleuzian-inspired analysis (rather than the use of isolated catch phrases) will give us better tools for understanding, critiquing, and engaging productively with 'cyberspace' and thinking through the issues of 'virtual' embodiment.

In thinking through the problems associated with virtual bodies, there have been two main trends. One eagerly anticipates technology that will allow us to escape the confines and limitations of the human body. The other argues for carefully and creatively thinking through our embodied relationship to technology. In what follows, I will briefly summarize the development of these trends from the hybrid origins of cyberspace to the emergence of posthumanism. This overview is meant to serve two purposes: first, to familiarize those who may not be well versed in these discourses with the contours of these debates, their major fault lines, and their place in a larger philosophical context; and second, to give some idea of where Deleuze's philosophical commitments might locate him in these debates, and of how his thought might be productively mobilized to re-think our evolving relationship to cyber technologies. The central claim is that Deleuze's thought does align with a certain strand of cyber and posthumanist discourses and that by situating his work appropriately in these debates, we can come closer to understanding and articulating the strange persistence of the flesh in 'virtual' environments.

Before continuing, some caveats. First, I am not concerned here with the use and deployment of the Deleuzian terms, like 'rhizome', that are most popular in cyber or techno-culture discourses. Instead, I am interested in the more fundamental question of where his philosophical commitments place him in the debates, and what they might add, particularly on the central question of 'virtual' embodiment. That is to say, this essay is directed not so much at how Deleuze is used in cyber theory, but at how he might be used. Second, though I speak of 'virtual' bodies, I do not engage with Deleuze's concept of the virtual, or attempt to theorize it vis-à-vis virtual reality (VR). As many have already noted, the use of a common term is misleading here. Furthermore, though I suspect there may be some fruitful connections to be made between these two 'virtualities', the complexity of Deleuze's concept of the virtual puts it beyond the scope of this paper. Third, the terms used here – particularly cyberspace and posthuman – are notoriously unwieldy, with many overlaps, interpenetrations, and contradictions. My own use of them will, I hope, be clarified throughout the paper. Finally, there is some difficulty in writing for two distinct audiences, those familiar with cyber and posthumanist discourses and interested in Deleuze, and those familiar with Deleuze but not well versed in cyber or posthumanist debates. For the former, the historical overview will be a needless summary, while the latter may wonder why it takes so long actually to get to Deleuze. However, I hope that in the end the rewards of putting Deleuze into conversation with these techno-cultural debates will justify the reader's patience.

Cyberspace: Hybrid Origins and the Dream of a 'Fleshless Ontology'

The genealogy or origin myth of cyberspace has by now been well established. And yet, it remains difficult to say exactly what cyberspace is – an idea, a place, a collection of technologies, the internet as we know it, or a dream yet to be realized? The difficulty of pinning down cyberspace can be traced back to its origins. The idea of 'cyberspace' has its roots in both science and science fiction, in theory and in popular media. It was a chimera from its conception and has remained equally elusive. On the scientific side, its lineage can be traced back to scientific developments following World War II and through the technological and scientific arms race of the Cold War. One commonly identified origin is Norbert Wiener's cybernetics theory. In the 1950s, repulsed by the horrors of the war, Wiener developed a theory of communications as a bulwark against entropy and chaos. An important element of this theory was the dissociation of medium, information, and meaning. Information was now seen as pure data, which could be translated from one medium to another without any loss of meaning. In the same time period (1950), Alan Turing developed the famous Turing Test to determine whether a machine had achieved sentience. Taken together, Wiener and Turing's work established a view of intelligence as separated and separable from the 'medium' of the body. This was made clear in Wiener's prediction that it would someday be conceivable to telegraph a human being (Wiener 1954: 103–4). Both Wiener and Turing's work would also be foundational to the developing field of artificial intelligence (AI). The concept of intelligence as the ability to process data, combined with Turing's idea that data could be broken down into a series of binary operations, supported the idea that intelligent machines could be created. For both Wiener and Turing, creating intelligence on a par with or superior to human intelligence had little or nothing to do with the body, which was regarded as a nuisance at best.

The subsequent evolution of computers and computer networks was, of course, fundamental to the emergence of theories of cyberspace. In the 1960s, the mathematician John von Neumann developed the underlying architecture for the computer as we know it, setting the stage for the emergence of the ubiquitous personal computer. In the depths of the Cold War, the American military contributed an important element of what would later become the internet, when military leaders imagined a distributed communications network that would ensure that the nuclear annihilation of one strategic location would not mean the destruction of crucial data. What finally emerged in 1973 was ARPANet (Advanced Research Projects Agency Network). This network was not used primarily by the military, but rather by academic researchers at Stanford and the University of California at Los Angeles (UCLA), among other universities (Conner 2004; Dery 1997: 5; Spiller 2002: 10–11). This network, with its military origins and academic application, would become a prototype for the internet.

Together, these scientific developments form one strand of lineal descent for what became known as cyberspace. However, the concept of cyberspace was first defined not in the scientific or academic realms, but in that of popular culture. It was in science fiction, film, television, and popular discourses that the effects and future of these scientific breakthroughs were debated, elaborated, and re-imagined. Science fiction, in particular, played a crucial role in shaping the popular image of cyberspace. A decade after the launch of ARPANet, William Gibson introduced the concept of 'cyberspace' in his canonical 1984 novel, *Neuromancer*. Here, cyberspace is imagined as a vast sea of coded information accessible to 'cowboys' who 'jack in' through computer terminals. Gibson's characterization of cyberspace was perhaps the single most influential factor in the initial characterization of cyberspace as a disembodied space. The body is referred to repeatedly, and derogatorily, as 'the meat' and the protagonist's inability to access 'the bodiless exultation of cyberspace' after suffering neurological damage is characterized as 'the Fall' (Gibson 1984: 6).[2] Gibsonian cyberspace is a 'space' where the non-material human intelligence can navigate, interact with, and 'hack' data. This vision of cyberspace was taken up by science fiction fans, scientific researchers, and cultural theorists. New research into virtual reality (VR) technologies promised to make Gibson's cyberspace a 'reality' by stimulating a 3-D environment that the user could navigate. It went even further by promising the user the ability to define and control this environment. As Gibson's idea of cyberspace percolated into the popular imagination and met up with ideas from VR research and video games, the idea of cyberspace evolved. It was imagined as a place where the user would be free of the material limits of his body, while also exercising an enhanced control over his virtual environment. In 1999, just over twenty-five years after the inauguration of ARPANet and fifteen years after Gibson introduced the term 'cyberspace', the continuing cultural relevance of cyberspace was re-affirmed in the block-buster hit, *The Matrix*. Here, recalling Descartes' evil demon, the simulated cyberspace, or 'matrix', is an illusion used by intelligent machines to keep mankind in bondage. A confused hacker named Neo becomes a potential savior through his ability to change and partially control the matrix with the power of his mind.[3]

As both *Neuromancer* and *The Matrix* testify, AI is a key theme of science fiction stories about cyberspace. The relation between cyberspace and AI in the fictive sphere is not surprising, given their mutual implications and shared origins in cybernetics, and it also plays a key role in the movement from cyber-specific theory to posthumanism. It is worth considering here because science fiction accounts of AI often reflect a set of anxieties about the boundary between human and machine. The emergence of faster, 'smarter' computers fed both the dream and the fear of machines that would be able to out-think and possibly come to dominate human beings.[4] Philip K. Dick's 1968 *Do Androids Dream of Electric Sheep?* (later made into the cult classic movie, *Blade Runner*) features a bounty hunter, Rick, whose job is to identify and then eliminate illegal androids. Increasingly sophisticated models that are programmed to pass the screening tests (a combination of a biometric lie detector and a Turing Test) make it difficult to tell android from human. After interacting and going to bed with one of the advanced models, Rick is nearly unnerved. Gibson's *Neuromancer* also imagines a situation in which human beings are frightened by the intelligent programs they have created and attempt to regulate and prevent them from becoming fully sentient, independent actors. In another nod to Turing, Gibson introduces the Turing Police, whose job it is to seek out and eliminate AI programs that threaten to achieve full sentience, as well as prosecute the human beings who allowed it to happen. The fascination with and fear of AI finds its latest expression in the TV series *Battlestar Galactica*, which begins with the attempt of cylons (a new name for androids) to wipe out the human race that created them. Biologically, at least on the surface and several layers down, these cylons are virtually indistinguishable from human beings. As in *Do Androids Dream of Electric Sheep?*, machine intelligence is wired into 'human' flesh. These fleshy robots raise the question of the body in another way. Instead of asking what happens when our intelligence escapes from the body into the machine, these fictions ask what happens to our humanity when machine intelligence finds its way into 'our' bodies. The dangers of AI and the potential treachery of humanoid robots reveal anxieties about the boundary between the organic and the inorganic, the human and the mechanical, which I will discuss in more detail later.

Together, scientific and academic research, science fiction and popular media have produced what Don Ihde would call a 'technofantasy', or technological myth, of cyberspace (Ihde 2002). This summary is a very brief account of some of the key factors in the development of that fantasy. From its beginnings, the technofantasy of cyberspace has been characterized by both the desire to escape the body and the belief that cyber technologies (however these are conceived) will make this escape possible – if not now, then tomorrow. In other words, the imaginary of cyberspace is invested in a notion of transcendence: specifically, transcendence of the body and its perceived material limits. Many critics, such Margaret Wertheim, have pointed out the religious, and specifically Christian, qualities of such thought (Wertheim 1999). Others, like Eric Davis, have noted its relation to Gnostic and magical thinking, with its focus on a non-material realm of spiritual knowledge (Davis

1994). Today, it has become a commonplace to note that the body–mind dualism of early cyber theory is essentially a redux of Platonic and Cartesian metaphysics, a point I will return to later. Whether the mind–body divide is traced to Christianity, Platonic Idealism, or the mechanistic Cartesian universe, it is clear that the technofantasy of cyberspace is not entirely new. Despite its radically progressive technological trappings, the technofantasy of cyberspace is firmly rooted in the kind of transcendence that has defined Western culture, religion, and philosophy for two millennia. This transcendent thinking produces what Carly Harper and Ingrid Richardson call the 'fleshless ontology of cyberspace'. As they observe, this means that '[t]he teleology of cyberspace, or the end towards which it progresses, is all about the final non-necessity of the body, or achieving a mode of existence that can do without the body' (Harper and Richardson: 2001). The techno-fantasy of cyberspace is that technology will finally deliver what philosophy and religion have only dreamed of – to free us at last from the earthly bonds of the flesh, with its hungers, needs, and limitations.

Waking from the Techno-fantasy of Cyberspace: The Long Morning After

When the internet entered the public domain in the late 1980s, it was often hailed as the harbinger of the imminent arrival of a fully immersive cyberspace.[5] It seemed that the 'teleology of cyberspace' was about to be achieved. In the heady years of the late 1980s and early 1990s, the internet was not always distinguished, at least in popular discussions, from VR or AI research. The merger of these distinct technologies in the popular imagination, with its roots in science fiction, is important for understanding some of the early discussions and predictions about the internet. Many early adopters and cyber theorists (by this time the subject had emerged as a field of inquiry) proclaimed that the internet would usher in a new era of human liberation. These predictions of liberation were invariably premised on the internet's supposed ability to transcend material constraints. It would democratize communication by removing physical barriers to participation. It would make universal access to information possible, by removing the costs of paper, printing, and mailing, and thus level hierarchies of knowledge. Most importantly, by offering a 'non-material' space for interaction, the internet would finally allow human beings to escape the narrow confines of a single body.

There are two significant senses in which it was predicted that we would become 'free' of our bodies. In one version, we would become 'free' of our material bodies by 'jacking in', like Gibson's space cowboys, to access a fully immersive 3-D environment. In this environment, it was imagined that we would be able to simulate any form of embodiment we could imagine (Seidler 1998: 20). Suddenly, men would be able to experience what it was 'to be' a woman, and vice versa. We could choose to inhabit any age, sex, race, or class we like, or none at all (Hayles 2002: 235). Nor would we be limited to the human form. Physical laws like gravity and the inability to fly would likewise be optional in this simulated space. This part of the fantasy of cyberspace is a pretty straightforward wish for escape into an alternate embodiment, or escape from embodiment altogether into a god-like perspective. The second form of anticipated liberation had more to do with being freed from the social and cultural categories applied to our bodies than with escaping from our bodies themselves. Even minus an immersive environment, it was argued that communication on the internet would make discrimination on the basis of race, sex, or gender impossible, or at least not as automatic, since nobody would 'really know' the race, sex, or gender of the person with whom s/he was communicating (Dery 1994b: 3, 7–8). Rawls's Veil of Ignorance would become more than just a thought experiment. All of the -isms that had fueled the Culture Wars would disappear once we entered the pure, bodiless space of the Net and could finally be judged for 'what we really were', or wanted to be, instead of on 'superficial' physical characteristics. Furthermore, optimists hoped that the ability to take on other embodiments, whether through full immersion or online 'performative' role-playing, would increase empathy and understanding. In both cases, our virtual bodies, whether composed of 3-D visual representations or words, would become accessories that we could discard and change at whim, and which we could shape to meet whatever aesthetic or social criteria we chose.

Throughout the 1990s, as internet use spiked, as the internet bubble swelled and burst, as VR technologies failed to deliver a fully 'immersive' experience, and as internet applications became increasingly commercialized, the utopian predictions of liberation began to look increasingly naïve. Issues of access, whether due to regional disparities or a gender gap, gave the lie to a dream of global, democratic participation. Race and gender, rather than disappearing on the Net, became key topics of concern. Issues of trust, identity, and 'virtual' violence, as well as 'virtual' sex and even 'virtual' rape, were heatedly debated. The technology itself remained frustratingly non-immersive. This internet was clearly not the cyberspace for which we had been waiting. Early euphoria gave way to more measured analysis and the myth of cyber-space began to break apart. Increasingly, critics questioned the notion that cyberspace could, or should, be thought of as a non-material realm that would allow us to transcend or escape the body. Critics like Robert Markley pointed out that internet technologies where not in fact 'free' or non-material, but actually required significant investment costs and the consumption of large amounts of material resources (Markley 1996: 55–78). Feminist critics questioned the effacement of bodies and whether gender play would actually produce change or merely reinforce stereotypes. Increasingly, the idea of the internet or cyberspace as a non-material, disembodied, and inherently liberating realm was found wanting. By the mid-1990s, the body, both virtual and material, had become a central site of cyber theorizing and debate.

Important pressure to re-imagine cyberspace and our embodied relation to technology came from the art world. Artists and theo-rists like Monika Fleischmann engaged in phenomenological studies that examined how the body actually interacts with technologies and environments. As founder of Art + Com (Berlin) and then head of MARS exploratory media lab (Sankt Augustin, Germany), Fleischmann brought together artists, computer programmers, architects, and sci-entists to imagine new environments and ways of interacting with technology. Inquiries like Fleischmann's led to an increased theoretical and scientific focus on the interface between body, mind, and machine. This approach recognized that, even in 'virtual' environments, the material body remained – after all, even Gibson's space cowboy had to hook himself up to a catheter if he wanted to spend a prolonged time in cyberspace. In a series of art projects and theoretical reflections, Fleischmann asked what the interfaces that we use (screens, keyboards) make possible and impossible. What senses do they privilege? How can we involve more of the body – and more of the brain – in our experi-ence of cyber technologies? Most importantly, Fleischmann introduced the concept of 'mixed-reality' to replace the term 'virtual reality'. This term was meant to indicate a more accurate understanding of our relation to cyber technologies, in which material bodies, their virtual representations, the human imagination, and computer hardware and software all interact to produce a reality that has both 'material' and 'virtual' elements (Fleischmann). The idea of mixed-reality is a theo-retically powerful tool because it allows us to think about the body as simultaneously taking part in, and being formed by, the 'material' and 'virtual'.[6] In doing so, it gives us a theoretical framework for talking about the physical aspects of computer–body interfaces, as well as the complex events and socially coded identities that emerge from their interaction.

Interventions by artists like Fleischmann, combined with the theoretical contributions of critics such as Robert Markley and Katherine Hayles, as well as an increasingly sophisticated popular discourse about technology, created a shift in the imaginary of cyberspace. A first crucial point was the establishment of the fantasy of cyberspace *as a fantasy*, and the exchanging of that dream for a rigorous phenomenological exploration of how human bodies interface with specific technologies. Central to this shift was a more complex conceptualization of the 'virtual' body. On the previous model, the 'virtual' body was either a visual representation of the user (an avatar) in a 2-D or 3-D virtual environment, or an imagined 3-D experience of simulated bodily awareness, in which the user's mind would fully inhabit and experience a 'virtual' body of her choosing. Following the shift, the 'virtual' body was increasingly seen not as a non-material representation of a human consciousness, but as that site where flesh, machinery, binary code, cultural codings, and imagination converge. On this view, the material body is no longer effaced, but becomes an important locus for understanding, theorizing, and critiquing cyber cultures and technologies. The focus is no longer on the split between the material body and the virtual body, or the representation – or non-representation – of the former by the latter. Instead, the emphasis shifts to the relation between material bodies, virtual bodies, and the material and cultural environments that variously form, define, constrain, or render them intelligible. The movement away from the techno-fantasy of cyberspace as a bodiless, non-material space has been slow and is far from complete. Importantly, as Fleischmann and Hayles argue, 'recovering' the body does not mean moving back to a pre-technological or purely 'human' past, but rigorously thinking through our relationship to and interaction with the technologies that shape our lives.

This brings us to cyborgs and posthumanism.

Becoming-Cyborg, Becoming-Posthuman

Perhaps the most important impetus for the critique of the dualistic worldview of early cyber discourses was Donna Haraway's 'Cyborg Manifesto' (Haraway 1991). First appearing in 1985, Haraway's manifesto was both prescient and provocative. It is one of the earliest, and arguably most powerful, examples of the shift away from a disembodied cyberspace. Haraway's main target was not the fantasy of disembodiment per se, but the underlying dualistic worldview that supported it. For Haraway, this worldview was associated with Enlightenment rationality and its subsequent deployment in Western science. Haraway's manifesto was a consciously feminist intervention in the history of science, including the technological realms of AI and cybernetics, usually reserved for geeky boys and the men they become. As a concept, the cyborg marks the attempt to think through the imaginary, socio-political investments of technology, as well as its material conditions and actual uses. Haraway describes the cyborg as 'a condensed image of both imagination and material reality' (Haraway 1991: 150), thus indicating something like Fleischmann's 'mixed-reality'. Unlike many early cyber theorists, Haraway readily avows her cyborg as a myth, but argues that it is a myth that is needed in order to resist and critique the old dualisms of Western thought (Haraway 1991: 154). Strikingly, and against the currents of her time, Haraway claims that we will not achieve the goals of a feminist politics by turning away from science and technology in order to recover a 'pure' nature, virgin and untouched by man's reason, and 'free' from the interventions of technology. Instead of the mother goddess, as representation of the 'pure' and 'whole' earth, Haraway offers the cyborg, an impure hybrid of flesh and machine. When Haraway insists that '[W]e are cyborgs. The cyborg is our ontology,' she means that we have always already been impure hybrids, that the boundary between human beings and nature, between human beings and technology, has always been more porous than Enlightenment rationality led us to believe. There is no going back to the Garden of Eden or to a Heideggerian Alpine forest free of technology. There has never been such a place. And even if there were, Haraway tells us, her cyborg would not be interested. Because she has no 'natural' origin, the Fall means nothing to her. Because she was not born into the nuclear family, not engendered of heterosexual relations, Oedipalized relations have no hold over her (Haraway 1991: 175–6).

Haraway's cyborg became an icon of cyber theory and its theoretical force is still felt over twenty years later. It also helped to usher in the era of 'posthumanism' first predicted by Foucault. Posthumanism reflects variously the belief that we have reached, are about to reach, or should actively seek the end of the human. The term, like postmodernism, is problematic because it is used to cover a range of contradictory positions. Also like postmodernism, it is not always clear what is supposed to separate our supposedly 'posthuman' era from the previous 'humanist' era (Ihde 2008: online). However, there are several elements that typify the kind of posthumanism proposed by Haraway: a critique of

Enlightenment humanism, a rejection of mind–body dualism, and the claim that our bodies and identities have always been formed in relation to technology, even when this technology was a simple stone hammer. For Haraway, these claims are interrelated. She argues that in setting the human at the center of the universe and dividing that universe into a superior mind and inferior matter, Enlightenment humanism fails to account for the fact that we are always already formed by and embedded in both nature and technology. Haraway's analysis lends itself to the conclusion that we have always already been 'posthuman', which is to say, we have always already been cyborgs.

The image of the cyborg, however, has also been taken up by another strain of posthumanism. Futurists like Ray Kurzweil and the AI and robotics researcher Hans Moravec argue that we are not nearly cyborg enough and urge us to dispose of the human body as an obsolete burden. In 1988, in an echo of Wiener's telegraph, Moravec predicted that technological advances would soon make it possible to 'download' human consciousness and save it on a computer (Moravec 1988: 109–10). Kurzweil imagines an approaching 'singularity' in which human biology will be fully replaced by stronger, faster machines (Kurzweil 2005). In a recent paper titled 'The Senses Have No Future' (1997), Moravec confirms Kurzweil's vision and argues that the only hope humans have for survival is to merge their consciousness with the superior speed, power, and flexibility of machines. Moravec's thesis is simple: the body is obsolete and must be transcended. This vision of posthumanism clearly revives the techno-fantasy of cyberspace, while expanding it to include a range of 'emerging' sciences. Here, the focus shifts from an immersive VR to AI, robotics, genetics, and neurobiology. However, the dream of a disembodied space, where embodiment can be simulated, remains. Moravec acknowledges that the 'download' of the human brain will require simulating proprioception, or a sense of the body in space, since the human mind cannot bear to exist in a vacuum. On his view, this simulated sense of being in a body will be sufficient for the work of the mind. However, ultimately, the need for such bodily simulation will mean that human beings are at a disadvantage and will inevitably lose the 'evolutionary' race with machines and fall into irrelevance and obscurity. He writes, 'As the cyberspace becomes more potent, its advantages over physical bodies will overwhelm . . . the whole becoming finally a bubble of Mind expanding at near light speed' (Moravec 1997).

Horrified by this vision of posthumanism, Katherine Hayles argues that Moravec makes a fundamental mistake when he assumes that the 'information' of human intelligence can be meaningfully separated from the material of the brain (Hayles 1999: 1).[7] She suggests that the desire to 'free' information from its medium, which can be traced back to Wiener, and the subsequent tendency to see ourselves as information waiting to be downloaded, is tied to a desire for immortality; free of the flesh, our memories encoded in the circuit board, we do not have to die. She recognizes the attraction of such a fantasy, and cautions, 'in the face of such a powerful dream, it can be a shock to remember that for information to exist, it must *always* be instantiated in a medium' (Hayles 1999: 13). Reaching back to Haraway's cyborg, Hayles argues instead for a posthumanism that explores and pushes the boundary of our relationship to technology, without ever forgetting or effacing the body. This view allows for imagining what the body might become in a 'posthuman' future of increasing machine–human hybridization, while resisting the mind–body dualism that has typified Western philosophy and science and makes Moravec and Kurzweil's fantasy of 'human' intelligence separated from 'human' bodies possible.

This all too brief summary indicates the two main tendencies in post-human debates. One, represented by Haraway and Hayles, argues for a critical thinking through of embodiment and our relation to technology. The other, represented by Moravec and Kurzweil, promises technology as escape and salvation. To a large degree, these two trends in posthumanism are an extension of the debates around embodiment in cyberspace. At the core of this debate is the question of the body and our human relationship to technology. If we wanted to categorize, we could say that Haraway and Hayles are aligned with those like Fleischmann, who advocate both theorizing and creatively intervening in our embodied relation to technology and a critical approach to the body's social and political codings. They reject transcendent or dualistic accounts and operate in a 'mixed-reality' paradigm. Moravec and Kurzweil, on the other hand, are aligned with tendencies in both science and science fiction to see the body as something separable from intelligence, and ultimately, as an inconvenience to be overcome. They re-enact the classic divide between a 'pure' realm of the mind and the inferior realm of the material body. They do not engage critically with issues of embodiment, because they have already decided that the solution is to get rid of the body. To be glib, we could call these two views the 'materialist' and the 'dualist'. The tension between these two views is not just a product of the techno-cultural debates of the late twentieth century, but stretches back through the history of Western thought. The mind–body divide that characterizes the 'dualists' is easily traced through Enlightenment rationality, Descartes, and finally, to Plato. As we have seen, it also has strong resonances with the transcendent religious thinking that characterizes Christianity. Though they may seem strange bedfellows, Moravec's 'pure mind' and Christian theology share the same world-view: one that has consistently devalued and effaced the material body in the name of a transcendent, non-material perfection. Like Christianity, this form of posthumanism promises us that we will only be truly happy and wise once we are free of the flesh. The worldview of 'materialist' posthumanism is messier and more complex, offering no final promises of bliss or salvation. Its philosophical lineage is less direct, has often operated on the margins, and still remains to be fully articulated.

Deleuze and Posthumanism: Resisting the Temptations of Transcendence

This brings us, finally, to Deleuze. Ann Weinstone has grouped Deleuze's work with the 'major philosophical and techno-scientific sources for progressive posthumanism' (Weinstone 2004: 10). I am wary of embracing the term 'posthuman' in relation to Deleuze's work. Its use to indicate mutually exclusive theoretical stances means that it risks meaning everything and nothing, while muddying the conceptual field. However, given its popular currency in cultural theory, this is probably a losing battle. If we want to situate Deleuze in regard to this discourse and ask whether he is a posthumanist, then I contend that the answer depends very much on which form of posthumanism we have in mind. It seems evident to me that of the two views outlined here (admittedly, with a speed and superficiality that risks caricature), Deleuze's thought would align quite well with the 'materialist', and would be vigorously opposed to the 'dualist'. That is to say, if by 'posthumanist' we mean that he questions Enlightenment rationality and the unity of the subject, while insisting on a form of critique that encompasses both material conditions and cultural codings, then it would be fair to call Deleuze a posthumanist. If we mean, instead, that Deleuze and Guattari's becoming-machine and machinic assemblages can be equated to Moravec's exhortations literally to 'upload' human consciousness into superior machines, then the term is not only inaccurate, but it also risks a gross misunderstanding of Deleuze's, and Deleuze and Guattari's, overall project.

However, as the last sentence indicates, the first question we face in deciding where to situate Deleuze and Guattari's work in the post-humanist debates is what to make of certain superficial resonances between some of Deleuze and Guattari's more ecstatic statements and a Moravecian image of merging with machines. How do we respond to those who see congruities between Deleuze and Guattari's machinic production, Body without Organs (BwO) and assemblages on one hand, and Moravec's merging of intelligence into machines on the other? Is Moravec's vision of mind merging with machine not just an example of the kind of impure minglings, assemblages, and cross-pollinations that Deleuze and Guattari urge us towards? Is it, in fact, not the inevitable result of Deleuze and Guattari's own de-privileging of the human and their blurring of the boundary between the organic and non-organic? In short, is Moravec's 'becoming machine' not a prime example of what it would mean to embrace a Deleuze and Guattarian ontology of becoming? A cursory reading of *Anti-Oedipus* and *A Thousand Plateaus*, or a chance encounter with select excerpts, might indeed leave one with the impression that Deleuze and Guattari are promoting a kind of 'becoming' that would ultimately transcend the 'merely' human body. The language is undeniably there: the talk of 'freedom' and 'liberation', the image of becoming almost anything other than human, the machinic assemblages. Taken out of context, phrases like 'the real difference is not between the living and the machine' (Deleuze and Guattari 1983: 285) might seem to support a Moravecian view.

The obvious first response is that what Deleuze and Guattari mean by machines, whether they speak of 'desiring-machines', 'social machines', 'organic machines', 'war machines', or 'machinic assemblages', is simply not what Moravec or Kurzweil means by machines. Deleuze and Guattari are not talking about computers, or steam engines for that matter, when they discuss whether there is a difference between the living and the machine (Deleuze and Guattari 1983: 285). 'Machines' offer Deleuze and Guattari a way to talk about the differential interactions of forces and processes of individuation that underlie, connect, and structure all entities, whether mineral, animal, or machine. This leads us to the longer response, which is that such a cursory, impressionistic reading misses the fact that Deleuze and Guattari's many 'machines' are part of a larger ontological critique – one, moreover, that is firmly situated in a materialist refusal of transcendence that is incompatible with a Moravecian worldview.

Deleuze laid out the basis of this ontological critique in 1968 in the first fully developed statement of his own thought, *Difference and Repetition*.[8] Hayles has identified the shift from humanism to the posthuman with a 'significant shift in underlying assumptions about subjectivity' towards a conception of the subject as 'an amalgam, a collection of heterogeneous components, a material-informational entity whose boundaries undergo continuous construction and reconstruction'

(Hayles 1999: 3). In *Difference and Repetition*, Deleuze lays the groundwork for just such an ambitious and fundamental shift in the conception of subjectivity. Situating his critique squarely against Aristotle, Plato, Hegel, and Kant, Deleuze argues against a representational metaphysics and epistemology that relies on the reification of categories and produces a dualistic and transcendent 'image of thought'. The shift that Deleuze proposes is nothing less than a complete re-evaluation of the Western philosophical canon. At the heart of this re-evaluation is a critique of 'the subject' and the logic of identity that makes this subject possible. Drawing on Duns Scotus, Spinoza, and Nietzsche, Deleuze calls into question the negations and either/or structures that efface real differences and argues for a mode of thought that does not subjugate difference to identity (Deleuze 1994: esp. 281–2). Instead, he offers a theory of forces that are differentiated by varying degrees of intensity. These differences in intensity produce more differentiations in an exponential process that finally produces entities that we recognize as discrete objects, individuals, and eventually, subjects. Deleuze's point here is that difference is prior to and produces individuals. This has two consequences: the individual is the result of a series of differentiations, not an essence; and as a contingent result of an ongoing process, the 'individual' (here we can fill in 'object', 'self', or any entity) is merely shorthand for a relatively stable state of affairs that is both partially determined by previous states and open to change. Another important point that will be relevant in Deleuze and Guattari's work, and in relation to posthumanism, is that on this ontological account there are no firm or absolute boundaries between one 'thing' and the next. Boundaries exist, as zones of consistency, but they remain permeable and open to transformation, or becoming other.

It is in *Difference and Repetition* that Deleuze introduces and argues for 'becoming' as a more accurate description of our ontological situation than Platonic 'being'. In his work with Guattari, 'becoming' is often taken as just a trendy catch phrase. Turning to *Difference and Repetition*, we see that 'becoming' is crucial to the fundamental shift in subjectivity for which Deleuze argues. Becoming refers both to the endless process of differentiation and to our relation to our own subjectivity. Deleuze's concept of becoming is indebted to Nietzsche, who advocates '[b]ecoming as inventing, willing, self-negating, self-overcoming: no subject but a doing, positing, creative' (Nietzsche 2003: 138). In displacing identity and being with difference and becoming, Deleuze argues for a new understanding of subjectivity as a process, a 'doing' that is at once creative and critical. In contrast to the unified Platonic or Kantian subject, Deleuze paints a picture of identity as decentered, distributed, and emerging from a series of highly complex interactions between pre-personal forces. The result is a subjectivity that is remarkably similar to what Hayles describes as 'posthuman'. Crucially, identity is revealed not as an essence, but as 'an amalgam of heterogeneous elements' that include biological and evolutionary processes, social and cultural codings, and accidents of history. The forms that life takes and the particular individuals and identities that arise are both determined to some extent *and* open to change or becoming other than what they are at any given moment. The self must be made, but it is always constituted in a context. This vision of subjectivity as emerging out of a process of becoming is resolutely materialist. If we have any doubt of this, we need only recall the source of the opposition between being and becoming. In the *Republic*, Plato rejects Heraclitean flux on the grounds that this material chaos, this becoming, obscures the unchanging, non-material truth of the Forms (Plato 1991).[9] In Platonic terms, becoming is 'not real' and 'not true'. Its materiality, its participation in the physical world of things and stuff and dirt and bodies, makes it incompatible with truth. At best, it is an imperfect representation of a 'pure' idea. When Deleuze returns to becoming, he returns to the founding moment of Western metaphysics and purposefully unleashes all the mess and chaos of material flux that Plato wanted to control by consigning it to 'mere representation'.

This vision of subjectivity remains remarkably consistent through Deleuze's work with Guattari until his late essay 'Immanence: A Life . . .'. In many ways, it anticipates much of the critical project of what I have provisionally identified as 'materialist' posthumanism. A better term might be 'immanent' posthumanism. Deleuze's philosophical commitments align him with those like Haraway and Hayles, for whom the critique of subjectivity spans both the obviously 'material' (biological processes) and the 'cultural' or 'social' codings that make identity intelligible. Though they are not 'material' in a physical sense, neither are they merely abstract nor transcendent, ahistorical truths. These social and cultural codings are always immanent to a particular situation or environment. Subtly, for each of these thinkers, these cultural and social codings have 'real' – that is, material – effects. For Deleuze, as for Haraway and Hayles, an immanent worldview that takes into account a range of heterogeneous forces is crucial to critiquing a form of subjectivity that, for various reasons, they find to be inaccurate, distorting, and even oppressive.

With this in mind, I would like to return to the question of the body in

Deleuze and Guattari's work. The main target of Deleuze and Guattari's critique in *Anti-Oedipus* and *A Thousand Plateaus* is the same logic of identity that Deleuze first targeted in *Difference and Repetition*. This logic depends on a strict separation between self and other, inside and outside, natural and unnatural, human and machine, and human and animal, to name just a few. Deleuze and Guattari systematically set about undermining this series of oppositions. In doing so, they repeatedly call into question the 'fact' of a unified, contained subject.

Traditionally, the boundary of the subject is identified with the boundary of the flesh; I end where my skin ends. This idea depends on a naturalized idea of the body as 'given' and obvious. Deleuze and Guattari, however, illustrate how the body must be constituted through 'codings', which are the result of the regulation, control, and interactions of various 'flows', including the biological, technological, and cultural. In *A Thousand Plateaus*, they use the example of the face or 'faciality' to discuss how a surface, itself the result of the convergence of a thousand tiny flows, is signified as something, as someone (Deleuze and Guattari 1987: 167–73). They ask us to be critical of the socially constructed, socially coded, but naturalized face and the underlying logic of identity that supports it. In doing so, they suggest that 'the body' is always more than its biological parts or fleshy boundaries. By opening the body beyond the limits of the flesh, to include its social and cultural codings, Deleuze and Guattari displace the body from what we traditionally think of as the 'material' realm, that of biology, while precisely insisting on its materiality. Braidotti clarifies this seeming contradiction when she writes that:

> The embodiedness of the subject is for Deleuze a form of bodily materiality, not of the natural, biological kind. He rather takes the body as the complex interplay of highly constructed social and symbolic forces. The body is not an essence, let alone a biological substance; it is a play of forces, a surface of intensities; pure simulacra without originals. (Braidotti 1994: 112)

The 'material' is not merely the biological. There is a whole range of forces that interact to form 'the body'. For Deleuze, these forces have always been 'material'. Unlike Moravec, Deleuze and Guattari's machines are not mobilized to do away with or escape materiality in a general 'becoming-machine'. Instead, as we have seen, 'becoming' has been, from the beginning, an indice for the recognition of materiality and material flux.

At the same time, drawing on Deleuze's earlier ontological analysis, Deleuze and Guattari insistently undermine the boundary between the organic and non-organic, the human and the machine, the human and the animal. The blurring or elimination of these boundaries has a strong relation to both forms of posthumanism that I have outlined above. It might also seem to support a Moravecian merging with machines. If there is no real difference between human and machine, then what is lost in merging them? The phrase 'no real difference' should be the first indicator that something is wrong here. For Deleuze and Guattari, the undermining of boundaries can never mean that there is no difference. Their point is more complicated: it is precisely because there are too many differences that these simple binary oppositions are insufficient. In undermining the boundary between man and machine, Deleuze and Guattari do not aim to efface their differences, but to reveal their inter-relation and the fact that 'calling into question the specific or personal unity of the organism' and 'calling in question the structural unity of the machine' are part of the same ontological critique (Deleuze and Guattari 1983: 284). Furthermore, in contrast to both a Moravecian posthumanism and some of their own most ardent supporters, Deleuze and Guattari recognize that there are material consequences of and limitations on our experimentations. Deleuze may repeatedly insist on the Spinozistic question, 'What can the body do?', but this does not mean that he believes that the body can do just anything. His theory of forces and intensities is firmly situated in what Hayles describes as 'the world of energy and matter and the constraints they imply' (Hayles 1999: 236). There is a significant difference between asking what the body can do and suggesting the body can do anything, or, recalling Moravec, doing away with the body altogether.

With this in mind, let us return to the question of where Deleuze's work fits in the cyber theory and posthumanist debates. Deleuze's project, from beginning to end, attempts to create a 'significant shift in underlying assumptions about subjectivity'. Hayles, following Haraway, identifies a critique of the liberal humanist subject as a crucial feature of posthumanism, and explicitly recognizes Deleuze and Guattari as being engaged in a similar project (Hayles 1999: 4). Arguably, Deleuze takes this project even further, by returning to the philosophical roots and habits of thought that make a Lockean subject possible. In contrast, Moravec's 'bubble of Mind' preserves key features of the dualist subjectivity identified with Plato and Enlightenment humanism, even as it promises to evolve past the human. As Chris Land observes with reference to Moravec's 'uploaded' brain, 'this figure of the post-human is surprisingly like the ideal of the liberal-humanist subject. Completely disembodied and obscenely rational, it is a pure will that has finally cut itself free of its puppet strings to become a self-contained master' (Land 2006: 122). Land has suggested the term 'transhumanism' as an alternative to distinguish a posthumanism that both critiques the liberal humanist model of subjectivity and affirms materiality, from that of Moravec, Kurzweil, and other futurists (Land 2006: 113). Weinstone uses the term 'progressive posthumanism'. Regardless of which term we prefer, what is clear is that Deleuze's philosophical commitments align him with the strand of cyber theory and posthumanism that not only insists on a critique of subjectivity and a thorough coming to terms with embodiment and materiality, but that also sees these two tasks as intimately interconnected.

Of course, establishing that Deleuze's work is more aligned with one form of posthumanism does not mean that there are not tensions. For example, Braidotti and others have already noted how Haraway's cyborg might challenge Deleuze and Guattari's famously troubled concept of 'becoming woman' (Braidotti 2006: 198; Braidotti 1994: 102–23). That said, it seems clear that there are significant shared philosophical commitments. Though I remain wary of the term, I would even suggest that Deleuze's ontology and the minor philosophical tradition that he identifies as an alternative to the dominant Platonic tradition could constitute a philosophical lineage for a posthumanism that resolutely resists the temptations of transcendence.

Conclusion: Beyond the Material–Virtual Divide

Where does this leave us in terms of thinking through 'virtual' bodies? In situating Deleuze in relation to debates in cyber theory and posthumanism, I have traced a line of thought that resists the techno-fantasy of escaping the body. This line of thought resists the fantasy of a 'fleshless ontology', not by returning to or shoring up the material body, but by revealing how the 'virtual' realm of cyberspace is always already formed by and implicated with material forces. In both the critical shift towards a cyber theory of embodiment and the materialist posthumanism that follows it, there is a recognition that what constitutes 'the body' spans both the 'virtual' and 'material' realms. In both 'materialist' posthumanism and Deleuze's work, this 'mixed-reality' view of embodiment is revealed to be part of a larger ontological critique that links the irreducibility of 'the body' to the biological body to a 'fundamental shift in assumptions about subjectivity'. In a 'mixed-reality' paradigm it no longer makes sense to talk about a 'virtual' body and a 'material' body. Instead, we turn our attention to a critical analysis of the relationships *between* our bodies, our brains, our environment, our identities, and the multitude of material forces that shape them. In conclusion, I would like to turn to the example of social networking sites to illustrate what this shift might look like in practice.

Social networking sites like Facebook or MySpace are a prime example of a 'mixed-reality' situation where 'virtual' and 'real' bodies mingle to produce identities that do not fully correspond to either. Through online profiles that consist of pictures, lists of preferences, lists of friends, and mini-blogs, users create online personas. The profile picture and other images that the user posts play a major role in establishing that persona. Users generally have the option of not posting a picture, or of posting a picture of something other than oneself, but in the online environments of Facebook and MySpace to do so would be considered odd – an indication that one is either unattractive or socially dysfunctional, or both. It would be very easy to take these images as acting as a more or less accurate representation of the 'real' body, and thus involved in an all too common and vicious form of representation. We might be tempted to launch a Deleuzian critique of representation, and there would indeed be plenty to say here. Certainly, the unofficial requirement to post a photo involves a good deal of 'facializing' and reterritorialization. (The images serve to categorize one as male or female, black or white, queer or straight, attractive or unattractive.)

This is all true and in a way too obvious. I would like to follow a different, perhaps counterintuitive, line of thought and argue that the work the images of bodies on social networking sites are doing is not merely representative, but also constitutive. I would argue that the nature of the sites and the way profile images are used complicates and undermines the representational schema (even as they participate in it). The nature of social networking sites is that they necessarily cross over the boundary between the online 'virtual' world and the 'real' or 'material' world. Theoretically, at least, most users know and will interact with most of their 'friends' in the real world at some time. Unlike early fantasies of cyber space, on social networking sites there is a mutual feedback between users' real-life experiences and activities and their online personas and interactions. Constant status updates and comments can shape how a person or event is perceived offline. Online discussions can lead to the organization of offline events, meetings, protests, or dates. Real-world events can in turn prompt a flurry of online comments and interactions. The nature and functions of social networking sites also mean that images are more than merely representational. In addition to the main profile picture, users have the option to upload additional pictures or picture albums. They are then able to 'tag' themselves and other users in each picture, creating a hyperlink between the image of each user and his/her profile. Other users are able to do the same, which means that a user is not necessarily the source of all of the images of herself that are linked to her profile. The representational schema is essentially reductive: x represents y. In contrast, the images that help form a user's persona on social networking sites are prolific, multiplying. The point of this proliferation of linked and tagged images is not to create a 'correct correspondence' with a given biological body in order to verify or solidify an identity. Instead, the proliferation of interconnected images actively supports the ongoing recreation or 'becoming' of all the online personas involved.

This process of 'becoming' parallels in many ways that described in *Difference and Repetition*. First, what these online identities can become is limited to a certain degree by the environment and forces in play: in this case, the categories each site offers (male or female, for example); social conventions and technological limitations (2-D, so many pixels, etc.); even the moods and inclinations of other users. Second, though the identities produced online are not reducible to biological bodies, they are formed in relation to them. This relationship, however, is not one of one-to-one correspondence, but a network of ever-shifting and increasing complexity. Third, the non-coincidence of the biological body, the signified bodily images, and the user's online identity means that it is difficult to 'locate' the self or the body. Finally, given this non-coincidence and the role that other users, social codings, and technological aspects play, we could say that the user is 'dispossessed' of her online self. She participates in its creation, but she does not, in the end, determine or possess it. I cannot elaborate on all of these parallels, or the questions they raise, here. But this brief sketch serves as just one small example of how a Deleuzian 'mixed-reality' ontology might help us to understand what is going on in contemporary cyber practices.

Ultimately, the implications of the mixed-reality paradigm extend far beyond cyber or internet technologies and practices. This is because the 'fleshless ontology' of cyberspace was never just about cyberspace. It reflected a dualistic worldview that has its roots in a long philosophical and religious tradition. As Haraway and others have insisted, it is this worldview that has dominated science and scientific inquiry. This is the Cartesian view, with its famous mind–body dualism. The shift in cyber theory to a mixed-reality paradigm and the articulation of a 'materialist' posthumanism are symptomatic of a larger shift in both our scientific models of inquiry and our cultural understanding of ourselves.

Developments in microbiology, genetics, and neurobiology increasingly reveal the Cartesian model to be insufficient to explain the complexity of relations, the mutual feedback loops and differential processes of individuation in a bacterium, a gene, or a neural network. In neurobiology, for instance, we find that the mind is not free of the flesh, but the result of a sublimely complex series of material processes, electrical impulses, chemical reactions, and the ongoing formation of neural networks, which both are influenced by behavior and influence it in turn. The brain is in the body, the body is in its environment, and the boundaries between are porous and engaged in a continual process of mutual informing. We note the same complexity in our online practices, in the creation of online identities and the proliferation and interconnection of social networks, as well as in the movement of political action from the 'virtual' into the 'real' and vice versa. Increasingly, in a range of techno-scientific and cultural fields, we are searching for an image of thought that is capable of explaining complex forms of relationality that span the old divide between 'mind and matter' or 'virtual and material' – one that can talk about determining factors, without falling into determinism; one that acknowledges the immanent materiality of the world without falling into a reductive materialism that is just one more offshoot of Cartesian mechanism; one that is sufficient to our dynamic, relational world.

Deleuze's philosophy offers this image of thought. His work is important for thinking embodiment and technology, precisely because his ontological account gives us a framework complex enough to get beyond the virtual–material divide. He reminds us that our bodies and our identities are never merely given, but must be constituted out of a range of incommensurable, heterogeneous forces. His work gives us a framework for talking about both the biological, physical processes and social and cultural codings that shape and produce our bodies and our identities. At the same time, he offers tools for creatively and critically intervening and challenging in these processes. This, indeed, is the force of his work with Guattari, and the source of its continuing appeal. The concepts they create together are an attempt to talk about how resistance, creation, and novelty can exist in this welter of partially determining, inter-related forces.

If Deleuze has anything to teach us about 'virtual' bodies, it is that they have never been virtual, if by virtual we mean non-material. This is why the techno-fantasy of escaping the body in a 'bodiless' cyberspace, or of a 'human' consciousness without a body, fails. What we are, to borrow a phrase from Douglas Hofstadter, is constituted in the 'strange loop' between our biological bodies, their virtual representations and significations, our physical and social environments, and the myriad processes that produce them. The idea that we could simply excise the body from this network and dispose of it like so much dead weight is an idea whose time has passed. Deleuze's work points us towards an understanding of the body – and by extension its social codings and implications for our subjectivity – that is sufficiently complex for our times. The flesh shows a strange persistence. Perhaps we are finally coming to understand it.

References

Braidotti, R. (1994), *Nomadic Subjects: Embodiment and Sexual Difference in Contemporary Feminist Theory*, New York: Columbia University Press.

Braidotti, R. (2006), 'Posthuman, All Too Human: Towards a New Process Ontology', *Theory, Culture and Society* 23:7–8, pp. 197–208.

Davis, E. (1994), 'Techgnosis: Magic, Memory and the Angles of Information', in *Flame Wars: The Discourse of Cyberculture*, ed. M. Dery, Durham, NC: Duke University Press, pp. 29–60.

Deleuze, G. (1994), *Difference and Repetition*, trans. P. Patton, New York: Columbia University Press.

Deleuze, G. (1995), *Negotiations*, trans. M. Joughin, New York: Columbia University Press.

Deleuze, G. and F. Guattari (1983), *Anti-Oedipus: Capitalism and Schizophrenia*, trans. R. Hurley, M. Seem, and H. Lane, Minneapolis: University of Minnesota Press.

Deleuze, G. and F. Guattari (1987), *A Thousand Plateaus: Capitalism and Schizophrenia*, trans. B. Massumi, Minneapolis: University of Minnesota Press.

Dery, M. (ed.) (1994a), *Flame Wars: The Discourse of Cyberculture*, Durham, NC: Duke University Press.

Dery, M. (1994b), 'Flame Wars', in M. Dery (ed.), *Flame Wars: The Discourse of Cyberculture*, pp. 1–17.

Dery, M. (1997) *Escape Velocity: Cyberculture at the End of the Century*, New York: Grove.

Dick, P. K. (1968), *Do Androids Dream of Electric Sheep?*, New York: Balantine.

Fleischmann, M., Fraunhofer Institute for Intelligent Analysis and Information Systems (IAIS), http://www.iais.fraunhofer.de/mars.html?L=1 (accessed May 30, 2009).

Gibson, W. (1984), *Neuromancer*, New York: Ace.

Hansen, M. N. (2006), 'Introduction', in *Bodies in Code: Interfaces with Digital Media*, New York: Routledge, pp. 149–81.

Haraway, D. (1991), 'Cyborg Manifesto', in *Simians, Cyborgs and Women: The Reinvention of Nature*, New York: Routledge, pp. 149–81.

Harper, C. and I. Richardson (2001), 'Corporeal Virtuality: The Impossibility of a Disembodied Ontology', *Body, Space and Technology* 2: 2. http://people.brunel.ac.uk/bst/2no2/Papers/Ingrid%20Richardson&Carly%20Harper.htm (accessed May 30, 2009).

Hayles, N. K. (1999), *How We Became Posthuman: Virtual Bodies in Cybernetics, Literature and Informatics*, Chicago: Chicago University Press.

Hayles, N. K. (2002), 'Escape and Constraint: Three Fictions Dream of Moving from Energy to Information', in *From Energy to Information*, Stanford, CA: Stanford University Press, pp. 235–54.

Hayles, N. K. (2005), *My Mother Was a Computer*, Chicago: University of Chicago Press.

Ihde, D. (2002), *Bodies in Technology*, Minneapolis: University of Minnesota Press.

Ihde, D. (2008), 'Of Which Human Are We Post?', *The Global Spiral*, http://www.metanexus.net/magazine/tabid/68/id/10552/Default.aspx (accessed April 25, 2009).

Jones, G. (1997), 'The Neuroscience of Cyberspace: New Metaphors for the Self and Its Boundaries', in *The Governance of Cyberspace: Politics, Technology and Global Restructuring*, ed. B. Loader, London: Routledge, pp. 46–63.

Kurzweil, R. (2005), *The Singularity is Near: When Humans Transcend Biology*, New York: Viking.

Land, C. (2006), 'Becoming-Cyborg: Changing the Subject of the Social?', in *Deleuze and the Social*, ed. M. Fuglsang and B. Sørenson, Edinburgh: Edinburgh University Press, pp. 112–32.

Lykke, N. (1996), 'Between Monsters, Goddesses and Cyborgs: Feminist Confrontations with Science', in *Between Monsters, Goddesses and Cyborgs: Feminist Confrontations with Science, Medicine and Cyberspace*, ed. N. Lykke and R. Braidotti, London: Zed, pp. 13–29.

Markley, R. (1996), 'Boundaries: Mathematics, Alienation, and the Metaphysics of Cyberspace', in *Virtual Realities and Their Discontents*, ed. R. Markley, Baltimore, MD: Johns Hopkins University Press, pp. 55–77.

Marks, J. (1998), *Vitalism and Multiplicity*, London: Pluto.

Marks, J. (2006), 'Information and Resistance: Deleuze, the Virtual and Cybernetics', in *Deleuze and the Contemporary World*, ed. I. Buchanan and A. Parr, Edinburgh: Edinburgh University Press, pp. 194–213.

Moravec, H. (1988), *Mind Children: The Future of Robot and Human Intelligence*, Cambridge, MA: Harvard University Press.

Moravec, H. (1997), 'The Senses Have No Future', *Proceedings of Der Sinn der Sinne International Congress*, Kunst und Ausstellungshalle der Bundesrepublik Deutschland, Bonn, Germany, February 2, 1997, pp. 319–35. Also available online: http://www.frc.ri.cmu.edu/~hpm/project.archive/general.articles/1997/970128.nosense.html (accessed January 12, 2010).

Nietzsche, F. (2003), *Writings from the Late Notebooks*, ed. R. Bittner, Cambridge: Cambridge University Press.

Plato (1991), *The Republic*, trans. B. Jowett, New York: Vintage Classics.

Seidler, V. J. (1998), 'Embodied Knowledge and Virtual Space: Gender, Nature and History', in *The Virtual Embodied: Presence, Practice, Technology*, ed. J. Wood, London: Routledge, pp. 15–29.

Spiller, N. (ed.) (2002), *Cyber_Reader: Critical Writings for the Digital Era*, London: Phaidon.

Sutton D. (2008), 'Virtual Structures of the Internet', in *Deleuze Reframed*, ed. D. Sutton et al., London: I. B. Taurus, pp. 27–44.

Weinstone, A. (2004), *Avatar Bodies: A Tantra for Posthumanism*, Minneapolis: University of Minnesota Press.

Wertheim, M. (1999), *The Pearly Gates of Cyberspace: A History of Space from Dante to the Internet*, New York: Norton.

Wiener, N. (1954), *The Human Use of Human Beings: Cybernetics and Society*, 2nd edn, Boston, MA: Houghton Mifflin.

Notes

1. See http://www.rhizome.org.
2. There is evidence that this characterization of the body as 'just meat', which has been taken as a defining aspect of a Gibsonian cyberspace, is meant to be the protagonist's 'naïve' view. After regaining his ability to interface with cyberspace and going through various reversals of fortune, Case, the protagonist, later recognizes a 'strength' in a former lover and realizes that, 'It belonged to the meat, the flesh the cowboys mocked. It was a vast thing, beyond knowing, a sea of information coded in spiral and pheromone, infinite intricacy that only the body, in its strong blind way, could ever read' (Gibson 1984: 239). It is striking that this passage occurs after Case has begun to interact with highly complex AI and security structures in cyberspace. The implicit comparison is between the body's 'vast sea' of information and the information of cyberspace. Here, the body, 'the meat', is revealed to be significantly more complex than cyberspace. This second revelation puts a different twist on the Gibsonian vision of cyberspace as something that is able to supersede, and eventually replace, the flesh. Perhaps we, like Case, are only now coming out of a long technological adolescence and becoming mature enough to recognize the complexity of 'the meat'.
3. *The Matrix* references science fiction pioneers like Gibson and Philip K. Dick, while also providing a vivid example of the classic Cartesian 'evil demon' or 'brain in a vat' problem. And yet, *The Matrix* complicates the traditional mind–body divide. It is worth noting that after waking up to realize he is effectively a 'brain in vat' Neo must first reclaim his physical body and come to terms with reality before he can enter, and conquer, the Matrix. While Neo is not bound by normal material limitations while inside the Matrix (he can fly and make death-defying leaps across urban rooftops), one scene makes it clear that what happens to his 'body' in the Matrix can have a direct effect on his material body. This increased sensitivity to the issue of material embodiment vis-à-vis cyberspace suggests that the intervening debates about cyber-corporeality in the 1990s had an effect on the techno-fantasy of cyberspace in the popular imagination.
4. It is not a coincident that this image of mindless, but physically powerful, automata emerged in the Cold War. It is a well-established fact that the robots, bugs, or aliens of science fiction were often barely disguised stand-ins for Soviet or Communist forces.
5. The technologies for the internet, as well as smaller academic or urban networks, existed as early as the 1970s, but a large-scale, commercial network did not emerge until the late 1980s and only gained widespread adoption in the 1990s. It is, therefore, impossible to pinpoint a single date or even year for the 'birth' of the internet.
6. For an overview of the relation of Fleischmann's 'mixed-reality' to the shift in cyber theory, see Hansen 2006: 1–22. Hansen claims that, with the shift to the mixed-reality paradigm, 'the "first generation" model of VR as disembodied hyperspace free of all material constraints simply no longer has any purchase in our world' (4). Given the trajectory that I trace from cyber theory to posthumanism, I would claim that Hansen's conclusion is overly optimistic. Unfortunately, the dream of being 'free from all material constraints' persists.
7. For those interested, Hayles gives an excellent summary of the history of cybernetics and the development of cyber discourses vis-à-vis materiality and the critique of Enlightenment humanism. See Katherine N. Hayles, 'Toward Embodied Virtuality', in Hayles 1999: 1–24.
8. Though *Difference and Repetition* (1968/1994) was written and published in French before *Anti-Oedipus* (1972/1983) and *A Thousand Plateaus* (1980/1987),

it was not published in English until well after the volumes co-authored with Guattari appeared. This delay may account for some of the trends in the Anglo-American reception of Deleuze and Guattari that overlook the ontological critique in favor of a 'radical' political or cultural critique, or at least see it as tangential, rather than essential, to the political-cultural project.

9. See, especially, Book IV, 436b–e, and Book X. This is the interpretation of Plato as a classic dualist, committed to a 'Two Worlds' theory, in which there is one world of material flux and another of ideal, non-material Forms. Though this is traditionally how Plato has been read, there is a range of other interpretations that attempt to finesse or even deny Plato's purported dualism. It is clear in *Difference and Repetition* that it is the classic interpretation of Plato, which has so deeply influenced Western thought, that Deleuze has in mind. His rare statements indicating that there is something profound in Plato, or Socrates, are directed at those places in the dialogues that seem potentially to undermine this dualism.

Chapter 7

'Be(come) Yourself only Better': Self-transformation and the Materialisation of Images

Rebecca Coleman

Be yourself only better.

(Premier Fitness)

[The] in-itself of the image is matter.

(Deleuze 2005a: 61)

The problem of the relationship between bodies and images, as it has tended to be posed in academic disciplines including, but not restricted to, media and cultural studies, concerns the problem of representation. That is, one of the dominant ways of conceiving the relationship between bodies and images is to understand the image as representing the body, with various degrees of success. As such, images are seen as capable of being decoded and deciphered, often for their ideological message and the kinds of norms they reproduce. This chapter suggests that this conception of the relations between bodies and images works within, and reproduces, a representationalist model which, in terms of the Deleuzian perspective developed here, is problematic. Drawing on Deleuze's work which attends to the affectivity and materiality of the image, I examine the way in which the relations between bodies and images can be understood as a mode of spectatorship which produces a particular set of impulses or inclinations. Taking as my focus the ways in which the prevalent cultural theme of self-transformation is organised through images, I suggest that images produce possibilities of embodiment, and become materialised in particular ways.

The chapter is an attempt to think through work on images and representation (Olkowski 1998; Marks 2000; see also O'Sullivan 2006) that has been deliberately developed in terms of 'alternative', non-representational or 'creative' works of art, and to consider whether and how such ideas might also be relevant to popular culture and, more especially, relevant to the theme of self-transformation which has often been critiqued for its reproduction of capitalist values. What is interesting – and perhaps what is so appealing – about the notion of self-transformation is its emphasis on the 'self' (or, as I will suggest, the body) as constantly in development. While there have been many arguments concerning how the contemporary theme of self-transformation produces a particular kind of (neo-liberal) subjectivity, and hence sets a particular standard that any transformation must aim to reach, this chapter explores instead how the appeal of transformation as a process in itself might be worthy of more attention and, in so doing, emphasises transformation as becoming.

Be(come) yourself, only better

My starting point here is the prevalence of the theme of self-transformation across a range of contemporary popular media sites. One example, a print advertisement for a Canadian fitness club, Premier Fitness, features a black and white photograph of a young, white, athletic woman along with the slogan, which is also trademarked by the company, 'Be yourself only better.' The woman is pictured mid-laugh, lifting weights, enjoying the process of becoming a better self through working on her body with a fitness regime. There is nothing particularly remarkable about this advert; its message, which seeks to link self-improvement with exercise and enjoyment, can be found repeated in many different media, including other promotional material for fitness clubs (fitness club chain Fitness First have also used the slogan 'be yourself . . . only better,' and have recently also announced a collaboration with Nintendo Wii to launch a new product called 'NewU'), healthy eating and exercise regimes (the British government's healthy eating programme is called 'Change for Life'), various self-help plans for success in business, spiritual, emotional or personal life, and adverts for self-improvement through higher education (the slogan for the University of Cumbria is 'Bring your dreams.' and is accompanied by another slogan, 'It's not where you are, it's where you're going'). What can be taken from these examples, and many more, is that the self is produced as a constantly transforming process; the Premier Fitness advert indicates that, in order to 'be', the self, and in this case the body, must become better.

   Part of what makes the theme of (self-)transformation interesting, then, is its very ordinariness, its reiteration across Western popular culture. The prevalence of this cultural theme has generated a good deal of academic attention which focuses on the ways in which self-transformation is a product of and a contributory factor in contemporary neo-liberal capitalism (for example, Salecl 2009). This is an economic and social system which, through a range of popular media, demands a 'better' self, through learning from the past and entering a more productive future. Writing about self-help books, for example, Jackie Stacey (2000) argues that:

> Addressed as the subject desiring change, readers are recruited to the project of self-transformation and self-improvement. Progress can be quickly achieved by the strategies laid out for the reader if they are willing to take the risk, face the truth, and understand themselves. These programmes typically lay out a plan for liberation from the follies of past lifestyles and habits through increasing self-knowledge and the wisdom that flows from it. (Stacey 2000: 137)

One important way in which the 'impulse' for self-transformation is being theorised is in feminist work on television make-over programmes. These programmes, which have become an extremely popular form of Western prime-time television, feature, as a general rule, a series of 'experts' (stylists, dieticians, cosmetic surgeons, dentists, life coaches, for example) 'working on' and improving a particular aspect of a woman's body in order to make her not only look but also 'feel better'.[1] In the British context, some programmes focus on encouraging the attainment of a healthy weight (whether that be by losing or gaining weight, as in the case of the Channel 4 programme, *SuperSize Versus SuperSkinny*), others on 'losing' years (Channel 4's *Ten Years Younger*, for example), improving self-confidence and bodily acceptance (*How to Look Good Naked*, Channel 4), and improving dress sense and style (BBC's *What Not to Wear* and ITV's *Susannah and Trinny Undress the Nation*[2]). Transforming the body, in these programmes but also in other media more generally (Featherstone 1991), therefore becomes perhaps the principal way in which 'the self' is improved.

This connection between the body and the self in media concerned with transformation is, for many feminists, symptomatic of 'post-feminist media culture' (Gill 2007). For example, in their analysis of US television make-over programmes *The Swan* and *Extreme Makeover*, Sarah Banet-Weiser and Laura Portwood-Stacer (2006) argue that the popularity of make-over programmes is inherently linked to the US tradition of beauty pageants, and also to the increasing dominance of a 'consumerist post-feminism', 'where a "celebration" of the body, the pleasure of transformation, and individual empowerment function as a justification for a renewed objectification of female bodies' (2006: 257). Discussing programmes which concentrate on 'making over' participants through cosmetic surgery, Banet-Weiser and Portwood-Stacer argue that there is an 'overt acknowledg[ment]' of 'the importance of *physical* transformation' in 'becoming a better "you"' (2006: 268).

> Over and over again [they suggest], the women undergoing surgery to improve their appearance state that they want to be beautiful as a *means* to the various ends of being more successful in their relationships, effective in their careers, respected in the communities, or prized for their femininity. [. . .] The underlying assumption made by these women, and thus by these programmes, is that appearance *is* one's character and capacity for achievement in all aspects of life. (2006: 268)

As an example of this subsuming of selfhood within appearance, they quote one participant in *The Swan*, who is explaining her involvement in the show: 'It is painful to wake up and know that you have a beautiful figure underneath a bunch of flab. I just want to be me again!' (Kimberly, quoted in Banet-Weiser and Portwood-Stacer 2006: 268).[3]

For Banet-Weiser and Portwood-Stacer, television make-over programmes document in detail this 'becoming me' through the (in this case surgical) transformation of the body. Indeed, they suggest that 'televised depictions of plastic surgery seem to leave nothing out' (2006: 265):

> The physical evidence of transformation, along with what appear to be the unadulterated expressions of pain by the subjects, provide unequivocal proof that change has taken place, and leave no room for doubt that the procedures depicted have resulted in a beautiful body. This mode of presentation not only naturalises a faith in the positive effects of plastic surgery, but also affirms a contemporary post-feminist ideology about individual transformation and the pleasure that eventually comes from constructing the perfect feminine body. (2006: 265)

Banet-Weiser and Portwood-Stacer are interested in how the medium of make-over television programmes specifically (help to) produce ideological values concerning normative versions of femininity (2006: 256–7). In particular, they understand make-over television programmes within the context of reality television more widely, which they suggest, through a range of techniques and conventions, 'promise [. . .] to give viewers a glimpse at "real" life, complete with flaws and everyday problems' (2006: 265).

Interestingly in terms of the argument I make here, and a point to which I return below, is Banet-Weiser and Portwood-Stacer's suggestion that with reality television, and make-over programmes in particular, there is a shift from 'the visual presentation of the *result* of a female liberal subjectivity' to the 'physical evidence of transformation' (2006: 265).

'[T]he *process* has become the product' (2006: 265, my emphasis). What is important about the contribution that these programmes make to the reproduction of feminine norms and the objectification of female bodies is therefore not only 'the reveal', where 'the new body/me' is uncovered, but also the process (including pain) through which this transformed self is constructed. What make-over television can be understood to do is display this process, not so much in order to expose the labour in itself, nor to demonstrate how this labour is disciplinary, but rather to organise and depict this labour as necessary for 'the pleasure that eventually comes from constructing the perfect feminine body' (Banet-Weiser and Portwood-Stacer 2006: 265).[4] The apparent emphasis on process is, in Banet-Weiser and Portwood-Stacer's terms, decidedly post-feminist in its distraction from 'a historical feminist emphasis on social change and liberation' (2006: 257) and in what Angela McRobbie (2004) has called post-feminism's 'double entanglement', seemingly 'taking feminism into account' whilst at the same time 'fiercely repudiat[ing], indeed almost hat[ing]' it (2004: 256).

McRobbie's argument about the double entanglement of post-feminism is part of a wider engagement with the ways in which post-feminist popular culture is both a consequence and productive of neo-liberal concerns with individualisation and self-transformation. Indeed, writing about the 'primarily female address' (2005: 100) of BBC television make-over programmes *What Not to Wear* and *Would Like to Meet*, McRobbie has suggested that neo-liberalism is at its most pernicious in relation to classed and gender individualism. Such programmes are part of neo-liberalism's encouragement of competition among women and '[p]ublic enactments of hatred and animosity [. . .] refracted at a bodily or corporeal level' (2005: 100):

> People are increasingly individualised, they are required to invent themselves, they are called upon to shape themselves to be flexible, to fit with the new circumstances where they cannot be passively part of the workforce but must, instead, keep themselves employable and adapt themselves and their skills for the rapidly changing demands of the labour market. (2005: 100)

McRobbie, drawing on Bourdieu, pays particular attention to the ways in which make-over programmes enact a 'symbolic violence' on their participants, and focuses on the class dimensions of this violence. Make-over programmes are, for McRobbie, part of a wider social process of 'female individualisation', where new social divisions are produced through 'the denigration of low class or poor and disadvantaged women through symbolic violence. What emerges is a new regime of more sharply polarised class positions, shabby failure or well-groomed success' (2005: 101). For example, she argues that on the original version of the BBC programme, *What Not to Wear*, the body language of its upper middle-class presenters 'indicates a leisurely approach to life and work, they sprawl over the sofa as they watch the video clips of the victims anxiously trying to choose an outfit and they laugh and giggle at their mistakes' (2005: 105–6). This is an example of what Bourdieu calls 'cultural intermediaries', 'authorities' who are able to draw on their (unconscious and embodied) cultural capital and express 'bodily displeasure at those who do not possess such good taste as themselves' (2005: 105). In so doing, class divisions are reiterated, in this case through gendered bodily appearance. For McRobbie, make-over programmes like *What Not to Wear* are

> self-vindicating on the basis that the victims are young adults; they are willing participants and submit themselves to being made over with great enthusiasm. This is popular entertainment which uses irony to suggest that it is not meant to be taken literally. However, this does not mean that there is no humiliation. Participants frequently dissolve into tears and there is 'panic mingled with revolt' as they are put through their paces, unlearning what is considered unacceptable and unattractive about themselves. (2005: 106–7)

Both McRobbie and Banet-Weiser and Portwood-Stacer draw attention to the make-over as part of the profusion of a 'liberal logic that celebrates disciplinary practices of femininity as "free" choice and individual pleasure' (Banet-Weiser and Portwood-Stacer 2006: 269).[5] Further, what is also emphasised is how these discourses are involved in processes of individualisation which implicate young women (McRobbie 2004), and young working-class women especially (McRobbie 2005), through popular culture: '[s]elf-help guides, personal advisors, lifestyle coaches and gurus, and all sorts of self-improvement TV programmes provide the cultural means by which individualisation operates as a social process' (McRobbie 2004: 260–1). Their analysis is thus concerned with pointing to how such programmes operate as a regulatory system for reinforcing classed and gendered inequalities. In this sense, these arguments contribute to social theory that, more generally, is concerned with pointing out capitalism's transformatory nature (see, as just a few examples, Lash and Urry 1987, 1994; Thrift 2008; Papadopoulos et al. 2008).

It is clearly important to note the relationship between the theme of self-transformation and contemporary capitalism. However, whilst drawing on this argument, and returning to it towards the end of the chapter, what I want to do here is change focus and consider not so much the content of these media images but rather what these media images might be understood to do. How might the 'willingness' of certain women to participate in (self-)transformation that McRobbie and Banet-Weiser and Portwood-Stacer identify be understood through a Deleuzian perspective? Taking such an approach, I suggest, attends not only to how the cultural significance of the theme of self-transformation reproduces particular social and cultural categories, but also to what it might be about these images that makes them so appealing. That is, while the work discussed above is concerned to point out the ways in which particular selves are, in complex ways, promoted to individuals through the ideological message of popular media, for example, a Deleuzian approach might instead emphasise the ways in which images of self-transformation become material through their affectivity. In this way, images are understood not so much as representations which have ideological effects on bodies, but rather as affects which resonate with bodies. As I will argue below, what is at stake in such an understanding is therefore not an analysis of the ideological meaning of an image but how (particular) images are taken up and lived out – materialised – by (particular) bodies as processes that are immanent to the transformation, or becoming, of those bodies.

Becoming

While social and cultural theory has long pointed to selfhood and identity as unfinished processes (for example, Hall and du Gay 1996), and the feminist work discussed above focuses on the self as a restricted project, the Deleuzian position I take up here highlights how (self-)transformation necessarily concerns and involves becoming. Deleuze's concept, or ontology, of becoming is well documented and entails a shift from conceiving the world in terms of Being to becoming: that is, from conceiving the world in terms of fixed, transcendent, autonomous entities to inter-connected processes. For Deleuze, whereas 'Beings' are conceived in terms of their static identity, as becomings, bodies are processes of transformation, 'never ceasing to become' (Deleuze and Guattari 1987: 277). As such, 'things' – bodies – cannot exist independently but rather are constituted through their relations with other things. The shift from Being to becoming, then, emphasises transformation not as a change from one form into another form – in the case of the examples discussed so far, not from the starting point of a body in need of improvement to an end point of a 'better' body – but as a process in itself. Indeed, as Deleuze and Guattari argue in their discussion of molecular becoming, 'a line of becoming has neither beginning nor end, departure nor arrival, origin nor destination . . . A line of becoming has only a middle' (1987: 231).

Deleuze and Guattari go on to suggest that

> becoming is not to imitate or identify with something or someone. Nor is it to proportion formal relations. Neither of these two figures of analogy is applicable to becoming [. . .]. Starting from the forms one has, the subject one is, the organs one has, or the functions one fulfils, becoming is to extract particles between which one establishes the relations of movement and rest, speed and slowness that are *closest* to what one is becoming, and through which one becomes. (1987: 272)

Becoming, then, is not a derivative process that involves identifying with or imitating something else in order to become like it. Such a model would belong to the world of Being, where there is a form that changes into a different form. Becoming is instead a process or a force of transformation in itself.

In shifting from a model of Being to becoming there is a move away from placing the subject–object binary at the core of an analysis of the world, and a conception instead of the centrality of bodies. Given their theorisation within Western philosophy as binary oppositions, as 'possessing' intrinsically oppositional 'qualities' (subjects as human and active, objects as artificial and passive, for example),[6] and of the identification of subjectivity with certain forms of standards (subjects as rational, conscious agents, for example), subjects and objects belong to the world of Being. However, bodies, in a Deleuzian sense, refer not necessarily to human entities but to a multiple and diverse series of connections which assemble as a particular spatial and temporal moment (Deleuze and Guattari 1987). A body is thus 'never separable from its relations with the world' (Deleuze 1988: 125). As such, the relations between a body and the world are mutually constitutive. It is not that a world necessarily precedes a body; nor is it that there is first a body and then a world. Thought in terms of the relations between a body and (popular) culture, it is not that a body is the consequence of the imposition of culture; nor is it that culture is the outcome of a body's activity. Instead, it is that bodies and the world are *immanent* to each other.

The concept of immanence is key to Deleuze's work and refers to an attempt to understand connections according to their own logics and processes. For Deleuze, '[a]bsolute immanence is in itself, it is not in something, to something; it does not depend on an object nor belong to a subject' (2001: 26). As a concept, immanence is an attempt to attend to the 'in itself' of a body, and Deleuze conceives of 'the plane of immanence' as a non-hierarchical 'surface' 'on which all bodies, all minds and all individuals are situated' (1988: 122). The plane of immanence, then, is an attempt to 'map' the connections between bodies, rather than to depend on what Deleuze calls a supplementary 'design', 'project' or 'programme' (1988: 122). Becoming is not definable by its form, or by smooth evolution (Grosz 1999), but is to be understood in terms of its movement as 'a complex relation between different velocities [. . .] A composition of speeds and slownesses on a plane of immanence' (Deleuze 1988: 123).

Immanence is therefore necessarily relational, or 'in-between'. The plane of immanence, despite being a flat surface, is thus not characterised by sameness or analogy but by multiplicity and difference. Indeed, it is the in-between which for Deleuze defines multiplicity: 'In a multiplicity what counts are not the terms or the elements, but what there is "between", the between, a set of relations which are not separable from each other' (Deleuze and Parnet 2002: viii). As an approach that prioritises relationality, difference is conceived not in terms of one thing being different from another thing (as in a model of Being), but as a force or power that produces new relations and new becomings.[7] An approach to images as representations tends to focus on decoding the content of images and on the effects that such images have on bodies. In this sense, I would suggest, bodies and images are understood according to a model of Being; they are separate entities, and bodies (as subjects) are seen to identify with or imitate standards set by the content of images. The transformation of a body is therefore from one form into another, in order to become like the image. In contrast to this approach, I want to focus on the ways in which the theme of (self-)transformation works through a logic whereby bodies and images are not separate things but are in constitutive relations. Thus, it is not so much that images are ideologically imposed on bodies, but that bodies – in the Deleuzian sense explored above – become in and through their affective and immanent relations with images. One way to explore these relations further is in terms of the ways in which a model of Being works through a representational logic which, according to Dorothea Olkowski (1998), a Deleuzian philosophy necessarily 'ruins'.

Representation

This 'ruin of representation' is for Olkowski 'the ruin of hierarchically ordered time and space' (1998: 2). For Olkowski, the 'system of representation, whether in the realm of philosophy, psychology, social and political theory, ethics, or aesthetics, operates by establishing a fixed standard as the norm or model' (1998: 2). Furthermore, she argues that such a fixed standard defines 'minority': '[t]he very meaning of minority is associated with falling below the standard of that norm, failing to represent that standard in all its perfection and completeness' (1998: 2). Given this link between representation, fixed standard and minorities, Olkowski points out that feminist arguments in particular, but also other 'minoritarian' work, have attended to and critiqued the representational norm. However, she suggests that the critique of representation in many cases 'do[es] no more than register a complaint against the norms of language, images, and social and political structures' because 'these analyses have operated with categorical generalisations: concepts neither abstract nor particular enough, which represent women merely in terms of pre-established, even naturalised, standards' (1998: 2). Partly, Olkowski is here suggesting that the representational model operates within an ontology of Being rather than becoming. That is, '[m]inorities are recognised as minorities because they deviate from representational norms, sometimes to the extent that they seem to make no sense at all' (1998: 3). The definition of minority according to a representational model, then, is one that is imposed on a particular kind of identity, subjectivity and/or embodiment. It is not immanent to that which is defined as minoritarian but rather exists prior and external to that which it captures, or endeavours to capture. As such, an approach that attends to how a minority is defined through a standard that is set from a majority, or 'molar' (Deleuze and Guattari 1987), position occupies itself with fixed standards, norms and outcomes, rather than, in Deleuze's terms, the immanence that is inherent to and creative of the becoming itself.

Olkowski's argument is therefore that, by focusing on representations of women, feminist work can reproduce a representational model. The representational model is the context through which an understanding of images as representations operates, although it cannot be reduced to this strategy.[8] Olkowski explains (through Deleuze's discussion of Aristotle) the distinction between a representational logic and a Deleuzian logic in terms of their conceptions of difference. She draws on Deleuze's *Difference and Repetition* (1994: 265–70), which suggests that a representational logic understands difference through a four-fold 'judgement' involving (i) identity; (ii) opposition; (iii) analogy; and (iv) resemblance. These four aspects of judgements are constituted by 'two elements':

> The first consists of the differences (conceived in terms of analogy) between species that are subsumed under the *identity* of a genus, or it consists of the genus that stands in relations of *analogy* with other genera. However, this abstract representation, in order to be a representation, insofar as it subsumes species, must also rely on what constitutes them, a second element, namely *resemblances* that presume the continuity of the sensible intuition in a concrete representation. (Olkowski 1998: 20)

Representational difference is concerned with classifying a 'thing' (a species, for example) in terms of a logic of Being, whereby things are identifiable according to a series of definitional categorisations and criteria. For example, a thing must be identifiable as a particular thing; it must have a recognisable identity which becomes apparent in opposition to something else. A thing is therefore, as Olkowski puts it, 'in relations of *analogy*' with other things. This analogy works through 'a second element' of representation where a thing is defined in terms of its resemblance to other things. The logic that underpins this representational understanding of difference operates through defining what things are in terms of whether or not things resemble each other.

Deleuze's (1988) argument in his essay on Spinoza and ethology is helpful in unpacking this representational notion of difference further. For Deleuze, ethology is an attempt to understand things not in terms of what they are but in terms of their affective capacities. Whereas a representational logic works through a classificatory system of Being, ethology instead studies the specific and changing relations through which the capacities of a body to affect and be affected by other bodies are produced. Deleuze argues that, with ethology, 'many things change. You will define an animal or a human being not by its form, its organs and its functions and not as a subject either; you will define it by the affects of which it is capable' (1988: 124).

> For example [he suggests], there are greater differences between a plow horse or draft horse and a racehorse than between an ox and a plow horse. This is because the racehorse and the plow horse do not have the same affects nor the same capacity for being affected; the plow horse has affects in common rather with the ox. (1988: 124)

What is emphasised in Deleuze's approach, then, is the difference which is immanent to bodies; the affective capacities of a body that are produced through the relations between that body and other bodies are necessarily specific. Difference is therefore not asserted through a prior and external system of representation (involving the fourfold procedure of identity, opposition, analogy and resemblance, for example) but rather can only be understood in its becoming.

For Olkowski, the 'effect' of a representational logic, given its basis in Being rather than becoming, is that '*difference* as a concept and reality' is erased' (1998: 20). The elimination of difference from a representational model means that difference, 'pure difference' in Deleuze's terms, can 'show itself at all as a concept and reality [. . .] only as a crack, a catastrophe, a break in resemblance or as the impossibility of claiming identity, opposition, analogy, or resemblance where reflection demands that they should occur' (1998: 20). This erasure of difference 'occurs [. . .] in the process of reflection, the *judgement* according to which these determinations are made and according to which difference is made to submit to representation' (Olkowski 1998: 20). Such a judgement might be understood to be the 'standard' on which representational accounts focus and which they also reproduce through this focus. Taking up Olkowski's argument therefore suggests that, in critiquing the neo-liberal standard of (self-)transformation and making an important complaint against a standard, feminist work on make-over television programmes does not attend to the difference, or immanence, of the transformation (of the women who affectively participate as either 'contestants' or audience).

For example, as well as the (re)production of a particular version of classed femininity (to which I return below), what is interesting about television make-over programmes, and media which engage with the theme of (self-)transformation more generally, is their direct relevance to an ontology of becoming. That is, the body/self that is transformed, or the 'me' that is uncovered and restored, is a body that is always in process. Indeed, picking up on Banet-Weiser and Portwood-Stacer's point that reality television emphasises process rather than finished product, I would suggest that the transformation that is 'encouraged' by popular media is necessarily an 'in-between' process, a becoming. Whilst the closing minutes of make-over television programmes are often devoted to 'the reveal' and to reactions of friends and family, there are also often scenes which return to the participant and observe the short-term maintenance, or not, of their make-over. Some programmes, such as *How To Look Good Naked*, also re-visit participants, asking 'do they *still* know how to look good naked?' The reveal is therefore not, in itself, the end of the transformation; these transformations are on-going projects.

The unfinished nature of the transformations at stake in contemporary culture might be a reason why so many advertisements draw on the promise of 'becoming a better self'. There is a necessary futurity with transformation, a becoming better, a becoming different, a becoming.

It is clearly important not to understand becoming as a process that is endlessly open; becomings are not unrestricted and a body cannot become what it wants (Coleman 2009). It is also not to ignore the past that is, in Stacey's terms, 'liberated [. . .] through increasing self-knowledge and the wisdom' (Stacey 2000: 137). While I have tried to emphasise the process – rather than the end points – of transformation in the examples I have discussed so far, it is plain that the women's bodies that are transformed in make-over programmes cannot become any-thing (even when they are transformed through cosmetic surgery). My argument here, then, is not that the particular kinds of transformation that are encouraged by popular media are unimportant. Rather, I am interested in shifting focus a little, away from what might be called the representationalist model and towards an attention to how the theme of transformation might be so appealing because of its resonance with the transformatory 'nature' of bodies themselves. This is not only to argue for an ontology of becoming, but also to place emphasis on the body, in a Deleuzian sense, rather than on the self, identity and/or subjectivity. For instance, drawing on Deleuze's work, Elizabeth Grosz (2006) suggests that 'we don't know what bodies are capable of' (2006: 191). She argues,

> This is not simply true because of our current forms of knowledge, the lack of refinement in our instruments of knowledge, but more profoundly because the body has and is a history and under the procedures of testing, the body itself extends its limits, transforms its capacities, and enters a continuous process of becoming, becoming something other than itself. This capacity for becoming other, or simply becoming, is not something that culture simply imposes on an otherwise inert nature but is part of the nature of nature itself. Becoming is what suffuses bodies from both outside (through the imposition of increasingly difficult tasks) and from within (through the unfolding of a nature that never was fixed and through the self-overcoming that is inherent in the very being and ontology of bodies). (2006: 192)

Understood in these terms, the 'becoming' involved in the cultural theme of (self-)transformation is not 'simply impose[d] on an otherwise inert nature' but becoming 'is what suffuses bodies'; bodies *are* becomings. This is a way of understanding the relations between bodies, images and culture outside of a model of representation. In this sense, popular cultural images are not an ideological imposition but rather a set of relations that, as I suggest below, materialise, or not, a particular set of impulses or inclinations.

The materiality of images

Grosz's argument about the becoming that is inherent to bodies is developed, in this context, in relation to questions of prosthetics and looking. This emphasis on looking is particularly helpful in exploring how the relations between images and bodies might be theorised according to both a Deleuzian and a feminist approach. For example, there is a great deal of work on female spectatorship of images, which, while emerging from a variety of perspectives including psychoanalysis and film theory (Mulvey 1989; Doane 1992; Stacey 1994), sociology (Lury 1998), and film theory, art history and visual culture (Betterton 1987, 1996; Kuhn 2002), draws attention to the ways in which the positioning of women's bodies in relation to images blurs the boundaries between subject and object, body and image, reader and text. While not attending to gendered difference, Deleuze's work on bodies and images also disrupts their positioning within a binary opposition, particularly through an emphasis on the affectivity and materiality of images. The quotation at the opening of the chapter indicates Deleuze's understanding of the image as 'matter' 'in-itself' (Deleuze 2005a: 61). In this sense, it is not that bodies and images are made of mutually exclusive 'stuff', but that images are material and materialised in certain ways. It is not that images, as representations, are of an inherently different order from bodies, and therefore have effects on bodies, but that bodies and images are in affective relations with each other and become through each other.

In *What is Philosophy?* (1994), for example, Deleuze and Guattari argue that the relations between art and bodies involve percepts, affects and sensations. A (great) work of art is a material which 'preserves' creativity: 'What is preserved – the thing or the work of art – is *a bloc of sensations, that is to say, a compound of percepts and affects*' (1994: 164). Sensation here occupies a double position, where it is both produced by and also productive of the work of art. While inherently part of the materiality of the work of art, sensation is 'in-between' the art work and the body that looks:

> Percepts are no longer perceptions; they are independent of a state of those who experience them. Affects are no longer feelings or affections; they go beyond the strength of those who undergo them. Sensations, percepts, and affects are *beings* whose validity lies in themselves and exceeds any lived. (Deleuze and Guattari 1994: 164)

This is an understanding of art, and the relations between bodies and images, which in Olkowski's terms 'ruins' a representational model through its emphasis on immanence and relationality. Indeed, Deleuze and Guattari suggest that '[a]s percepts, sensations are not perceptions referring to an object (reference): if they resemble something it is with a resemblance produced with their own methods' (1994: 166).

As an 'in-between', sensation is not an effect of an image on a body but rather is the affective relation between an image and a body. Deleuze explains sensation in his book on Francis Bacon (2005b) as 'Being-in-the-world':

> as the phenomenologists say, at one and the same time I *become* in the sensation and something *happens* through the sensations, one through the other, one in the other. And at the limit, it is the same body which, being both subject and object, gives and receives the sensation. As a spectator, I experience the sensation only by entering the painting, by reaching the unity of the sensing and sensed. [. . .] sensation is not in the 'free' or disembodied play of light and colour (impressions); on the contrary, it is in the body, even the body of an apple. Colour is in the body, sensation is in the body, and not in the air. Sensation is what is painted. (Deleuze 2005b: 25–6)

Sensation is the body 'entering' the image, and the image entering the body. Sensation cannot involve one autonomous entity (a subject) looking at another autonomous entity (an object): 'What is painted on the canvas is the body, not insofar as it is represented as an object, but insofar as it is experienced as sustaining *this* sensation (what Lawrence, speaking of Cézanne, called "the appleyness of the apple")' (Deleuze 2005b: 26).

Looking, in this sense, can be conceived as the affective relation between a body and an image. Looking is the materialisation of the image. This is a becoming *of* the image in a body, but where that body is not autonomous from that image. It is not a body becoming in resemblance to the image (an image being ideologically imposed on a body, for example), but becoming as an immanent process. As Deleuze and Guattari argue, '[w]e are not in the world, we become with the world; we become by contemplating it. *Everything is vision, becoming*' (1994: 169, my emphasis). For my purposes here, then, in its theorisation in relation to vision and looking, becoming is, fundamentally, a mode of looking that makes impossible an attempt to define the boundaries between bodies and images. Indeed, discussing the kind of spectator that Deleuze's work on cinema suggests, Richard Rushton (2009) argues that 'for Deleuze, the spectator is *fused with* the film; there is no spectator who watches (and listens to) a film, for the spectator is only ever *formed by* watching (and listening to) a film' (2009: 48). This 'absorption' into the film, according to Rushton, produces for the spectator '*the possibility of being another being*' (2009: 50).[9] To look is to materialise the image and to become something else.

Inclination, looking and becoming

The looking conceived through a Deleuzian approach involves 'vision' as a multi-faceted sense. That is, as Laura Marks (2000) argues in the context of film, the mode of looking that a Deleuzian approach proposes is multi-sensory, a 'haptic visuality'. Marks defines haptic visuality in distinction to 'optic visuality', a mode of perception which 'depends on a separation between the viewing subject and the object' (2000: 162). As such, for Marks:

> [w]hile optical perception privileges the representational power of the image, haptic perception privileges the material presence of the image. Drawing from other forms of sense experience, primarily touch and kinesthetics, haptic visuality involves the body more than is the case with optical visuality. (2000: 163)

Haptic visuality is thus a multi-sensory embodied experience of an image and, importantly, 'emphasises the viewer's *inclination* to perceive' (Marks 2000: 162, my emphasis) what Marks calls 'haptic images'. Drawing on Deleuze's notion of 'optical images' in his work on cinema, and altering this to become her concept of 'haptic images', Marks defines haptic images as affective images 'connect[ed] directly to sense perception' that 'forces the viewer to contemplate the image itself instead of being pulled into narrative' (Marks 2000: 163). Haptic images are in this sense immanent, rather than (only) being organised to make sense through a 'supplementary' narrative structure. The point of haptic visuality is that while any images might be haptic – affective, immanent – it is not necessarily the case that viewers will be inclined to perceive them as such. Haptic visuality, as an attention to this inclination, can therefore be understood as interested not so much in the content of an image but in what that image does: that is, in the kinds of inclinations that images produce, and the kinds of embodiment that images might encourage and produce.

In conceiving the relations between bodies and images outside of a representational model, then, it is not that the specificity of the kinds of embodiment that images promote is neglected. A focus on the affects and sensations that the relations between bodies and images can and do produce can be concerned with, in Marks's terms, the inclinations towards which the materialisation of images tends. This is what Olkowski argues are the 'two directions' demanding attention after 'the ruin of representation': first, the creativity of difference and becoming, and second, 'with just as much urgency, [. . .] the social and political forces of fascism and capitalism, which make use of all the powers of representation for their own ends' (1998: 189). A Deleuzian position, then, does not lose sight of the force of (in this case) capitalism in directing the becoming of bodies through popular media images towards their own ends. In light of the earlier discussion of feminist work on make-over television programmes, what might be suggested through an ontology of becoming is that the creativity of multiplicity and difference inherent to becoming is restricted through the organisation of images according to certain standards (of a successful, liberal and middle-class femininity, for example). In contemporary popular culture, there is an inclination towards the affectivity and immanence of images of (particular kinds of) self-transformation. And, crucially, as Celia Lury (1998) has argued in the context of photography, the encouragement of particular ways of seeing is the encouragement of particular ways of life.

At the same time, however, what it is also important to recognise – and what is highlighted through the Deleuzian approach developed here – is the issue of creativity, which can be overlooked in approaches that, for strategic reasons, focus primarily on standards and the replication of normative values. What seems especially significant about the theme of self-transformation is its suggestion of the creative becomings that are inherent to bodies. Creativity in this sense refers to the ways in which becomings are involved in the making of something new, where this 'new' is not necessarily disconnected from the 'old' or the past (see Coleman 2009). Indeed, in the self-help books that Stacey discusses, in order to transform into a 'better' self, the past must be engaged with and learnt from. Creativity is the taking up of the spirit or force of, in the terms of this chapter, an image, to become not like it but with it. It is to repeat the image, not in terms of identification and resemblance, but through materialising the affectivity of the image into something new. Of course, it could be objected that materialising images of self-transformation is not the creation of something new but the reproduction of the same old ideological values, and it is generally the case that Deleuze's work has been taken up in relation to art which in some way critiques, explicitly or not, a capitalist system. However, this would be to miss the creativity that is implicated in images that I have pointed to so far, as well as the empirical experience of those bodies that are moved by and with such images. This is crucial to note when, drawing on what feminist work on make-over television has pointed out, images of self-transformation seem to appeal most strongly to working-class women.

For example, in their methodological discussion of their empirical research with women about their viewing of and responses to reality television, Bev Skeggs et al. (2008) argue that, while the middle-class respondents tended to distance themselves from the programmes and to offer 'considered responses' (2008: 15) of their engagement with them, '[t]he working class participants responded to the "reality" television participants as if they were "real" – not representations' and 'demonstrat[ed] empathy and judgement through personal experience and ultimately *immanently positioning themselves* with the unfolding drama' (2008: 13). For these authors, concentrating on the ways in which the working-class women 'get carried away' (2008: 15) with the image is a method of capturing the affective relations between the programmes and the viewers (2008: 17) which become materialised in embodied practices. These women are not independent from reality television but rather are 'absorbed' in it, become through it. Taking up this argument, then, I would suggest that, for working-class women, images of self-transformation are not responded to through a distant or considered mode of spectatorship but rather are experienced and materialised, affectively and immanently. As such, it seems important to attend not only to the ideological content of such images, but also to what these images do, how they become materialised in and as particular bodies. These are, fundamentally, creative becomings, not least because for the women who are engaged, as viewers or participants of the programmes, there is what Grosz terms the 'suffusion' of the body 'from both outside' and 'from within' (2006: 192), the engagement with popular culture as part of the impulse to become. Focusing on 'getting carried away' with popular media images of self-transformation, then, might suggest that these images are 'haptic' not only in their affectivity but also in their reverberation with the inclination for a body to become something else.

Acknowledgements

I would like to thank Debra Ferreday for the many ways in which she has engaged with the ideas that feed into this chapter.

References

Banet-Weiser, S. and L. Portwood-Stacer (2006), '"I just want to be me again!" Beauty Pageants, Reality Television and Post-Feminism', *Feminist Theory* 7: 2, pp. 255–72.

Betterton, R. (1987), *Looking On: Images of Femininity in the Visual Arts and Media*, London: Pandora.

Betterton, R. (1996), *An Intimate Distance: Women, Artists and the Body*, London: Routledge.

Coleman, R. (2009), *The Becoming of Bodies: Girls, Images, Experience*, Manchester: Manchester University Press.

Deleuze, G. (1988), *Spinoza: Practical Philosophy*, San Francisco: City Lights.

Deleuze, G. (1994), *Difference and Repetition*, trans. Paul Patton, New York: Columbia University Press.

Deleuze, G. (2001), 'Immanence: A Life', in *Pure Immanence: Essays on A Life*, New York: Zone, pp. 25–33.

Deleuze, G. (2005a), *Cinema 1: The Movement-Image*, London: Continuum.

Deleuze, G. (2005b), *Francis Bacon*, London: Continuum.

Deleuze, G. and F. Guattari (1987), *A Thousand Plateaus: Capitalism and Schizophrenia*, London: Continuum.

Deleuze, G. and F. Guattari (1994), *What is Philosophy?*, London: Verso.

Deleuze, G. and C. Parnet (2002), *Dialogues II*, London: Athlone.

Doane, Mary Ann (1992), 'Film and the Masquerade: Theorising the Female Spectator', in *The Sexual Subject: A Screen Reader in Sexuality*, London: Routledge, pp. 227–43.

Featherstone, M. (1991), 'The Body in Consumer Culture', in *The Body: Social Process and Cultural Theory*, ed. M. Featherstone, M. Hepworth and B. S. Turner, London: Sage, pp. 170–96.

Gill, R. (2007), 'Postfeminist Media Culture: Elements of a Sensibility', *European Journal of Cultural Studies* 10: 2, pp. 147–66.

Grosz, E. (1999), 'Becoming . . . An Introduction', in *Becomings: Explorations in Time, Memory, and Futures*, ed. E. Grosz, Ithaca, NY: Cornell University Press, pp. 1–11.

Grosz, E. (2006), 'Naked', in *The Prosthetic Impulse: From a Posthuman Present to a Biocultural Future*, ed. M. Smith and J. Morra, Cambridge, MA: MIT Press.

Hall, S. and P. du Gay (eds) (1996), *Questions of Cultural Identity*, London: Sage.

Kuhn, A. (2002), *Family Secrets: Acts of Memory and Imagination*, London: Verso.

Lash, S. and J. Urry (1987), *The End of Organised Capitalism*, Cambridge: Polity.

Lash, S. and J. Urry (1994), *Economies of Signs and Space*, London: Sage.

Lury, C. (1998), *Prosthetic Culture: Photography, Memory and Identity*, London: Routledge.

McRobbie, A. (2004), 'Post-Feminism and Popular Culture', *Feminist Media Studies* 4: 3, pp. 255–64.

McRobbie, A. (2005), 'Notes on *What Not to Wear* and Post-Feminist Symbolic Violence', in *Feminism After Bourdieu*, ed. L. Adkins and B. Skeggs, Oxford: Blackwell, pp. 99–109.

Marks, L. (2000), *The Skin of the Film: Intercultural Cinema, Embodiment, and the Senses*, Durham, NC: Duke University Press.

Mulvey, L. (1989), *Visual and Other Pleasures*, Basingstoke: Macmillan.

Olkowski, D. (1998), *Gilles Deleuze and the Ruin of Representation*, Berkeley, CA: University of California Press.

O'Sullivan, S. (2006), *Art Encounters Deleuze and Guattari: Thought Beyond Representation*, New York: Palgrave Macmillan.

Papadopoulos, D., N. Stephenson and V. Tsianos (2008), *Escape Routes: Control and Subversion in the 21st Century*, London: Pluto.

Pitts, V. (2003), *In the Flesh: The Cultural Politics of Body Modification*, Houndmills: Palgrave Macmillan.

Rushton, R. (2009), 'Deleuzian Spectatorship', *Screen* 50:1, pp. 45–53.

Salecl, R. (2009), 'Emotions in Times of the Collapse of Liberal Capitalism: From Rational Choice to Magical Thinking', unpublished paper presented at 'Emotional Labour' symposium, Centre for Gender and Women's Studies, Lancaster University, 3 April 2009.

Skeggs, B., N. Thumin and H. Wood (2008), '"Oh Goodness, I *am* Watching Reality TV": How Methods Make Class in Audience Research', *European Journal of Cultural Studies* 11:1, pp. 5–24.

Stacey, J. (1994), *Star Gazing: Hollywood Cinema and Female Spectatorship*, London: Routledge.

Stacey, J. (2000), 'The Global Within: Consuming Nature, Embodying Health', in *Global Nature, Global Culture*, ed. S. Franklin, C. Lury and J. Stacey, London: Sage.

Thrift, N. (2008), *Non-Representational Theory: Space, Politics, Affect*, New York: Routledge.

Notes

1. While these programmes do occasionally feature male participants, the vast majority of participants are female and the programmes themselves draw on the ideas and conventions of the 'make-over' that have been central to 'women's media', including magazines, television and novels.

2. *Susannah and Trinny Undress the Nation* is a spin-off from the original BBC programme, *What Not to Wear*, which featured Trinny Woodall and Susannah Constantine as presenters (as discussed below in terms of McRobbie's work). Following a move from BBC to ITV, 'Susannah and Trinny''s new programme addresses not only style but also an improvement of the lifestyles and relationships of heterosexual couples and 'tribes' of 'problem' women (for example, 'dog lovers' and 'sex bombs'), through certain kind of self-help discourse (see http://www.itv.com/Lifestyle/Fashion/TrinnyandSusannah/default.html; accessed 11 January 2010).

3. In this sense, then, the suggestion is that while selfhood is authentic, appearance is not. See Coleman (2009) for an alternative means of understanding the relationships between selfhood and appearance.

4. In the context of Banet-Weiser and Portwood-Stacer's interest in post-feminism, what is so significant about reality television's emphasis on the process of transformation is its seeming appropriation of feminism's intention to record and make explicit the labour, including the pain, that goes into the production of normative femininity. The suggestion seems to be that pain is necessarily inauthentic and negative. This might be in contrast to other feminist work on body modification, tattooing, ritual, for example, which argues against an understanding of these, often painful, processes of self-transformation as mutilative and pathological (see, for example, Pitts 2003). I am grateful to Debra Ferreday for elucidating this point to me.

5. For example, Banet-Weiser and Portwood-Stacer argue that '[a]ll make-over programmes are about becoming a better "you" by making better purchases and adopting better lifestyle habits [. . .]. Cosmetic surgery shows not only capitalise on this ideological climate where the consumption of medical procedures rather

than (or in addition to) a new haircut or a new pair of jeans is normalised' (Banet-Weiser and Portwood-Stacer 2006: 269).

6. It is important to note here that the critique of subjects and objects as necessarily oppositional entities is not exclusive to the work of Deleuze (and Deleuze and Guattari). Indeed, there is a strong trend in feminist theory on women's spectatorship of images that points to how women are positioned as both subjects and objects. See Coleman (2009) for a discussion of how this theory might work in relation to a Deleuzian approach.

7. The 'new' that is involved in difference is significant in terms of my argument and will be returned to below.

8. Indeed, Olkowski is keen to establish that 'the ruin of representation' does not do away with critique of representations – this is in many ways strategically helpful to minoritarian politics - but that it creates new modes of engagement and draws attention to 'what else' images might involve (see, for example, 1998: 11). In a similar vein, Simon O'Sullivan argues: 'It is not as if [deconstruction] is itself a bad thing. [. . .] it might be strategically important to employ deconstruction precisely to counteract the effects – to disable – a certain kind of aesthetic discourse (again, deconstruction operates here as a kind of "expanded ideological critique"). Often, such critiques, that inhabit the object of criticism (in this case discourses of representation), are the only way to strategically engage with an enemy, at least at first, but after the deconstruction the art object remains. Life goes on. Art, whether we will it or not, continues producing affects' (2006: 41).

9. Rushton argues that the term 'absorption' is preferable to the more currently popular 'immersion' because '[t]he mode of absorption is one in which the spectator *goes into* the film – that is, is absorbed in or by the film – whereas in the mode of immersion the film *comes out* to the spectator so as to surround and envelop her/him' (2009: 49). While immersion for Ruston leaves the body 'intact', absorption produces the possibility of the body entering into another world and becoming otherwise.

Chapter 8

An Ethico-Aesthetics of Heroin Chic: Art, Cliché and Capitalism

Peta Malins

the drug addict . . . look at the representations of these bodies in fashion . . . this culture is really completely schizoid! . . . all these heroin ads . . . these bodies that are leaking . . . the junkie body leaks all over the place . . . Deleuze would have very hard things to say against this junkie thing.

(Braidotti, no date)

A thin, semi-dressed young woman kneels awkwardly, her body twisted and bent forward over the side of an armchair in what appears to be a fairly dingy lounge-room. Surrounding her, and taking up most of the photograph, is a grimy red carpet, marked with what seem to be cigarette burns. The woman's exposed feet are covered in dirt and her face is shiny, as though coated in a fine layer of sweat. The photo's strange angle creates a sense that the room is spinning, and accentuates the gravitational weight of her thin, unsteady body as she tries unsuccessfully to push herself up. The unusual framing also suggests that the photo has been taken by an amateur (a friend of the woman, perhaps) rather than by a fashion photographer. In fact, aside from the designer underwear the woman is wearing, the image – by UK photographer Corinne Day – has little to suggest that it is a fashion advertisement at all.

During the 1990s, documentary-style images such as this – with models looking thin, anxious, bruised, doped-out and unwell – became commonplace in fashion magazines. Along with Day, artists such as Steven Meisel, Bettina Rheims, Paolo Roversi, Mario Sorrenti and Juergen Teller[1] all began to draw on the grungy aesthetics of drug use to generate interest in, and value for, consumer goods. Produced at a time when glossy, well-lit images of healthy, smiling, curvaceous women dominated mainstream fashion photography (Harold 1999), such images are conspicuously bleak. The fashion models are photographed in seemingly 'everyday' postures and locations; rarely are they in the centre of the image and seldom do they look at the camera. The images tend to be overexposed, emphasising the starkness of their location, and generally do not appear to be touched up in any way. The settings – usually shabby rooms in cheap rental apartments – seem to be as much the subject of the photographs as the models themselves, and the designer clothes or accessories being worn seem to recede into the background.

Dubbed 'heroin chic' by the popular media, such advertising was widely condemned for 'glamorising' and promoting drug use, for 'exploiting' disenfranchised drug users, and for making light of 'the serious issue' of addiction (Ashton 2002: 14). A decade later, several perfume advertisements, including those for Dior's *Addict*, Yves Saint Laurent's *Opium* and Gucci's *Rush*, have generated similar responses (FVR 2002). According to at least one campaign advocate, 'there is nothing sexy, pleasurable, attractive or alluring about this exploitation!' (FVR 2002: unpaginated).

Yet surely there is. Surely it is the sublime, libidinous, abject pleasures circulating through and around such advertisements that make them so very appealing to advertisers and consumers alike. But how is it that the drug-using body, a body so abjected, stratified in everyday life, can be rendered so productive, so saleable, in these advertising assemblages? What can these assemblages tell us about art and capitalism, and about the relationships between art, capitalism and ethics? Most importantly, what implications do these assemblages have for minoritarian bodies and their relations with others?

Most academic commentary on heroin chic imagery has, like the public and media commentary, been negative (see, for example, Giroux 2000 and Halnon 2002). Here, however, the focus has tended to shift from concerns about the potential of such images to encourage drug use or anorexia, to concerns about their potential to produce offensive, middle-class imitations and appropriations of lower-class poverty, suffering and drug use. What tend to be left out in both analyses, as Harold (1999) notes, are the potential becomings which take place in between drug user and consumer: becomings which constitute neither an imitation or appropriation of drug use nor an actual use of drugs, but a transformational trajectory between the two. References to drugs in advertisements do not necessarily rely on consumers identifying with the drug object, practice or experience, but rather depend on their investment in the possibility of becoming-other: an investment in the potential for sensing and perceiving in new ways; experiencing chaos and vertigo; and connecting to the outside (Fitzgerald 2002a). Such becomings may indeed be overcoded by movements of imitation, or stratified as actual drug use, but they may also lead elsewhere: to new and perhaps more ethically positive bodily relations.

In this chapter I explore the extent to which heroin chic images might be understood as productive of bodily transformations. To do so, I draw on Deleuze's (2003) and Deleuze and Guattari's (1994, 1987) writings on art, capitalism and ethics in order to re-read drug-referenced advertising and explore its ethico-aesthetic capacities. I suggest that heroin chic images do indeed contain an ethico-aesthetic potential, but that this capacity is severely curtailed by two different forces: that of the cliché and that of capitalism. To be truly revolutionary, art needs not only to dismantle the clichés which striate it, but also to find a way to bypass the capitalist axiomatics which co-opt and convert it.

The Powers of Art

Art, for Deleuze and Guattari, is less about creating forms than about generating sensations. Its power or strength lies in its capacity to render perceptible forces which would not otherwise be sense-able or knowable. It does so through the production of what they term 'percepts' and 'affects' (Deleuze and Guattari 1994). Percepts are found in the artwork itself. They can be understood as non-signifying nodes of sensation: an intensity of colour, a texture or contrast. Affects, by contrast, emerge in the connection between the artwork and the body. They can be thought of as non-signifying, impersonal movements of sensation, felt by a body as it encounters the world: a shiver, a heat, a sudden thumping of a heart. Percepts do not in themselves narrate a story or represent something else; they simply create sensation. Likewise, affects are not emotions; they are not in the first instance processed cognitively, nor are they given a category or name such as 'fear' or 'sadness'. Instead they are felt directly by the body: across the skin, along the nervous system, creating often imperceptible shifts in register, temperature or bodily posture. They are, as O'Sullivan notes, 'passages of intensity, a reaction in or on the body at the level of matter' (2006: 41).

Art brings percepts and affects together to produce specific assemblages, or 'blocs', of sensation (Deleuze and Guattari 1994). The strength of art, for Deleuze and Guattari, lies in its ability to compose percepts and affects in such a way that new modes of perception are made possible. Everyday perception is always already locked into specific habitual relations of signification, representation, subjectivity and emotion, and so one of the primary goals of art is to render perceptible forces and vectors which are otherwise imperceptible. In the paintings of Cézanne, for example, Deleuze finds a skill for 'rendering visible the folding force of mountains, the germinative force of a seed, the thermic force of a landscape' (2003: 57), while in Van Gogh he discovers 'the unheard-of force of a sunflower seed' (57). Likewise, in cinema, Deleuze does not look for layers of meaning and signification but instead examines its capacity to render visible and audible forces such as movement (1986) and time (1989). And in literature Deleuze pays attention not to the emotions and forces it narrates, but to the emotions and forces it makes palpable through the very language or style it deploys. The strength of all art, as Deleuze and Guattari suggest, is its capacity 'to make perceptible the imperceptible forces that populate the world, affect us, and make us become' (1994: 182).

Examining the work of Francis Bacon, Deleuze (2003) finds in it an exceptional capacity for rendering visible otherwise imperceptible forces which act upon the body. Bacon's paintings often depict a human or animal figure which has been distorted, its contours blurred or smudged or extended unnaturally. His figures are never deformed beyond recognition, but only to the extent that full and comfortable 'recognition' is precluded. In his *Three Portraits Triptych 1973*, for example, Bacon presents each figure sitting awkwardly on a chair. Their faces are smudged and misshapen and their bodies contorted. Their twisted legs appear to merge with their shadows, as though leaking out from their bodies and running into a puddle on the floor. In another of Bacon's portraits, entitled *Portrait of George Dyer Talking (1966)*, the figure sitting on a chair is even more contorted, its body a lumpy bundle of flesh and muscle, with one leg tucked up uncomfortably. Its head seems to be undergoing a kind of becoming-animal: a merging between human and chicken (beak, comb). For Deleuze, these paintings can be understood to be rendering visible the very real forces of discomfort felt by a body forced to sit on a chair – or talk – for hours on end. He writes:

> Bacon's Figures are not racked bodies at all, but ordinary bodies in ordinary situations of constraint and discomfort ... what fascinates him are the invisible forces that model flesh or shake it ... the relationship not of form and matter, but of materials and forces – making these forces visible through their effects on the flesh. (2003: x)

Deleuze sees in Bacon's works a powerful rendering visible of the body itself – freed from the stratifications, significations and subjectifications of everyday life. He sees, in other words, a rendering-perceptible of the invisible forces that surge through the stratified and organised body:

the forces proper to the body without organs. In Bacon's *Triptych May–June 1973*, we see the forces at work upon a body sitting on a toilet for a long time, or vomiting into a basin – forces which contort the body, deforming it, forcing its eyes closed, its mouth open, its back hunched. As Deleuze notes:

> we witness the revelation of the body beneath the organism, which makes organisms and their elements crack or swell, imposes a spasm on them, and puts them into relation with forces – sometimes with an inner force that arouses them, sometimes with external forces that traverse them. (2003: 160–1)

Bacon later brings together an eruption of internal and external forces in his two drug-referenced paintings: *Henrietta Moraes (Lying Figure with Hypodermic Syringe) (1963)* and *Version No. 2 of Lying Figure with Hypodermic Syringe (1968)*. Both versions present a female figure lying on a bed with a syringe needle sticking into an outstretched arm. Yet the forces traversing each figure differ remarkably. Where the force of the drug in the first image is one which relaxes a body, freeing it of stratification, in the second image the force of the drug is one which simultaneously deforms and rigidifies, bringing forth the body without organs at the same time as it draws forth all the stratifications of habit and social sanctioning. Referring to this second version, Deleuze writes that it 'is less a nailed-down body ... than a body attempting to pass through the syringe and to escape through this hole or vanishing point' (2003: 17–18). This is a body attempting to escape its striations, its identity and representational consistency: attempting to connect to an outside.

The power of art is its ability to offer up these forces of the future: forces outside of current modes of perception and corporeality, 'an excess not somehow beyond the world but an excess of the world' (O'Sullivan 2006: 40). In doing so, art has the capacity to make possible new ways of being and relating: new ways of folding the self. This is the power of art and also its ethics. Art enables the formation of new bodies: bodies which perceive in new ways, which are composed in new ways, and which have the potential to connect to others in new ways. Art does not address a pre-existent audience, but instead creates its own audience: an audience with new perceptual capacitates, and new potentialities for living (Zepke 2005: 4). This is the ethico-aesthetic[2] potential of art, and it is what Deleuze and Guattari are referring to when they say that art has the power to bring forth a 'people to come' (1994: 218).

But what sorts of future people do heroin chic and other drug-referenced advertisements bring forth? Can they be thought of as an art, and if so, what forms of perception do they make possible?

Heroin Chic as Art

The woman now lies on her side on the floor of the room, her head resting on a cushion taken from the seat of the couch. The cooler exposure of this second image changes the tone of the grimy carpet beneath her, and emphasises the cold white edge of the fireplace behind her. Although lying down, she still does not look comfortable; her legs are crossed and twisted awkwardly, seemingly cramped for space near the wall. She is wearing little more than a pair of jeans, while her bare left arm stretches out along the carpet, the crook of her arm facing up. Her lips are slightly parted, her eyelids are darkened, and her gaze is unfocused and vacant. Again, the photo's strange angle creates a sense that the room is spinning, and that the woman has given in to the distorted pull of gravity.

Day's photos do, in many ways, render perceptible invisible forces which can act upon a body. They draw attention to the force of a body's weight pressing down upon the heels of the feet; the force of shoulder-blades pulling tense against skin; the force of rough carpet rubbing up against toes, ankles, knees. Perhaps they also draw attention to the forces of heroin: its capacity to soften and weaken the muscles; distort proprioception and time; bring on a sleepiness; or induce a cold sweat during withdrawal. In encountering these images, one can become aware of one's own weight, one's own eyes and skin, one's own posture, one's own perception of time and space. One can perceive the relation between the body and its surroundings, and between the body and its potentiality, in new light. These deterritorialisations of perception carry with them an ethico-aesthetic capacity. As Harold has argued, it is the very 'unruly' corporeality of the heroin chic body which 'perform[s] an ethical function . . . [for such] bodies do not adhere to reason, [and as such] require one to make ethical responses without the safety-net of a moral map for guidance' (1999: 74). They require, in other words, that one engage with the body – one's own body and the bodies of others – in new ways, no longer based on Enlightenment ontologies of reason and rationality.

There are, however, at least two types of force which can be understood to limit the ethico-aesthetic potentials of art, including that of heroin chic. The first of these, which Deleuze explores in his work on

Bacon, is that of the cliché, which must be actively dismantled if art is to become a repetition of difference rather than sameness. The second, which Deleuze and Guattari explore in their collective works, is that of capitalism, which, on the one hand, accelerates the creative potentials of art but, on the other hand, reduces its capacity for connecting to an outside. I will examine each in turn and explore the extent to which they haunt heroin chic imagery and limit its ethico-aesthetics.

The Dangers of the Cliché

Despite its smooth appearance, an artist's 'empty' workspace is, as Deleuze (2003: 10–11, 86–7) points out, always already 'full': heavily striated by a range of historically embedded clichés, which limit aesthetic possibilities. Certain forms, tones and features are always already more likely than others to appear, and these delineate the canvas according to a prior set of probabilities. Deleuze focuses on four representational clichés: those of illustration (reproducing that which is already visible); narration (trying to communicate a set story or meaning); figuration (using symbolism to convey meaning and significance); and faciality (the production of a stratified identity through representation of a particular, recognisable 'face'). These four forces shape what it is possible to see, think and do artistically. They limit the ways in which an artist can imagine the world, and as such, the forms of art they can produce (O'Sullivan 2006: 63).

The first thing an artist must do, therefore, is to smooth out, or deterritorialise, their workspace in order to enable new modes of perception to emerge (Deleuze 2003: 86). Yet representational clichés are extremely difficult to dismantle; it is not sufficient simply to cover them over or work around them, nor does parody suffice. Instead, the dismantling of clichés requires active, purposeful effort (87, 89). Examining the work of Bacon, Deleuze identifies a range of successful strategies which can be employed to dismantle the cliché (3–7, 99–100). These include the use of isolation (rendering a figure or body alone, as a means of beginning to dispense with illustration and narrative); the use of asignifying traits (marks or fields of colour that have no representational or meaningful function); and the creation of scrubbed out or blurred zones along the edges of a figure (which work to disrupt figuration, illustration and faciality by dismantling the recognisability of the figure or face itself).

In contrast to the fashion photography of the time – a field of reference dominated by glossy, stylised images of meticulously made-up models, where fantasy and artifice are *de rigueur* – heroin chic images such as

Day's are disruptive precisely because they seem to act as illustrations, as representations of a 'real' world beneath and beyond fashion. By diagramming some of the forces which can impact upon any body, including those of fashion models, these images begin to dismantle the clichés of beauty and perfection which are embedded in the fashion industry. However, to the extent to which they appear as a kind of documentary realism, they fail to disrupt the cliché of illustration – a representational form which reaffirms the world as it supposedly 'is': a world which is recognisable, familiar and knowable.[3] The apparent simplicity of the photographic method – in which a camera exposes a film to light from the world outside it – works to obscure the many ways in which photographers are involved in the construction of images, choosing not only the location and subject of their photo but also, amongst other things, the framing, angle, posture, lighting and mood. It also tends to obscure processes of photo manipulation and selection, in which certain forms and representations of 'reality' are made visible and knowable, while others are discarded. Through its allusions to realism, documentary-style photography tends, more than any other form of photography, to obscure its own processes of construction and cultural production (Fitzgerald 2002b). Such images thus fail to render visible the forces of construction which shape all photographs and, more importantly, fail to disrupt the assumption that there is a truth or reality which can be represented in the first place.

Many heroin chic images also fail to break with the cliché of narration. Images have the capacity to generate a story or narrative sequence not only through their connection to other images in a series, but also – more importantly – through the way in which they are internally constructed. One of the most common methods is the use of a 'recognisable' setting or a collection of 'recognisable' objects to signify or suggest a storyline. In one of Juergen Teller's drug-referenced fashion photographs entitled *Charlotte Rampling, Paris (2001)*, for example, a woman in a cocktail dress and high-heeled shoes lies slumped forward on a couch, her dress partly unzipped, one shoe on the floor. Her posture and disarray, combined with the photograph's dim lighting and the presence of a lampshade and sagging couch, suggest that she has arrived home – or possibly to a cheap hotel – after an evening of partying, and that her extreme tiredness and/or intoxication (perhaps alcohol, perhaps another drug) has prevented her from changing out of her clothes and making it to bed. Although such narratives may be highly ambiguous, and will certainly differ between (and within) individual viewers, they tend to reduce an image to a limited 'range' of interpretive possibilities.

They also shift the force of the image away from the production of non-conscious sensory hæcceities and affects, to the production of conscious, linear narratives, meanings and truths.

Figuration is another form of cliché that haunts many heroin chic advertisements, which tend to rely on certain visual codes and symbols to represent signs of drug use. These symbols are figurations: clichés which stand in for, and signify, particular forces. Such coded references work to the extent that they reproduce – or cite – an established history of coded drug representations in documentary photography, media and film (Fitzgerald 2002b). The documentary photography of artists such as Larry Clark, Nan Goldin, Eugene Richards, Susan Watts and John Raynard has been particularly influential in this regard (2002b), as have popular films such as *Trainspotting*, *Pulp Fiction*, *Drugstore Cowboy* and *Christiane F.* The use of an outstretched arm – with the crook of the elbow facing upwards or toward the camera – has, for example, become a common technique through which to suggest injecting drug use. Another common way in which drug use is suggestively made 'visible' in advertising imagery is through the application of codes of 'disease' or 'illness' to the body (Hickman 2002: 122). These include the darkening of the subjects' eyes; the addition of bruises, scabs or abscesses; the drooping of the eyelids; and the sagging of the head, hunching of the body or holding of the stomach. Although such figurations do not necessarily signify drug use, they resonate with a general tendency to link drug use to a kind of primitive desire (Fitzgerald 2002b) and to a desire lacking in reason, rationality and will-power (Keane 2002).

The use of such figurations is also tied to the production of particular clichéd forms of faciality. As Fitzgerald (2002a) argues, such faciality has important ethical implications for the ways in which drug-using bodies can be 'recognised', perceived and connected to. He writes:

> There is a tendency in drug photography to attempt to make images of dark, seedy, secret worlds. This can have the effect of Othering the subject, or making them different through exoticising them . . . thus a certain safety or distanciation can occur between the reader/watcher and the subject. (374)

The diseasing of the body in drug-referenced advertising thus has important implications for an ethics of bodily relations. The concern here is not that certain photographs or representations might offend drug users, or might present them incorrectly, but rather that certain representations might limit the potential for drug-using bodies to connect with other bodies. This in turn reduces the potential for other connections, such as those of empathy and compassion. The concern is, in other words, not a moral one, but an ethico-aesthetics.

Breaking with the Cliché

Amongst the heroin chic fashion images of the 1990s, very few attempts at actively breaking with representational clichés can be discerned. Mario Sorrenti's work stands out in this regard. In many of his photographs, as in Bacon's paintings, a figure is presented alone, centred in the image and surrounded by a field of uniform, saturated colour. Instead of trying to represent a known and knowable word, such images work to separate perception from the actual in order to open it out on to the field of the virtual. By isolating the figure, such images circumvent the tendency to convey force through a story or sequence of events. Instead of telling a story, they focus on conveying a mood or a force, drawing attention to the capacities of the body for affecting and being affected.

In Mario Sorrenti's *Keren (1995)*, for example, a young woman wearing a black t-shirt and pale blue singlet and underpants is framed by a soft greenish-grey backdrop. Her slender figure is slumped forward on a stool, her upper body propped up by her elbows pressing into her thighs. Her head hangs down, as though the effort to raise it for the photograph might have been too great. She looks more unwell than exhausted, her uncomfortable position on the tiny stool suggesting a need, rather than desire, to sit down. The stillness of the image, with its uniform colour, does not seem at all tranquil. It is as though the room is in danger of spinning, its potentiality pressing like a weight against her head, her stomach, her body.

By isolating the figure, the forces upon the body are able to come to the fore: the numbing of muscles, the soft heaviness of the arms and eyelids, and the strange contortioning of the body as it tries to reposition itself or hold itself together. Perhaps these are the forces of a drug, or of anorexia. Ultimately they are forces which would act upon any body which was forced – as in Bacon's paintings – to 'sit for hours on a narrow stool' (Deleuze 2003: x): forces of gravity, exhaustion, dizziness; the pressure of elbows against thighs; the weight of the head hanging forward. What is important is not that the body sitting on the stool has been depicted as though it were a body under the influence of – or withdrawing from – a drug such as heroin, but that it makes visible a force which is common to both (57).

In Sorrenti's *Francis Bacon I, II, II, IV (1997)* series, a photographic technique similar to Bacon's scrubbing has been used to dismantle the clichés of illustration and faciality. Each figure is again isolated within fields of uniform colour (black backdrop, pink triangle of floor), and again supported in the image by nothing more than a stool. Like Bacon's figures, these are bodies which are in presented processes of becoming: becoming-animal, becoming-imperceptible. No longer bounded entities, their bodies are in the course of disintegrating, merging with the floor, the wall, or leaving the image altogether. These photos bring to the fore the corporeal potentiality of bodies: the ways in which they can affect and be affected.

During the 1990s and early 2000s, a range of other bodies-in-becoming appeared in fashion magazines alongside those of heroin chic. Advertisements tapped into themes of gender, sexuality, masochism, bodily prosthetics (becomings-horse, becomings-dangerous), anorexia, bulimia, self-harm, suicide, accidents, disasters, crime, death and murder. Like heroic chic's figures, these bodies work to render perceptible extreme forces upon the body – forces of gravity, of *potentia*, the force of flesh falling on hard concrete; the force of a hand pushed against the back of the mouth; the force of the stomach flexing; the force of a body trying to escape from itself, to leak out from its confines ('Why not walk on your head, sing with your sinuses, see through your skin, breathe with your belly' (Deleuze and Guattari 1987: 151)); the force of ropes pulling along skin, metal spikes pressing against flesh; the force of a drug upon the body.

As with the figure in Bacon's *Version No.2 of Lying Figure with Hypodermic Syringe (1968),* some of the extreme figures presented to us in mid-1990s fashion photography can be understood as bodies attempting to escape the confines of their corporeal existence. They are bodies which are leaking out in all directions, moving fast toward their limit-points: toward schizophrenia, overdose, unconsciousness, death. Through them, the body's capacity for disintegration and deterritorialisation is made sensible, palpable. Deleuze writes:

> Beyond the organism, but also at the limit of the lived body, there lies what Artaud discovered and named: the body without organs . . . It is an intense and intensive body . . . traversed by a wave that traces levels or thresholds in the body according to the variations of its amplitude. (2003: 44–5)

This body without organs is the invisible, desiring force of all bodies. It is the force of the virtual: the force of an outside of perception and sensation and which opens on to the future. It is the body un-actualised, or pre-actualised: the body in its virtual form.

To the extent that it effectively breaks with representational clichés, heroin chic advertising can therefore be thought of as generating substantial artistic and affective force. By rendering perceptible invisible forces upon the body – such as those of drug use, desire, exhaustion, dizziness and nausea – they have the potential to disrupt our perception of the body and its relationship with the world. More specifically, notes Harold (1999: 72), they have the capacity to challenge a range of modern assumptions about the self and the body. They do so, first, by demonstrating the body's fluid, porous nature. The body here can no longer be understood as unified and autonomous, but must be understood as intimately related to, and affected by, the world around it. Heroin chic images also have the potential to dismantle modernist ideals of reason and rationality; a body affected by invisible forces, desires and passions is not one which can be governed by a rational free will. Such images thus work to deterritorialise the very idea of an enduring self or identity, illustrating instead 'the self's position within a fluctuating nexus between always-changing, always-becoming identities' (72).

Combined, these movements of deterritorialisation also have the potential to shift the ways in which a social ethics can be understood and enacted (Harold 1999). To the extent that they demonstrate the power of bodies to differ from themselves, heroin chic's images might be capable of promoting a kind of ethics based on our mutual capacity to differ, to become-other, rather than an ethics or morality based on our essential sameness or human-ness. As Harold argues:

> An ethical framework that accounts for corporeality . . . might encourage an engagement with others based not on the other's degree of similarity to ourselves and our ideals . . . [but rather] this irreducible otherness that simultaneously connects us. (75)

Such an ethics connects bodies through their difference – through their power of differing – rather than through their sameness to one another. As such, it enhances the potential for new inter-personal relations to form.

Yet most heroin chic advertisements are limited in these artistic, ethico-aesthetic functions. Many, as we have seen, fail to disrupt the clichéd forms of representation, and as such, have difficulty launching new becomings and lines of flight. And even where drug-referenced advertising succeeds in breaking with cliché, there is yet another force which must be taken into account – that of consumer capitalism. As Roffe notes:

> Even once an artwork breaks free of the gravity of the territorial cliché, there remains the other subversive movement: that of capitalism . . . which

threatens to strip the artwork of its distinctiveness in order to submit it to the commodity form. (2005: unpaginated)

The Dangers of Capitalism

the derelict zones of drug use are the engines of late capitalism, not because they are abject, but because they are moments of difference where desire seeks to escape bodily limitation.

(Fitzgerald and Threadgold 2004: 416)

One of the most interesting things about capitalism is that it tends to operate through, and thrive upon, the production of deterritorialised flows (Deleuze and Guattari 1987: 453). Flows of money, of goods, of labour and trade; flows of information, language and art; flows of desire and identity: all are produced and supported within sites of capital. Unlike the State, capitalism thrives upon on the capacity, and desire, of bodies to become-other. Through sites of capitalist consumption, for example, bodies are increasingly able to mutate: to transform their identities, their behaviours, their organisation and their potentials. As Massumi notes, 'subjectivity is being disengaged from the plane of transcendence of "human" being, becoming an immanent abstract machine of mutation' (1992: 135). Capitalism cares very little for the categories of identity, morality, reason and rationality that otherwise pervade the social strata. You can see and say and be and do almost anything in relation to sites of capital, so long as you do not interrupt the flows (Colebrook 2002: 65).

In relation to sites of capital, then, remarkable possibilities seem to open up for becomings-other: for deterritorialising the body and its relations with the world. The *becoming* body, write Fitzgerald and Threadgold (2004), 'is both beautiful, fear instilling and a source for productive capital in modern capitalist societies' (415); it is 'a most valuable site as it is at once both marginal and central to the production of capital' (415).

Such becomings and deterritorialisations, however, cannot be separated from the movements of reterritorialisation, which are also an essential part of the operation of capital. As Patton suggests, 'capitalist societies simultaneously reterritorialise what they deterritorialise, producing all manner of "neoterritorialities"' (2000: 97). For while capitalism is busy destratifying bodies and codes, it is also simultaneously engendering extreme forms of stratification, producing, for example, rigid striations of wealth and poverty, and first and third worlds (Deleuze 1995: 172–3).

These seemingly opposing forces of deterritorialisation and reterritorialisation are not at all incompatible. As Deleuze and Guattari make clear, capitalism's becomings – like all becomings – are always double, involving not only a line of deterritorialisation, but also an equal and opposite movement of reterritorialisation (Deleuze and Guattari 1987: 10). One reason – perhaps even the primary reason – why capitalism is so successful is because it has mastered the coordination and modulation of the two forces deterritorialisation–reterritorialisation (Deleuze and Guattari 1987: 492). The question of the success of capitalism, then, is not one of 'freedom' versus 'constraint', observe Deleuze and Guattari, 'but of the manner in which one masters the flows' (1987: 462). Contemporary globalised capitalism is increasingly perfecting the speed of transference between deterritorialisation and reterritorialisation, such that the pulsating movement from one to the other happens at an ever-greater efficiency and speed. As Deleuze and Guattari note, 'at the complementary and dominant level of *integrated (or rather integrating) world capitalism*, a new smooth space is produced in which capital reaches its "absolute" speed' (492).

Rather than code bodies according to qualitative values (gender, sexuality, ethnicity, etc.), capitalism increasingly tends to code bodies in ways that are quantitative; its aim is to regulate and direct flows (consumption, trade, profits, etc.) rather than to judge them. In other words, it focuses less on coding bodies in terms of hierarchical molar identities and categories, and more on coding them in terms of their functional capacity to effect flows of capital: that is, in terms of their exchange, rather than moral, value.

Sites of capital are increasingly adept at harnessing the desiring-potentials of minoritarian, nomadic and deterritorialising bodies. Thus we see, in relation to capitalism, the simultaneous production and suppression, release and containment, exploitation and censorship of minoritarian bodies. The cultural and bodily becomings-other of young people, the poor, ethnic minorities, anorexics, drug users: all are increasingly harnessed to market goods. At the same time, the suppression of minoritarian groups and movements is increasingly tied to the threat they pose to capitalist axiomatics and flows. In many 'producing' nations, for example, workers protesting against their conditions are often violently crushed by a totalitarian State acting in the direct interests– and with the cooperation and support– of large multinational corporations (Deleuze and Guattari 1987: 472). We also see minorities in 'consumer' nations – protesters, the homeless, drug users – regularly suppressed or 'moved on' in the interests of maximising flows of capital.

The extent of these violences, which includes violence against all sorts of minoritarian bodies (third-world producers, ethnic minorities, indigenous bodies, women, children, animals, forests), is also often obscured by the 'freedoms' offered within spaces of 'first world' consumer capitalism, at least for those who have the capacity to consume (Deleuze and Guattari 1987: 447; Deleuze 1995: 173).

The deterritorialising potentials opened up by heroin chic fashion advertisements, therefore, cannot be separated from the territorialisation and stratification of minoritarian bodies, nor from the obscuring of these territorialisations. For our ability to think beyond the logic and aesthetics of capitalism, and to develop successful forms of resistance to the sorts of harms it entails, is itself continually undermined by capitalism, which is increasingly taking over responsibility for the production and circulation of philosophy, art and politics (Deleuze and Guattari 1994). As Deleuze notes, 'The current political situation is very muddled. People tend to confuse the quest for freedom with the embrace of capitalism. It seems doubtful that the joys of capitalism are enough to liberate a people' (2006: 379). Art's involvement with capitalism, therefore, does more than simply divert the energy of artists; it also helps to launder unethical corporate brands, giving them a cleaner, brighter – and more 'revolutionary' – public image, at the same time as diverting attention from substantive issues of politics and ethics (387–8).

Yet can revolutionary, artistic flows not also potentially be produced from within sites of capital? Because they work in and through the decoding of flows, capitalism does indeed necessarily engender unexpected lines of rupture and flight: lines which are capable of forming revolutionary 'war machines' and challenging both the state and capitalism (see, for example, Patton 2000: 7). Capitalism, as Deleuze and Guattari suggest, 'gives rise to numerous flows in all directions that escape its axiomatic' (1987: 472–3); it is 'leaking all over the place' (Deleuze 2004: 270); 'its lines of escape are not just difficulties that arise, they are the very conditions of its operation' (270). Although most of the escaping flows are captured by the State or reterritorialised by capitalism (i.e. harnessed in advertising and marketing), some do have the potential to gather momentum and link up with other flows to form broader, revolutionary movements of resistance or escape. To this deterritorialising affect, Bennett (2001) gives the term 'enchantment'. She argues that 'part of the energy needed to challenge injustice comes from the reservoir of enchantment – including that derived from commodities' (128). These moments of deterritorialised enchantment, including those offered through capitalist consumption and advertising, enable a kind of ethical posture or energy which is necessary for the formation of an ethics (128).

Bennett's argument that an ethics can – perhaps even must – emerge from a kind of joyous deterritorialisation or 'enchantment' is an important one. It is from such an ethico-aesthetics, rather than from ethical or moral imperatives, that it becomes possible to bring forth a 'people to come' (Deleuze and Guattari 1994: 218). While I agree with Bennett that such an ethico-aesthetics is possible within capitalist advertising, I am less optimistic about the extent to which such sites can offer these revolutionary potentials. As Deleuze and Guattari admit, 'all decoded flows, of whatever kind, are prone to forming a war machine … But everything changes depending on whether these flows connect up with a war machine or, on the contrary, enter into conjunctions or a general conjunction that appropriates them' (1987: 459). To the extent that an advertising image constitutes an 'art' that has been produced under the conditions of a consumer capitalism – designed such that the deterritorialised flows that it engenders are channelled toward, rather than away from, capitalist consumption – its range of creative possibilities (its virtual potential) is reduced, and its capacity to launch revolutionary deterritorialisations is diminished. The forces of stratification and violence which are a 'complementary' part of capitalism's deterritorialisations are more likely to be obscured than rendered visible through its vision. Certainly advertisements do work in 'unpredictable' ways (Bennett 2001: 113, 115), but sites of capital are, as I noted earlier, extremely good at appropriating escaping flows. They may not always succeed, but in most cases they do.

Although I agree that it is possible for an ethical and political posture to emerge from within commodity cultures (such as advertising), I believe that it is more crucial that art finds non-capitalist sites – or at least sites which constitute cracks or fissures within or between capitalist relations – from which to launch its lines of flight. Rather than oppose capital, revolutionary forces must constitute 'decoded flows that free themselves from this axiomatic' (Patton 2000: 105), and through which other ways of connecting and perceiving become possible. It is, as Deleuze and Guattari suggest, 'by leaving the plan(e) of capital, and never ceasing to leave it, that a mass becomes increasingly revolutionary' (1987: 472).

Breaking with Capital and Clichés

During the 1990s, the billboard 'jamming' and advertisement 'spoofing' group called *Adbusters* produced an activist, sabotage-style advertisement aimed at drawing attention to the fashion and heroin chic's negative impact on women. Rendered in black and white, the image presented a very thin, naked young woman hunched over a toilet vomiting, followed by the words 'Obsession: For Women'. With its clear referencing in both style and wording to a Calvin Klein perfume advertisement, the image carried with it no ambiguities; its message – that the fashion, cosmetics and advertising industries are producing bulimia and body-image problems amongst women – is clear.

This type of parody, which involves overcoding advertising images and messages with more 'truthful' messages regarding the 'hidden' ethical and health implications of consuming that brand or product, might seem to be a useful way of drawing attention to existing social relations. However, to the extent that it operates through a commitment to ideals of 'truth', which capitalism itself has so long ago dispensed with, it has a limited capacity to challenge the techniques of subversion and deterritorialisation favoured by contemporary advertising. As Harold notes:

> while the advertising sabotage articulated by Adbusters is not without some rhetorical value, it does little to address the rhetoric of contemporary marketing – a mode of power that is quite happy to oblige subversive rhetoric and shocking imagery . . . despite its deconstructive sensibility, parody . . . perpetuates a commitment to rhetorical binaries – the hierarchical form it supposedly wants to upset . . . parody, as negative critique is not up to the task of undermining the parodist's own purchase on the Truth as it maintains a hierarchy of language and the protestor's role as revealer. (2004: 190–1)

Parody is, by nature, reactionary, negative and oppositional, and as such does little to generate an alternative deterritorialising force of becoming or enchantment. It also does little to break with cliché (Deleuze 2003: 89). In order to escape the grasp of capital and cliché simultaneously, while none the less generating a force of active becoming, activist interventions need to shift away from simple information provision and critique to more positive, creative forms of production. Consider, for example, the 'pranking' forms of activism suggested by Harold (2004). Unlike parody, pranking involves creative and artistic performances, interventions and installations which operate to deterritorialise perception. A good example Harold gives is the *Biotic Baking Brigade*'s 'cream-pie-to-the-face' manœuvre in which – reminiscent of old-style vaudeville pranks – cream pies are publicly launched upon the faces of prominent neo-liberals and corporate leaders. Another, more pertinent example given is *INFKT*'s creative alter-tobacco campaign which challenged the influence of the cigarette industry in a very different way to the dominant 'Just Say No' campaigns. Acknowledging that 'Nike's provocation to "just do it" has proven far more compelling to young people than . . . [the] message of abstinence ever could be' (203), *INFKT* harnessed young people's 'anti-authoritarian attitudes' by encouraging them to take part in deterritorialising tobacco company claims. Instead of telling young people not to smoke, *INFKT* encouraged them to sabotage tobacco ads. The acts of sabotage themselves operated very much like those of Adbusters' campaigns, but the crucial difference is that the *INFKT* campaign involved activating the desire-flows of young people to be part of the prank. Such strategies work, as Harold (2004) suggests, 'less through negation and opposition, than by playfully appropriating commercial rhetoric, both folding it over on itself and exaggerating its tropes' (189). In doing so, such strategies are able – in the same way as capitalism – to harness the desire-flows of the media and the consumer public.

The strength of pranking interventions such as these lies not in their ability to draw attention to the 'realities' of consumption, but in their ability to deterritorialise the relations of power that flow through capitalist assemblages: 'by layering and folding the rhetorical field [it] addresses the patterns of power rather than its contents' (Harold 2004: 209). They involve 'an artful proliferation of messages, a rhetorical process of intervention and invention, which challenges the ability of corporate discourses to make meaning in predictable ways' (192). Pranking thus constitutes what Deleuze and Guattari would call a minor practice (1987: 106, 361). Such a practice will, as O'Sullivan notes, 'precisely stammer and stutter the commodity form, disassembling those already existing forms of capital and indeed moving beyond the latter's very logic' (2006: 73).

An Ethico-Aesthetics of Bodies

Deleuze's work suggests an appreciation of the ways in which the deterritorialising body, including that of the injecting drug user, can generate flows of desire and enable potentially revolutionary shifts in perception. His work also compels an awareness of the ways in which representational clichés can operate to stifle these artistic potentials, and the extent to which sites of capital can co-opt and restratify their revolutionary movements. Although heroin chic images contain within them potentials for becoming-other, their context as fashion advertisements renders them far more likely to obscure, rather than render visible, the forms of violent exploitation and oppression of minoritarian bodies, including of drug-using bodies, which are an inextricable part of contemporary capitalism. And to the extent that these images reproduce a range of representational clichés, which generate a particular drug-user faciality, they also work to stratify the ways in which drug-using bodies can be perceived, understood and connected to.

Together, these forces of stratification – capitalism and the cliché – impact on the bodily capacities of those who use drugs, particularly those who use drugs in public urban space. In relation to urban capitalism, the marginalised body of the drug user tends to be judged less according to a moral code, and more according to an exchange potential: evaluated in relation to the flows of desire it might engender on the one hand and the flows of profit it may block on the other. And these evaluations are increasingly based on particular clichéd perceptions of drug-using bodies. As urban spaces become increasingly tied to consumer capitalism – as advertising billboards, giant TV screens, café seating, retail shops and privately owned 'public' squares proliferate – relations between bodies, spaces and flows of capital become increasingly important. In many cities, for example, we see how intensive policing operations are often spurred on by retailer complaints to the media about the negative impact of drug users on sales (Fitzgerald et al. 1999: 73–5, 85). The policing of drug-using bodies in city space, particularly during major city events, also cannot be separated from attempts to maximise flows of tourism and retail consumption (Malins et al. 2006). Drug-using bodies are often well aware, in a bodily sense, of these ways in which urban space is shaped by flows of retail capital, and tend to negotiate spaces of consumption by performing their bodies (dress, comportment, body shape) in particular ways (521–2). Others keep away from such spaces in order to avoid surveillance and police attention, preferring instead to use drugs in parks or universities, or at home (Malins 2007: 160).

For many critics of heroin chic, the problem with the images is that they present drug use and the drug-using body as objects of aesthetics, rather than of ethics. Giroux, for example, writes: 'Within the postmodern world of heroin chic fashion photography, the "other" is cast as an object of aesthetic consideration, a source of sensations rather than a serious object of moral evaluation and responsibility' (1997: 25). What such an approach misses is that ethics and aesthetics are – and must be – connected. An embodied ethics does not emerge from rational judgement and moral reasoning, but from sensory, affective becomings, generated through an ethico-aesthetics. As Bennett suggests, we need an aesthetic, affective impetus if we are to develop a positive ethical life and to garner the energy and creativity to launch revolutionary movements of change.

Simply drawing attention to the problems with consumption, and telling people not to consume certain products, images or substances for ethical or moral reasons, are strategies which will remain limited in their capacity to shape behaviour. Consumption is not a 'rational' event but an embodied one, involving both conscious and non-conscious processes. People enjoy consuming, be it products, images or drugs. Consumption generates and enables the same kinds of desire-flows and becomings as those which enable life to flow (Fitzgerald 2005: 569–71). Attempts to block these desire-flows are often corporeally resisted. As Bennett notes, 'The fear that changing the infrastructure of consumption would entail the end of pleasure in consumption' might well, for example, 'be one source of cultural resistance to the adoption of more eco-friendly ways of life' (2001: unpaginated, note 14). Promoting asceticism, cynicism and negativity will only go so far in challenging existing modes of consumption, and will do little to promote ethico-aesthetic 'styles of life' (Deleuze 1995: 100).

Government shock-tactic anti-drug campaigns, for example – which present drug use in entirely negative terms, display extreme images of the effects of drug use, and call for people to be 'reasonable' by abstaining from drugs – are likewise problematic. On the one hand, they are likely to generate the same kinds of desire-flows as those on which heroin chic advertising trades. On the other hand, by simultaneously calling upon bodies to refrain from experimenting with those lines of flight and desire-flows, they are likely to deaden, rather than inspire, ethico-aesthetic modes of engagement with drug use – not only by those who consume drugs, but also by the people around them. A more effective strategy must involve a shift from asceticism to an ethico-aesthetics in which ethically positive forms of drug consumption are rendered more affectively pleasurable. Doing so will involve not simply oppositional critique, but also the active creation of alternative opportunities for creativity, 'enchantment' and becomings. Heroin chic offers a sample of the kinds of ways in which the body-in-becoming has the capacity to generate an ethico-aesthetics. Through similar kinds of creative enchantment, harm minimisation might be able to engender an optimism and an openness to new encounters: movements which are likely to enhance rather than diminish the capacity of bodies to affect the world and to be affected by it.

Acknowledgements

I would like to thank Kirsty Duncanson, Jane Gardam, Mark Halsey, Anna Hickey-Moody, Barbara Huneter, Nesam McMillan and Alison Young for their insightful feedback on an earlier draft of this chapter.

References

Ashton, R. (2002), *This is Heroin*, London: Sanctuary.
Bennett, J. (2001), *The Enchantment of Modern Life: Attachments, Crossings, and Ethics*, Princeton: Princeton University Press.
Braidotti, R. (no date), 'Interview with Rosi Braidotti', downloaded 16 May 2002 from http://users.skynet.be/nattyweb/RosiInt.htm.
Colebrook, C. (2002), *Gilles Deleuze*, London: Routledge.
Deleuze, G. (1986), *Cinema 1: The Movement-Image*, trans. H. Tomlinson and B. Habberjam, Minneapolis: University of Minnesota Press.
Deleuze, G. (1989), *Cinema 2: The Time-Image*, trans. H. Tomlinson and R. Galeta, Minneapolis: University of Minnesota Press.
Deleuze, G. (1995), *Negotiations*, trans. M. Joughin, New York: Columbia University Press.
Deleuze, G. (2003), *Francis Bacon: The Logic of Sensation*, trans. D. Smith, London: Continuum.
Deleuze, G. (2004), *Desert Islands and Other Texts 1953–1974*, trans. M. Taormina, Los Angeles: Semiotext(e).
Deleuze, G. (2006), *Two Regimes of Madness: Texts and Interviews 1975–1995*, trans. A. Hodges and M. Taormina, New York: Semiotext(e).
Deleuze, G. and F. Guattari (1987), *A Thousand Plateaus: Capitalism and Schizophrenia*, trans. B. Massumi, London: Athlone.
Deleuze, G. and F. Guattari (1994), *What is Philosophy?*, trans. G. Burchell and H. Tomlinson, London: Verso.
Fitzgerald, J. (2002a), 'A Political Economy of "Doves"', *Contemporary Drug Problems* 29, pp. 201–39.
Fitzgerald, J. (2002b), 'Drug Photography and Harm Reduction: Reading John Ranard', *International Journal of Drug Policy* 13, pp. 369–85.
Fitzgerald, J. (2005), 'Illegal Drug Markets in Transitional Economies', *Addiction Research and Theory* 13: 6, pp. 563–77.
Fitzgerald, J., S. Broad and A. Dare (1999), *Regulating the Street Heroin Market in Fitzroy/Collingwood*, Melbourne: Victorian Health Promotion Foundation.
Fitzgerald, J. and T. Threadgold (2004), 'Fear of Sense in the Street Heroin Market', *International Journal of Drug Policy* 15, 407–17.
FVR (2002), *Faces and Voices of Recovery Campaign Website*, downloaded 12 November 2003 from: http://www.facesandvoicesofrecovery.org/DIOR_NEWS.HTM.
Giroux, H. (1997), 'Heroin Chic, Trendy Aesthetics, and the Politics of Pathology', *New Art Examiner* 25, pp. 20–7.

Giroux, H. (2000), *Stealing Innocence: Youth, Corporate Power, and the Politics of Culture*, New York: Palgrave.
Guattari, F. (1995), *Chaosmosis: An Ethico-aesthetic Paradigm*, trans. Paul Bains and Julian Pefanis, Bloomington: Indiana University Press.
Halnon, K. (2002), 'Poor Chic: The Rational Consumption of Poverty', *Current Sociology* 50: 4, pp. 501–16.
Harold, C. (1999), 'Tracking Heroin Chic: The Abject Body Reconfigures the Rational Argument', *Argumentation and Advocacy* 36: 2, pp. 65–76.
Harold, C. (2004), 'Pranking Rhetoric: "Culture Jamming" as Media Activism', *Critical Studies in Media Communication* 21: 3, pp. 189–211.
Hickman, T. (2002), 'Heroin Chic: The Visual Culture of Narcotic Addiction', *Third Text* 16: 2, pp. 119–36.
Keane, H. (2002), *What's Wrong With Addiction?*, Melbourne: Melbourne University Press.
Lai, A. (2006), 'Glitter and Grain: Aura and Authenticity in the Celebrity Photographs of Juergen Teller', in *Framing Celebrity: New Directions in Celebrity Culture*, ed. S. Holmes and S. Redmond, London: Routledge, pp. 215–30.
Malins, P. (2007), 'City Folds: Injecting Drug Use and Urban Space', in *Deleuzian Encounters: Studies in Contemporary Social Issues*, ed. A. Hickey-Moody and P. Malins, London: Palgrave, pp. 151–68.
Malins, P., J. Fitzgerald and T. Threadgold (2006), 'Spatial "Folds:" the Entwining of Bodies, Risks and City Spaces for Women Injecting Drug Users in Melbourne's Central Business District', *Gender, Place and Culture* 13: 5, pp. 509–27.
Massumi, B. (1992), *A User's Guide to Capitalism and Schizophrenia: Deviations from Deleuze and Guattari*, Cambridge, MA: MIT Press.
O'Sullivan, S. (2006), *Art Encounters Deleuze and Guattari: Thought Beyond Representation*, London: Palgrave.
Patton, P. (2000), *Deleuze and the Political*, London: Routledge.
Roffe, J. (2005), 'Art, Capitalism, Local Struggle: Some Deleuzean Propositions', *Drain Mag* 3, downloaded 22 April 2006 from: http://www.drainmag.com.
Zepke, S. (2005), *Art as Abstract Machine: Ontology and Aesthetics in Deleuze and Guattari*, New York: Routledge.

Notes

1. A good source of much of this photographic work is *The Archaeology of Elegance: 1980–2000 - 20 Years of Fashion Photography* (2002), ed. Marion de Beaupre, Stephane Baumet and Ulf Poschardt, New York: Rizzoli International. Another good source is *Fashion: Photography of the Nineties* (1996), ed. Camilla Nickerson and Neville Wakefield, Zurich: Scalo.
2. Although it was Felix Guattari who first explicitly referred to the idea of an 'ethico-aesthetic paradigm' (1995), the link between ethics and aesthetics is one which, I believe, runs implicitly throughout Deleuze and Guattari's collective works. For both thinkers, the practice of ethics cannot be separated from aesthetics and embodied sensation, and from what Deleuze, following Foucault, also refers to as 'ways of existing' or 'styles of life' (1995: 100). Ethico-aesthetics is thus concerned with the ways in which – through art, language, music, architecture, science, social relations and other forms of creativity – we can enact more ethically positive forms of subjectivity, thought and life. 'Ethically positive' here should be understood not as a specific pre-determined end-point, but as a relative term designating a mode of life which is more open, uncertain and rich with possibilities than that which otherwise exists. Practices of ethico-aesthetics therefore

involve opening on to difference by increasing, through aesthetics, the capacity of bodies to affect and be affected in new ways.

3. Referring specifically to Teller's work, Lai (2006) notes that realist images such as these fail to destabilise the fashion industry because they instead work to recoup consumers who are otherwise jaded by the artifice of fashion advertisements. Through Teller's realist images, such consumers are re-connected to the fashion industry – made to feel as though the world of glamour and high fashion is not so removed from their world after all.

Chapter 9

Multi-Dimensional Modifications

Patricia MacCormack

In *What is Philosophy?* Deleuze and Guattari posit that a concept comes from a problem. A problem is an impasse between two discourses. The problem describes the space-between, a refusal of the need for one discourse to colonise the other, a disagreement where creation is the resolution. Heavily modified bodies in Western culture offer a multi-conceptual entity. They represent the impasse between philosophy (the need to create) and sociology (the need to reflect), between volition and fashion, between signification (modifications which symbolise, which mean something) and asignification (modifications which deterritorialise traditionally signified flesh), and between flesh and self (in what ways modifications de-gender and de-racialise the body). This chapter will explore the modified body as an in-between, a concept which negotiates and transgresses discourses of signified flesh and subjectivity to create a new concept of the body as liminal. These bodies allow us to navigate the plasticity of the regime of signification through which the body emerges – what Deleuze and Guattari call signifiation – and the concrete materiality of marked flesh, which involves actual pain. Bodily modified people share nothing as a 'tribe' except their status as in-between; thus the space they occupy comes to mean more than the essence of their being modified bodies.

Body and Skin

The most prevalent and obvious way in which modified bodies have emerged in discourse is as an object of analysis. Traditional biunivocal expressions of the signified body are renegotiated. Racial alterity becomes tribal primitivism in the marking of the body. But as this chapter will attend to the modified body in Western culture which is marked by external forces, imagining volition in the signifiation of the body, territories such as race and gender, by which the signified body emerges, themselves recede in the face of the body as a hermeneutic object which has suddenly, in the moment of marking, created the binary of the modified and the non-modified. The modified body in this chapter will deal primarily with the body that has been volitionally tattooed or pierced, scarred and impregnated with surgically implanted non-human extensions such as coral horns and metal sub-dermal objects. It will focus on modifications as visually perceptible events and so, for the sake of space, will not address modification play such as flesh-hooking, corset training and other modifications designed for experience rather than marking. While attending to other forms of modification, I will not be dealing with such modifications as plastic surgery, as the tattooed/scarred/ pierced/coral–metal implanted body presents the body as despot because the significations of these modifications, rather than presenting a hyper-active fulfilment of the organized capital body that much plastic surgery facilitates, seem more unstable multiplicities even when they are directed toward fashion or fetishisation of transgression. Covertly the 'corrected' body which is created through surgery performed on 'deformities' could be seen as eroding already present despotic modifications and, while I absolutely resist any claim that the 'deformed' body should celebrate its alterity in the face of its everyday oppression, it is interesting that such bodies are surgically modified toward a non-deformed body, even if that disfigurement or deformity has no physiological threat of harm. The dialectic configuration of the marked and the unmarked fails to address the marking of all territorialisation performed upon and organising bodies by which subjectivity becomes viable. Analysis of the marked and modified body as a noun organises that body. I will argue that the modified body can be a means by which bodies in proximity can be made to unravel, and the encounter of any other body with the modified body as a plane of indiscernible affectivity creates, beyond a body to study, or even a Body without Organs, an event of art, body as concept, not object, a baroque body, a body where textual inscription extends the flesh rather than presents a fascist regime that empties the body and inevitably the modified body as mobilising thought. The modified body, while tactically being positioned with another body, does not differentiate two bodies, the body in relation with itself and ultimately the non-modified and the modified. While concepts involving 'looking at' or 'in relation to' modified bodies are given, modified bodies described as skin create relation as an inflection, a between and a band, so entities may be considered as less than one and more than two. The encounter, more than the bodies encountering, is privileged.

The Western modified body has been sociologically categorised as modern, primitive, fashionable, extreme (an unstable matter of degree more than essence), representative of self-expression, a mark of subcultural belonging, but problematically other, where the relation between body and observer is fiercely maintained: 'you will be organized, you will be an organism, you will articulate your body – otherwise you're just depraved' (Deleuze and Guattari 1987: 159). The invocation of the modified body which begins with the article 'the', or especially 'your' and 'their', shows the condition of possibility of the modified body as something to be spoken about or which speaks as the Other. Deleuze and Guattari see letting go of the demand for what they call The Other Person to speak (so one can subsequently speak about the other person) as creating both disarticulation and *n* articulations. This also creates an irrefutable relation without speaker and spoken about as well as polyvocal expression as experimentation. The worst thing the modified person can say is nothing. Silence insinuates guilt or ignorance. The demand for the other to speak is a demand for an appropriate answer to pre-formed categorisation. 'When they come across an object, they change it, by sleight of hand, into a relationship, language or representation . . . a little bit of naivety is better than suspicion' (Serres 2008: 41). The modified body is often taken as a spectacle but when this body unravels discursively from object within which a subject is contained and expressed to superject planes it is felt, it invokes tactility of sight, skin as textured veil not revelation, is sensorial, aural; the senses become consistency. The marking(s) encountered in silence as epistemologically not enough and sensorially too much are what Lyotard calls *dispositif* – zero that refuses the act of explanation, knowledge, law and all other expressive techniques which impose on desire 'forever deferring, representing and simulating everything in an endless postponement, we libidinal economists affirm that this zero is itself a figure . . . where of course several libidinal positions are affirmed together' (1993a: 5). Zero folds inside within outside and alters the dissipations and organisations of desire. Collapsing senses and internal/external dialectics can be created when we allow the modified body to be an activating modification. Of the scar as an active sign Deleuze says,

> a scar is a sign not of the past wound but of 'the present fact of have being wounded'; we can say that it is the contemplation of the wound . . . There is a self wherever a furtive contemplation has been established, whenever a contracting machine capable of drawing difference from repetition functions somewhere. The self does not undergo modifications, it is itself a modification. (1994: 77, 78–9)

Thinking the active synthesis of the larval self Deleuze offers with the dispositif allows the self inflected and separate from the mark as a zero simultaneous with elements of reflection as imagination, memory as creation and a zero time of experiencing the mark which does not seek history as vindication nor future as intent. The mark is external to the self in that it provides a dispositif catalysing active contemplation and also modification-self. Furtive contemplation comes as stealth and silence but never as repression or ignorance. Saying nothing of the tattoo is a mode of silence which is as voluminous as signifying explanation but so too is the equally active constitutive drained contemplation of 'I don't care about the modification, it is just there.' The modification is never its own thing from moment to moment and the modified-self emergent is a differing between-time.

The modified body need not be object, problem or even self-expressive subject but can be explored through Deleuze and Guattari's idea of the concept when referring to The Other Person. Deleuze and Guattari posit The Other Person as a concept.

> The concept of The Other Person as expression of a possible world in a perceptual field leads us to consider the components of this field for itself in a new way. No longer being either subject of the field nor object in the field, the other person will become the condition under which not only subject and object are redistributed but also figure and ground, margins and centre, moving object and reference point, transitive and substantial, length and depth. (1994: 18)

The modified body, however, should not be understood as another object which is spoken about in the context of this chapter. Without wishing to regress into standpoint politics, I am/have a heavily modified body and, through analysis. a modified body can become other to itself through the disanchoring which occurs in being told what one's body is and why it has been modified. Additionally, the creation of modified bodies as a unified category forces a homogenised relation with those with which one has nothing in common. So The Other Person can be understood as a minoritarian becoming. The creation of relations with other modified bodies need not make those bodies the same, but 'a concept also has a becoming that involves its relationship with concepts situated on the same plane' (Deleuze and Guattari 1994: 18). Modification is a plane of consistency over a collective group. Creating relations through this consistency can offer the possibility of what Deleuze and Guattari call an inter-kingdom politics, which at the same time expresses Guattari's notion of a finite existential territory. Here a connection can be made between the collectivisation of modified people as 'modern primitives' and Deleuze and Guattari's discussion of primitivism and segmentarity: 'Primitive segmentarity is characterized by a polyvocal code based on lineages and their varying situations and relations, and an itinerant territoriality based on local, overlapping divisions' (1987: 209). Primitives have no centralised State mechanisms. The modern primitive cannot be centralised by sociology, capitalist consumption, tribal fantasies or fetishised transgression, although all of these have been attempted through regimes of observation, analysis and signification. The very opening lines of the seminal tome *Modern Primitives* posit them as an enigma, and Vale and Juno cite Nietzsche's demand that through the illogical comes good (Juno and Vale 1989: 4). I resist the term, as it has associations with co-opting non-Western tribal practices and runs the risk of turning tribality into commodity. However, the term itself as contradictory creates at least two which none the less inflect within each other and offer at least a first step in the proliferation of vocalisation beyond the body which is and the body which is not modified. The mark as dispositif takes modification outside of cultural temporality or contracts time into a single space. It neither refers nor defers but is undeniably and voluminously present, encroaching upon everything and saying nothing except creating a re-fascination with a body – flesh-text as theory, what Deleuze calls self as question (1994: 77). 'What does the theoretical text offer its fascinated client? An *impregnable* body, like a thief, a liar, an imposter who can never be caught' (Lyotard 1993a: 246, original emphasis). The silent subject whose body speaks for itself only does so through an imperceptible language or one which involves attending to languages heard with more than the ears, just as the eyes feel the modified skin and the viscera encounter the skin as an aesthetic affect. The modified body is an imposter without an original it co-opts, a thief of the desire for knowledge and of the apprehension of signification and a liar through speaking neither truth nor lie, nor indeed anything at all. Both body and encountering body know nothing of their own or the other body except that something happens when the relation inflects both into one libidinal band.

Modified bodies diverge through the other elements of their minoritarianism so they create an activism of bodies with one shared disorganising principle that neither takes away from nor ignores other principles of alterity. Similarly but beyond the scope of this chapter, modification can be shared between those who have chosen to be modified (although the notion of volition here is problematic) and those who are considered abnormal versions of the majoritarian body – bodies which are variously

'diffabled' and 'deformed'. A politics of minoritarian flesh beyond signifiation occurs as these bodies experience irrefutable daily difficulties as a
result of their bodies, just as being tattooed and pierced hurts (whether
for pleasure or as by-product) and are also useful: for example, in the
use of piercings or temporary modifications for sado-masochistic play.
This does not necessitate a binarisation of the real flesh from the signified body but it does make one put one's flesh on the line in minoritarian
becomings, evinced when the tattooed and pierced body is continually
asked in a troubled way by the non-modified 'did it hurt?' – or more
strangely long after the act, 'does it hurt?' or 'is it permanent?' These
questions show the material elements of the body which becomes traitor
to the self. As Scarry so beautifully articulates, the body in pain registers as one's body split into the body as subject and the self acted upon,
one's body hurting oneself (I am not hurt, my body hurts me). Scarry
points out that pain is inexpressible and unmakes the world (1985). Pain
occurs simultaneously with any imagined volition in creating a body
as what Roy Boyne has called the 'citational self' (1999: 209). While
Scarry's exploration of pain during torture involves a very different
ethics, both her and modification's incarnations of pain dematerialise
regimes of signifiation, particularly of the inside and outside and self
and flesh, but also attest to the inexpressibility of pain which catalyses
these dematerialisations. The material elements of being modified as
act, encounter and body emphasise being marked as being touched, the
body unravelling as skin while multiplying itself as single plane through
subcutaneously filling the entire volume of the body with pain, pleasure:
inevitably intensities beyond description.

Drawing/Writing

'Paintings, tattoos or marks on the skin embrace the multi-dimensional-
ity of bodies' (Deleuze and Guattari 1987: 176). Deleuze and Guattari
define the primitive shamanistic body and voice, in opposition to the
Christ-head or facialised body, as operating through two paradigms
resistant to the signified Western Christ-body. The first collapses ani-
mality, corporeality and vegetality. The second is their organisation of
fragile and precarious powers (1987: 176). Becomings begin as inter-
kingdom, toward becoming-imperceptible, through zones of relation
without imitation or hierarchical filiation and equivalence. Some very
obvious examples in cultural manifestations of certain modifications
can be applied to the first part of this idea. The marking of the body
with animal patterns is a relatively common form of tattooing – lizards,

zebras and cats, in particular. The zebra stripes create trajectories which, without orientation from starting point to finishing point, envelop and allow a body in zebra intensities to emerge. These stripes exhibit a becoming-zebra. The power of the zebra as being striped is the most dazzling of zebra intensities, and the movement of perception the stripes create, as the eyes follow lines leading to nowhere except other lines, demands a body that moves or must be moved around to see them and a body that, like a zebra, stands disinterested until, when aware of being perceived, flees in self-preserving terror. The observer could then be said to be becoming-lion if expressing predatory signification, or creating a shared zebra threshold, not because the observer has their own stripes but, like optical illusion which hypnotises the eyes with the confusion of striped lines, all bodies residually can be perceived through trajectories which move the eyes around the body without alighting on punctuating signifying organs. The zebra-tattooed body has no genitals, face or gender, just stripes. The cat, usually big cat, body performs cat-intensity functions. The tiger's stripes are similar to zebra functions, although awareness of perception is met not by fleeing but with a roar, and orange saturates in a different way to black and 'unmarked'. (Zebra bodies are rarely tattooed with white, as white is a notoriously difficult ink in terms of both showing up on skin and maintaining its colour.) Leopard intensities share their kingdom with spots that dazzle the eyes after looking at the sun. Leopard spots are not circles, but spirals which do not connect, multi-coloured and of varying sizes. Domestic cats offer many varieties of pattern expression, but lines, blocks of colours and the creation of a muzzle area constitute these re-orientations of perception not only through pattern but also through texture from smooth skin to fur. Often cat people receive sub-dermal metal receptacles into which whiskers are screwed. Similar proliferation of modifications can be seen in the bifurcated tongue of Eric Sprague, the Lizard Man. Contact lenses and other modifications make the becoming-cat more than just a 'tattooed body', the tattooing being one dimension of selected modification. It is almost fortunate that these becoming-cat people (I think here specifically of Dennis Avner, The Stalking Cat) never look even vaguely like a cat. Resemblance gives way to hybridity and both cat and human terms are lost, neither half and half (no convincing cat part and no longer majoritarian human) nor exchanged. The modifications in these examples include, together with their inter-kingdom becomings, the expression of alternate powers, precarious because the becomings never become and the questions posed fail to give an answer; perception of these bodies itself is inter-kingdom. This can be taken further when considering tattoos which are abstract blocks, shapes and lines that cover the body but have no resonance with other recognisable kingdoms (seen in such tattooed bodies as The Great Omi and The Enigma). The more extreme of these modifications are tattooed on the face, most often not with the face of the animal but of the pattern itself, because primitives 'have no face and need none' (Deleuze and Guattari 1987: 176). The encroachment of tattoos on to the face moves the body from a coupled machine to a complex machine. The face seems the final frontier of tattooing. There are problems with these examples, however. They do have a residual immobilisation of the becoming-element which orients the becoming as a finality – there may be no moving on from the zebra or cat. But the most difficult problem comes from exemplifying. My mentioning certain tattooed individuals suggests, by having an example, that imagining the becoming is vindicated and possibly authorised by either the tattooed body or my application of this body to becoming. One reason why the invocation of these bodies is important, however, is that the permanence of these markings and their coverage will affect the daily real lives of people. Without wishing to bifurcate the real from the theoretical, I contend that the everyday resistance to or even fetishistic celebration of heavily tattooed bodies (and this is not limited to becomings-animal but all heavy modification) is an irrefutable phenomenon. Bodies tattooed with symbols, pictures, designs and other images which do not orient toward an inter-kingdom element are equally met with a demand for vindication, be it a demand for speech or insipid prejudice. So the necessary evil of speaking of exemplary bodies is outweighed by what heavily modified bodies must encounter everyday as minoritarians.

> Let us now draw or paint. Isolate if you can, the chance encounters of corners or folds, the small secret zones in which the soul, to all extent and purposes, still resides . . .. observe on the surface of the skin, the changing, shimmering, fleeting soul, the blazing, striated, tinted, streaked, striped, many coloured, mottled, cloudy, star-studded, bedizened, variegated, torrential swirling soul . . .. Tattooing, my white, constantly present soul blazes up and is diffused. (Serres 2008: 23)

Serres claims consciousness comes when the body is tangential to itself. Modification thought as affective power allows the modification for and in itself to unravel. Demarcation between skin and modification is one form of perception through signifying punctuation – there *it* is. But when understood as a plane of composition, the modification becomes a plane of immanence which is one point of perception of the plane of consistency of the modified body; the modification distributes the body differently and no longer demarcates itself from the skin. Serres uses qualities over forms. The qualities are all adamantly unstable and unlimited. Modifications can be taken as nouns – the tattoo, the piercing, the branding, the implant – annexed to or added on to the body. Serres's words reference the adjectival qualities of drawing and painting that dissipate and disappear. When we encounter a more traditional tattoo, such as a symbol or picture, the skin cannot be denied as part of the image, just as the canvas and the paint form the painting. Their materiality includes its own adjectival states. The tattoo may represent something, for the perceiver, for the tattooed person, annexed to external referents. This is not why the tattoo is art and why it always exceeds all who encounter it as such. Deleuze and Guattari state of two forms of oil painting, 'The distinction clearly does not come down to "representational or not", since no art and no sensation have ever been representational. In the first case sensation is realized in the material and does not exist outside its realization' (1994: 193). Neither skin nor tattoo, implant nor implanted site represents. They are all-too-visceral encounters, examples of putting one's flesh where one's mouth is, so to speak. The modification as question performs affective adjectival and sensorial functions when not in need of an answer, but additionally is always beyond itself in relation to another. The soul defined by Serres is inherently a touch, which means that perception and relation are essential in any event of art, including the self when, as asemiotic desiring-desired consistency, it emerges as its own art event.

In Kafka's *In The Penal Colony* the apparatus writes an ultimately fatal tattoo upon and in the criminal. But the apparatus is itself the tattoo upon the flesh of its creator. The creation of a new body is the criminal cured and killed through the moment he knows himself, as his crime is formed by his tattoo. The apparatus creates that body. The creator created the apparatus as a writing of his own body through his creation, defining himself through his tattoo(ing) as apparatus of self. But, like a tattoo, the corporeal reorganising machine is part of, an expression by, but ultimately exceeds, its wearer. The apparatus consumes its maker, its signifying function, like any tattoo; it misbehaves, becoming at turns pointless and fatal, and the maker accepts that it is a permanent marker of what he has chosen to wear as a badge of who he is. The problem is that the machine – The Harrow – performs a repetitive function, the aim of which is to reiterate, collapsing flesh, self and word, as one sentence resistant to interpretation, imagination, dissipation. Serres's description of affective qualities and potentials of the tattooed body teem with vitalistic and effulgent intensities; a relation of fascination, wonder and joy is created and we chase the intensities, never apprehending but irrefutably occupied by them. The harrow performs precisely that – it harrows, demanding comprehension but, like all signification, there is no moment of clarification. Signification harrows. Specificity, quality and relation are unified without deviation. The machine performs a fascist operation; the machine which signifies is all there is. Modification, depending on perception, risks colonising and slaughtering the body through a sociological or psychological mechanisation of the modified self – the discursive machine precedes and resists the art-event of the modified body but the body is no less corporeal and the event of self no less material. Deleuze and Guattari state of Kafka's story:

> it is less a question of presenting this image of a transcendental and unknowable law than of *dissecting the mechanism* of an entirely different sort of machine, which needs this image of law only to align its gears and make them function together with a 'perfect synchronicity'. (1986: 43)

Synchronising modification, psychology, sociology and techniques of self as limited to regimes of signification dissects the body, performing exsanguinated by discourse. But, like the criminal's harrowed body, the modified body bleeds. Corporeality as art is what Lyotard, in his discussion of *The Penal Colony*, calls *sanguis*, which 'nourishes the flesh. It gives its hue of blueness, its pinkness ... the infinite juxtaposition of nuances that drive the painter and philosopher crazy' (1993b: 180). This craziness is love.

Love and Modification

> We thus come back to a conclusion to which art led us: The struggle with chaos is only the instrument of a more profound struggle against opinion, for the misfortune of people comes from opinion.
>
> (Deleuze and Guattari 1994: 206)

Modification manifests new folds of flesh by proliferating encounters with skin. These encounters are localised at points of modifications as events, to the body in which they reside, to other bodies and through consistencies of time as qualities of intensity and speed. Modification precedes and exceeds perceivers and comes first as sensation, encouraging all flesh to come forth as art when it catalyses a refolding of the body as experienced differently. Deleuze and Guattari note that biunivocalisation expresses the body as a single substance through selection from and coalescence of limited binaries or, more correctly, isomorphic terms – male/not male, white/not white and modified/not modified.

Modifications can certainly be gendered and racialised. Stereotypically, there are 'feminine' tattoo images and bodily sites for modification. (Interestingly, the genitals are usually not a site for either gender.) While gendering tattoos usually deals with form and place, racial considerations of modification on Western bodies are affected more through intensity and saturation – the contrasts between skin and modification depending on hues of skin, keloiding of scar and modification. But the first binary is the modified/non-modified and these further considerations follow. A single body contemplates its own modified folds, and those areas not modified are not the background or empty space but, by virtue of not being modified, become voluminous qualities of their own. 'With cosmetics, our real skin, the skin we experience, becomes visible . . . we never live naked in the final analysis, nor ever really clothed' (Serres 2008: 34, 38). Like cosmetics, modifications always involve imagining their own absence just as empty skin involves the presence of modification. Both form and relations of these are perceived through potential modulation, so Serres speaks not of 'with' and 'without' but each plane attenuating and modulating its powers. The whole body emerges as teeming with art, unmodified skin's proximity to modification and vice versa, the bleeding of the outlines of tattoos that occurs over time which makes this differentiation difficult, and also the skin as potential site and thus teeming with possibility but also its own qualities of organising the chaos into a canvas which has no bare space.

The body is a series of sites, unmodified, modified or perhaps the struggles between the two as folds of each other. Receding from the demand for speech, explanation or at worst vindication through the opinions of modification in the West, all planes of the flesh shine with their own qualities of colour, texture, movement, porousness. Body 'art' makes the entire body art because all folds demand attention. The need for an artist in modification should also not be forgotten. Art attends to creating art from chaos but the result is the opposite of the mapping of this chaos by determined co-ordinates – Deleuze and Guattari rethink science, philosophy and art as always including 'an *I do not know* that is positive and creative, the condition of creation itself and that consists in determining *by* what one does not know' (1994: 128). Modification emphasises all bodies as aesthetic events which can experience and are experienced through zones or folds of proximity.

Modified bodies can emerge as both art and philosophy. Philosophy's object is, according to Deleuze and Guattari, constituted not because of what it is known or true, but 'Interesting, Remarkable or Important' (1994: 82). The very question 'why', asked of the modified or the modification (usually involving the modified having to re-ask themselves at every question, contemplating these zones and not simply contemplating or asking but attending at all), makes the modification attend to its pre-modified state (bare skin, without holes), which is always also a demand for absence. Certain interesting conundrums occur. What is the affective relation between a modification and the eyes of the body when it is imperceptible without a mirror, such as one on the back or face? What of modifications which are forgotten, because one's modifications often surprise when they are perceived anew, as a smudge or 'what's that?' mark, or as a re-experience when another witness attends to them? The eyes, as the modification, unfold and re-fold the sensorial encounter. The modification can be very uninteresting to the modified subject, and the perception can come from folding with the perception of the observer where the modification itself catalyses the fold but is not part of its new constitution. 'The' modification contemplated can be 'modification' as verb and that it is interesting and remarkable is why modifying practices are important. Stereotypes of the modified –crusty activist punks, radical transgressives, sexual outsiders, various subcultures and especially we who just like them – inevitably create, as Lingis would call it, the community of those who have nothing in common. These bodies are verified through being made minoritarian collectives. Collections of tattoos and piercings, branding and implants coalesce independent of bodies and form their own activism. Modification creates its own philosophy as its own art. The modified subject emerges as Deleuze and Guattari's conceptual persona. Activism and political mobilisation are created through the sharing of a singular intensity by many who may have nothing else in common. Politics is what Deleuze and Guattari would call an inter-kingdom becoming. While collectivism as a discourse which imposes power limits the body to being only modified, the modification as dispositif flees the subject to collect as a politic. This is necessary as the collective demands renegotiating the body art/philosophy of modification because activism is needed most crucially where 'real-life' bodies are at risk of misfortune through opinion. Returning to Deleuze and Guattari's definition of art, modification, unlike race or gender, may be conceived as coming from will and experienced as opinion through taste. But however unfashionable or paranoid the claim may seem, tattooed bodies still experience malignant treatment and oppression in most social contexts, spanning oppression coming from the act of address demanding accountability to violence. Perception of modifications can create a relation of what Deleuze and Guattari (after Blanchot) would call friendship and Lyotard and Serres love. 'The philosopher is the concept's friend: he [*sic*] is the potentiality of the concept' (Deleuze and Guattari 1994: 5). Modifications offer nothing *a priori* and in order to be philosophers we must create each modification as its own concept based on its importance. In this way mobilising discourse, including the modified body as both philosopher and conceptual persona, in relation with the many folds of self and with each, potentialises a new creative relation. The permanence of the mark for which it is maligned and celebrated is an event of thought which is made permanent depending on our relation with it. It is permanent and not permanent, not as a matter of presence or absence but art event and encounter. To be friend to modification involves being friend to self (as the modified body is always taken as specificity), neither lacking nor reducible to its perceived intent, but a kind of remembered present which is also renewed as dissemblance. This act of friendship is to be friend to subjectivity as concept. Experimenting the subject constitutes the third and most crucial of Guattari's three ecologies, the others being social relations and environment (2000: 28). The subject here is both self and the subject as the abstract notion or element of address, both philosophical and political. The modified self as conceptual persona is involved in an activism in which we may not wish to participate, but conceived as a particular kind of necessary encounter. The self contemplates the modified self, the observer contemplates the modification, and the self contemplates self as observed self while contemplating the observer. These foldings and refoldings can seduce away from knowledge to thought and subjectivity to activist and aesthetic modification. The third element, the self as other person in relation to another person and who is encountered as modified by that person, dissipates the modifications in flesh, of self, into a social relation and the plane of skin and activism become the environment – of art and of concept, of friendship and love. Guattari maligns signification as a social(ogical) terror massacring the body (1996: 29). The desire for asemiotic perception of and as bodies and revolutionary consciousness means 'we want to open our bodies to the bodies of other people, to other people in general. We want to let vibrations pass among us, let energies circulate, allow desires to merge, so that we can all give free reign, to our fantasies, our ecstasies' (1996: 34). Guattari sees the bodies lived in reality as material of desire because of their materiality, because they can bleed, rupture, suffer and die and because signification can hurt while it oppresses. He does not see aestheticised bodies as more or less revolutionary than women's bodies but part of similar tactics.

When feminism and modification coalesce, a further micro-interkingdom politics occurs (MacCormack 2006: 64–5). The body as a site of play means that modifications are always fantasies. Even modifications which are most adamantly spoken of as symbols of self exceed the self, and thus hurl the self into a kind of sacrifice to the modifications' excesses. Through this vitalistic sacrifice the self disappears at the moment it becomes friend to modifications as concepts. Signification perpetuates what Serres calls the order of death, whereas opening to thought as potentiality comes from the order of love: 'the ecstasy of existence is a summation made possible by the contingency of the other . . . in fact it is an art of love' (2008: 29). Modification may be silent but it is most frequently adamantly present when a tattoo is visible, when an implant or piercing grows and stretches, and even if removed leaves a hole as its own form of modification. Tattoos may be described as beautiful, ugly, palatable, vulgar, odd, abstract, symbolic – all of these and everything else because they add and multiply affective qualities, speech, relation, desire. Modifications are phenomena that are too recent to be inserted comfortably into corporeal indices. As modern aesthetic, decorative and visceral, modifications, through their escapes from other reified epistemologies which constitute the body, offer becomings to come. They engage, because they are real things on real bodies which remind us of the body as materially constituted by signification but also desire, and activism, revolution and liberty, a negotiation of both as same, yet too often the flesh is forgotten or purely abstracted. Our fascination with modifications invokes them as 'loved with the most demanding impatience' (Lyotard 1993a: 52) for something we know will never arrive and this itself is an element of the love modifications elicit.

References

Boyne, R. (1999), 'Citation and Subjectivity: Toward a Return of the Embodied Will', *Body and Society* 5: 2–3, pp. 209–25.

Deleuze, G. (1993), *The Fold: Leibniz and the Baroque*, trans. T. Conley, Minnesota: University of Minneapolis Press.

Deleuze, G. (1994), *Difference and Repetition*, trans. P. Patton, New York: Columbia University Press.

Deleuze, G. and F. Guattari (1986), *Kafka: Toward a Minor Literature*, trans. D. Polan, Minneapolis: University of Minnesota Press.

Deleuze, G. and F. Guattari (1987), *A Thousand Plateaus: Capitalism and Schizophrenia*, trans. B. Massumi, Minnesota: University of Minnesota Press.

Deleuze, G. and F. Guattari (1994), *What is Philosophy?*, trans. H. Tomlinson and G. Burchell, New York: Columbia University Press.

Guattari, F. (1996), *Soft Subversions*, trans. D. Sweet and C. Weiner, New York: Semiotext(e).

Guattari, F. (2000), *The Three Ecologies*, trans I. Pindar and P. Sutton, London: Continuum.

Juno, A. and V. Vale (1989), *Modern Primitives: An Investigation of Contemporary Adornment and Ritual*, San Francisco: Re/search.

Kafka, F. (2003), *The Metamorphosis and Other Stories*, trans. D. Freed, New York: Barnes & Noble.

Lingis, A. (1994), *The Community of Those Who Have Nothing in Common*, Indianapolis: Indiana University Press.

Lyotard, J.-F. (1993a), *Libidinal Economy*, trans. I. Hamilton-Grant, Indianapolis: Indiana University Press.

Lyotard, J.-F. (1993b), 'Prescription', *Toward the Postmodern*, ed. R. Harvey and M. S. Roberts, London: Humanities.

MacCormack, P. (2006), 'The Great Ephemeral Tattooed Skin', *Body and Society* 12:2, pp. 57–82.

Scarry, E. (1985), *The Body in Pain*, Oxford: Oxford University Press.

Serres, M. (2008), *The Five Senses: A Philosophy of Mingled Bodies*, trans. M. Sankey and P. Crowley, London: Athlone.

Chapter 10

Dance and the Passing Moment: Deleuze's Nietzsche

Philipa Rothfield

Nietzsche's Image of Thought

According to Deleuze, the image of thought in Nietzsche does not bear upon truth or falsity but draws instead upon the nuances of evaluation and interpretation. Deleuze depicts Nietzschean thought as that which produces movement, bursts of activity, rather than something that simply and inertly pictures or represents the world. The figure of activity persists in Nietzsche's work and in Deleuze's reading of it. Inasmuch as a text activates, inasmuch as a cluster of concepts can indeed provoke movement, Deleuze's Nietzsche aims to provoke a better kind of life. This Nietzsche discerns life, through evaluating and selecting certain kinds of activity over others. It asserts a form of life whose commitment is to all that which is affirmative.

The affirmative type is not us. We are not affirmative types. This is nothing personal. It is just that the positive value of Nietzsche's thought locates itself apart from the structures of the self. Deleuze makes it clear that, from a critical point of view, the self is a sick, pathological structure which has no ongoing future. Somewhat paradoxically, what does endure is difference, or more precisely, the activity of differentiation. This is becoming, and its endurance is what Deleuze dubs the being of becoming, whose perpetual form is the eternal return.

For Deleuze, Nietzsche's thought is organised around two central themes, force and power – or rather, forces and their relations, power and its productions. Nietzsche's genius, according to Deleuze, lies in transforming our understanding of power, away from the one who wills, *qua* person or individual, and towards 'an event, that is, to the forces in their various relationships in a proposition or phenomenon, and to the genetic relationship which determines these forces (power)' (Deleuze 1983: xi).

Not the self but an event. Not the doer, rather the deed. Is there any room here for a notion of the body? To speak of 'the body' would seem to suggest some sort of identity, a thing perhaps or some combination of body and mind, sentience and sensibility. However conceived, and its conceptualisation can take many forms, the body as a concept nevertheless implies the existence of an ongoing identity. And indeed, our experience suggests likewise.

While Deleuze attributes a conception of the body to Nietzsche's work, it is a form of corporeality which defies any predication of embodied subjectivity as we might know it. The body in Deleuze's Nietzschean text – *Nietzsche and Philosophy* – continually reaches out towards that which is not yet, towards the different. Bataille posed difference in relation to subjectivity:

> *In risk*, I now perceive a movement that, rather than relating the individual's present to his or her future, connects it to *a person who doesn't yet exist*. In this sense risk doesn't assign action to the serving of an agent but serves a still inexistent person. And in this regard it exceeds 'being's limits'. (Bataille 1992: 143)

In Bataille's world, the movement beyond the identity of the individual in the present begs to differ. It achieves its summit by transgressing the bounds of identity, by 'lacerating' the self.

Deleuze's Nietzsche is more sanguine, though no less demanding. While Bataille risks the self through excess, Deleuze rejects the value of subjectivity altogether, by distinguishing between consciousness and the body:

> To remind consciousness of its necessary modesty is to take it for what it is: a symptom; nothing but the symptom of a deeper transformation and of the activities of entirely non-spiritual forces. (1983: 39)

For Deleuze, the subject functions in a particular fashion, constantly reverting to type. By contrast, the body differs. It is part and parcel of that which produces difference. This wilful, corporeal concept drives towards differentiation, encompassing, producing, indeed provoking change. Like Bataille's risked self, the body becomes other than itself. This is its type.

If we were to take up Deleuze's suggestion that thought for Nietzsche is less about truth and falsity and more about the provocation of movement, what to say about this body-thought which – 'projectile-like' – is already *in* movement?[1] For Deleuze, the body in Nietzsche is no more than a momentary distillation of related forces. It exists in the passing moment, while reaching towards a future which is not itself. Although the passing moment is never still, it nevertheless embodies a power and potential for change. This is its corporeal form.

Movement Selection

It is thanks to Nietzsche, Deleuze writes, that 'philosophy has a new relationship to the arts of movement; theatre, dance and music' (1983: xiii). Nietzsche's philosophy gives creative life to thought itself; 'to think is to create' (1983: xiv). Whether thought's creations have, so to say, artistic merit, is a question of evaluation. Deleuze, like Nietzsche, was very particular on this matter of evaluation. High and low, noble and base, these are the unambiguous terms that Nietzsche chose to distinguish between the productions of human culture. They convey an approach towards philosophy which is critical of the ways in which particular ideas and values have come about. This is an approach which takes sides rather than accepts thought as given.

Deleuze distilled Nietzsche's philosophy, away from an apparent series of 'capricious aphorisms and pathological fragments', and towards a systematic interpretation which makes much of the distinction between active and reactive force (1983: ix). Although 'we' are constitution- ally drawn to the perspective of that which reacts, Deleuze harnesses Nietzsche's admiration for the activities which shape life. Deleuze dwells on affirmation, becoming active and the ongoing reproduction of diver- sity, posed in relation to the eternal return, a figure as far away from the human as we could imagine. The body takes on a new significance in this context. It forms and reforms as often as forces meet, passing through a series of transformations in a roiling sea of chance. If there is little to recognise from the point of view of lived subjectivity, this is not the fault of the body, for *all* activity in the Nietzschean sense necessarily escapes consciousness (1983: 41).

One of the features of Deleuze's reading of Nietzsche is a clear dis- tinction between (reactive) consciousness and unconscious agency. This bears upon our understanding of the body in Nietzsche. It puts subjectivity in its place whilst elevating the body, crediting it as the source of ontological elaboration (movement to come). As Deleuze notes, however, this body is not a 'site' as such. It is neither a corporeal substance nor a sentient identity. To that extent, it is not the body as we know it.

I am interested in the movement arts, in dance and in dancing. Although one might speak of dance in general terms, at the level of culture writ large, there is a sense in which culture is always expressed as a specific mode of existence, as a form of particularity (cultural specificity). We could construe this in the following manner:

> Culture, according to Nietzsche, is essentially training and selection . . . It expresses the violence of the forces which seize upon thought in order to make it something affirmative and active. – We will only understand the concept of culture if we grasp all the ways in which it is opposed to method. Method always presupposes the good will of the thinker, a 'premeditated decision'. Culture, on the contrary, is a violence undergone by thought, a process of the formation of thought through the action of selective forces, a training which brings the whole unconscious of the thinker into play. (Deleuze 1983: 108)

Every culture implies a history (or genealogy) of constraint: that is, the selection of certain relations of force which are expressed via the vicissitudes of (cultural) training. Deleuze calls this the 'force of thinking'. It represents a mode, a history of thought shaped through each culture's style of 'selective violence' (1983: 109). Although these forces are by their very nature unconscious, they nevertheless take hold of thought and shape it. Viewed in this way, culture is an activity that produces certain fields of thought, which Deleuze has elsewhere called 'the working thought' (1983: 23). Art is the creation of thought in the field of culture. Culture creates. The artist is one product of that creation: 'The species activity of culture has a final aim: to form the artist, the philosopher. All its selective violence serves this end' (1983: 109).[2]

Dance also selects. It espouses aesthetic and kinaesthetic values.[3] Dance is embedded within social and cultural milieus, according to which bodily practices are thought and bodies think. These practices form the unconscious of the thinker; they shape the working thoughts of the dancer. They are what Bourdieu gestured towards with his concept of the *habitus* (Bourdieu 1990). In Nietzsche's thought, this is signified through the notion of training and selection. Dance is a form of culture in this Nietzschean sense. It is shaped and it shapes. The dancer is an end-product of this selective process, trained in specific ways via the unconscious activities that delineate the particular field and style of dancing. These fields are in turn situated within the lived, cultural everyday that informs the working thoughts at play within each kind of movement art. There are large differences between the ways in which the cultures of dance are lived and produced. These are social, cultural and spiritual, physical and affective, as well as kinaesthetic. Because dance is itself a mode of selection, any discussion of its working thoughts will be informed by its history and path of selective violence.

Thinking Through the Body

In what follows, Deleuze's work on Nietzsche will be discussed with a particular focus on his account of the body, its constituent forces, the will to power and sensation. Deleuze's notion of the body in Nietzsche's thought will be oriented towards the activity of dancing, thought as distinct histories of thought, each of which selects, trains and produces according to its own kinaesthetic and other forms of value.[4] I understand dance as a form of life which espouses its own values and according to which we might in turn evaluate this philosophical account of the body. There is a difference between giving an account of dance according to a Nietzschean conceptual framework and the practical evaluations implicit in dancing itself. This difference concerns the power of interpretation. For Alphonso Lingis:

> What interprets is not a contemplative spirit both impotent to act on things and omnipotent to charge them with its meanings; what interprets is power, is Will to Power, and there can be no such thing as absolute power, solitary power. And if it takes power to interpret, to give sense to, to orient, it is because the being interpreted is itself a force, affirming itself, generating divergent perspectives. (1985: 44)

To what extent does the imposition of a philosophical framework upon a field of practice divert that field's own wilful, working thoughts? To what extent can a form of culture insist upon its own evaluations, its own selections?

Deleuze writes that thought can create in two ways. On the one hand, it inspires 'practical evaluations which evoke a whole atmosphere, all kinds of emotional disposition in the reader. Like Spinoza, Nietzsche always maintained that there is the deepest relationship between concept and affect' (1983: xii). This is thought's 'projectile-like' action (xiii). The philosophical thought gives a perspective on life.[5] It depicts life, proposing a certain kind of value for it. The proposition reaches out towards and espouses life. But, on the other hand, thought can also organise life. It selects, constrains and produces. The shape of thought rendered through culture is itself a form of life, a mode of existence temporally realised through specific patterns of training and selection. In writing about dance, these two modes of thinking come together.

Interpreting Nietzsche

According to Deleuze, Nietzsche realised 'the hour had come' for the body to be reevaluated (1983: 39). Nietzsche writes: 'What dawns on philosophers last of all: they must no longer accept concepts as a gift, nor merely purify and polish them, but first *make* and *create* them, present them and make them convincing' (1967: 220, §409). A new concept of the body thus arises, that of a momentary body, the product of chance, a meeting of forces. The body in Nietzsche's thought consists of forces in relation: 'dynamic quanta, in a relation of tension to all other dynamic quanta' (1967: 339, §635). This pertains to and describes any kind of body, whether political, social, physical or human (Deleuze 1983: 40). However brief its tenure – and bodies last only as long as their constituent forces remain in relation – we need to be clear that the body is not a place where things happen.[6] It is rather the happening of things, an event or action whose constituent elements combine in terms of 'a power relationship between two or more forces' (Nietzsche 1967: 336, §631).

The relation between forces which comprise each and every body is characterised by struggle. Each body represents the momentary crystallisation of forces whose mutual tension unfolds according to relations of dominance: 'In a body the superior or dominant forces are known as *active* and the inferior or dominated forces are known as *reactive*. Active and reactive are precisely the original qualities which express the relation of force with force' (Deleuze 1983: 40; original emphasis). The relationship between superior and inferior forces represents a form of hierarchy between forces articulated through relations of domination. Dominance does not destroy or absorb the difference between forces. To obey a superior force means to function in relation to that which dominates. Thus, reactive forces remain distinct, while posed in relation to superior forms of activity. Reactive forces adapt (with respect to) rather than disappear or merge. While forces could be said to have quantity – 'dynamic quanta' – their quantity emerges as a matter of difference between them. Both quantity and quality thus arise within and according to relations of difference. According to Nietzsche: 'It is a question of a struggle between two elements of unequal power: a new arrangement of forces is achieved according to the measure of power of each of them' (1967: 337, §633).

Deleuze makes much of the fact of difference between forces, of difference in the origin of things rather than an initial identity which yields subsequent identities. Difference signifies struggle between possibilities, between differing perspectives that remain so even as one force dominates another, as one possibility takes hold. While the relational aspect of struggle thought in quantitative terms indicates relations of domination and subjugation, qualitative difference between forces indicates a distinction between the *manner* in which forces relate to each other. Each differential relationship of force embodies a diversity of perspectives upon the one event. Qualitative difference between forces is an important factor in the Nietzschean universe: 'The art of measuring forces raises the whole question of interpreting and evaluating qualities' (Deleuze 1983: 43). It is a question all philosophers must address.

Quality and quantity arise together in the differential relationships found between forces. While that difference never disappears, it is possible to look at it as nevertheless comprising a mutual relationship, a singular moment of an ongoing movement. The rejection of primary identity in favour of relational difference produces a distinctive and unusual conception of the body. Deleuze writes:

> There are nothing but quantities of force in mutual 'relations of tension' (VP II 373/WP365). Every force is related to others and it either obeys or commands. What defines a body is this relation between dominant and dominated forces. Every relationship of forces constitutes a body – whether it is chemical, biological, social or political. Any two forces, being unequal, constitute a body as soon as they enter into a relationship. (1983: 40)

The body is thus conceived as a series of evolving, differentiated states which are themselves constituted by a plurality of distinct, though related, forces. Although chance underlies their meeting, there is nevertheless a principle that represents the generation of these successive corporeal states: that is to say, the vicissitudes of their meeting by which new bodies emerge. It is not a principle in the sense of an overarching or underlying law; rather it is something which manifests in the particularity of each successive corporeal formation. Nietzsche calls this principle the will to power. Deleuze argues that it is something that needs to be incorporated into our understanding of force.

The will to power concerns two interrelated matters: the momentary relationship of difference between forces and the emergent product of that relationship, the body. Deleuze writes of these matters as a question of synthesis on the one hand, and genesis on the other (1983: 52). The will to power is synthetic. It offers a (double) perspective on relations of force:

> Forces in relation reflect a simultaneous double genesis: the reciprocal genesis of their difference in quantity and the absolute genesis of their respective qualities. The will to power is thus added to force, but as the

210 Deleuze and the Body

differential and genetic element, as the internal element of its production. (1983: 51)

The will to power inheres in this antagonistic encounter between forces. It is a principle of connection (synthesis) between forces which concerns but does not erase difference. Indeed, it is via this difference of force that the will to power is able to pursue its genetic role (1983: 53). The will to power is the principle which concerns the ways in which forces meet and impact upon one another, thereby creating further relations of force. It is that which actively generates the ensuing product of their meeting – the 'genealogical element' in the production of bodies (1983: 52).

By construing the will to power as a generative potency, Nietzsche was able to account for the way in which the world unfolds. The will to power represents the impetus behind emerging events (bodies). The will to power is contingent inasmuch as forces meet by chance, but it is also determining with respect to that chance moment. It represents the creative moment elaborated in the concrete instance. It is

an essentially *plastic* principle that is no wider than what it conditions, that changes itself with the conditioned and determines itself in each case along with what it determines. The will to power is, indeed, never separable from particular determined forces, from their quantities, qualities and directions. It is never superior to the ways that it determines a relation between forces, it is always plastic and changing. (1983: 50)

Because the will to power is only what it is in the particular and in the multiplicity of particulars, Deleuze claims that it 'reconciles' empiricism. This is an empiricism which is elaborated via the dynamic instance. Indeed, the will to power lies at the heart of the dynamic instance, for it is internal to each and every body. It functions as 'the internal element of its production' (51). It is creative and productive, part and parcel of the relations between forces inherent in all bodies but also representative of 'that which wills'. It is the genealogical principle of emergent corporeality and therefore becoming. It is both determining but also determined by the forces which it both synthesises and shapes. Hence the choice of the term, will (determining), but also the suggestion of plasticity (determined in the particular) – 'fluent' as well as 'seminal' (53).

This notion of fluidity or plasticity is important. The will to power is not an individual expression of abstract potential whose form is given prior to its specific elaboration. It is, rather, engaged, situated and activated. Lingis signals the responsive dimension of the will to power by dispersing life itself in a field of forces (1985: 51). He writes:

But for Nietzsche the force, the power of the will, does not come out of the sovereignty of an ego, the sovereignty of self-consciousness; rather, it comes out of the fact that the Will to Power is fundamentally receptive and *continually draws force from the universe*, from the dispersed, the distance, the different, and the beyond. It owes its force not to the sovereignty of the self-conscious ego-formation, but to its *essentially receptive, affective nature*. (1985: 50–1; emphases mine)

As the will to power drives, it also draws upon – 'its sensitivity yields its activity, its power and its will to power, and its will to power makes it sensitive' (1985: 51). The will to power's sensitivity does not derive from lived subjectivity. It is not a perceptual, experiential capacity belonging to the human subject. It is a form of sensitivity found in the dynamism of the concrete, a sensitivity that makes possible the generation of new forms, new bodies, through syntheses of force. Deleuze writes of this matter in terms of the will to power's 'capacity for being affected', a capacity manifested in each passing moment (1983: 62). The ability to be affected concerns the extent to which forces are able to engage. It arises through relations between forces, for it is the relation itself that exhibits sensitivity.

The capacity to be affected is not an inert faculty. The will to power's sensitivity – which resides in particular bodies/relations of force – goes hand in hand with the ability to produce or generate. Deleuze adapts sensation away from subjectivity and locates it in a 'history or process of sensible becoming' (1983: 63). Sensibility is thus allied with the emergence of sensation. The association between sensation and sensibility means that sensation is found in the body – it is sensibility as it arises in the course of becoming. Deleuze puts it thus:

> Given two forces, one superior and the other inferior, we can see how each one's capacity for being affected is fulfilled necessarily. But this capacity for being affected is not fulfilled unless the corresponding force enters into a history or a process of sensible becoming. (1983: 63)

Sensation and sensibility thereby belong to the world. They arise in the passing moment and inhere in the myriad becomings of the body. Sensation in the body does not belong to the subject. Sensation or feeling belongs rather to a sensibility of forces that is expressed in the genesis and emergence of their relations with one another. Feeling (for power), affect and sensation are thus discerned in the body, in each body, but also in the context of other, emerging bodies, in the 'becoming of forces' (1983: 63). The sensitivity of the will to power can also be construed as a measure of corporeal power. Deleuze refers to Spinoza's view that:

212 Deleuze and the Body

'The more ways a body could be affected the more force it had. This capacity measures the force of a body or expresses its power' (1983: 62). A body's ability to engage with other bodies is an indication of its force and power.

Dancing as a Mode of Activity – The Master Type

How well does this account of the body, its forces and sensations, sit with the activities implicit in dancing? Is the body of the dancer at one with this Deleuzian analysis of Nietzschean corporeality? The Nietzschean perspective is dynamic to its core. In one sense it is well adapted to the movement arts for they exemplify the dynamic instance, both as the passing moment and as the passage of becomings. The Nietzschean account draws attention to the inherent dynamic which produces movement according to a series of singular instances – which Deleuze calls sensible becomings. While the dynamic principle is an overarching concept, it is to be found only in the passing moment, in the dancing itself. And its power derives from, is 'dispersed' in, the universe. The will to power is not an abstract potential. It is what it is *in* movement. The will to power is determining and plastic; it 'changes itself with the conditioned and determines itself in each case along with what it determines' (1983: 50). Dancing is similarly determined and determining in the concrete instance. The two-fold aspect of the will to power – both receptive and determining – speaks to the sense in which all dancing is inherently improvisational.[7] While improvisation commonly refers to a sub-species of contemporary dance (as the work of a subject who 'produces' movements in the moment), there is a sense in which every passing moment of movement – every emergent body – makes a particular use of those available forces to which it is related: by engaging the bodies (and their implicit forces) which lie to hand. The plasticity of the will to power is one aspect of this improvisation. It captures the responsiveness of the will to power in dancing to that which is available, to the related forms of force which meet by chance in the moment. The genetic aspect of the will to power is its second facet: utilising what lies at hand actively to produce that which emerges, the new bodily formation. Each body or concatenation of bodies ensues as a result of this productive, improvisational activity. Improvisation lies at the crossroads of chance; it takes up and produces what follows. The dancing lies in the flow from meeting to meeting, in the successive simultaneity of action predicated upon response.

The notion of availability and its utilisation aims to capture the sense in which the dancing body (or the multiple bodies which make up the dancing body) draws upon those forces to which it is related. These are finite and particular at any given moment. The take-up of specificity implicit in improvisation exemplifies Deleuze's distinction between 'all of chance' and its concrete particularity:

> But all forces do not enter into relations all at once on their own account. Their respective power is, in fact, fulfilled by relating to a small number of forces ... The encounters of forces or various quantities are therefore the concrete parts of chance, the affirmative parts of chance and, as such, alien to every law [. . .] (1983: 44)

What I call improvisation is an affirmative relationship to the concrete moments of chance to be found in the passing moment of dance. In Nietzschean terms, it is the enjoyment of difference and the assertion of interpretive authority upon that difference. Improvisation represents a duet with the world of sensuous becomings – it is the moment-by-moment activity whereby one body becomes another.

Every push out of the floor involves multiple relations between the foot and the floor, between the pushing of the foot and the resistance of the floor. The foot has to find the floor in each moment of the push-off. The push is active but the nuances of the push, its direction and forms of contact, arise from a series of mutual and momentary engagements between foot and floor. The foot is not a single vector of force applied to a constant surface area. The foot itself is a living, complex body with multiple exertions and qualities, some pouring directly into the ground, some at angles to the floor, each with various qualities of flesh and bone pressed into the surface of the floor. The softening of legs into the floor, prior to pushing off, allows gravity to exert itself upon a receptive body. Then the push can utilise the power inherent in a softened limb, making something of its contact with the ground, pushing into the floor to provoke an upwards thrust along the dancer's torso. As the push yields subsequent movement in a dancing body, as the dancer's body is propelled forwards or upwards or along, the qualities of the foot's touch upon the floor alters depending upon the arrangement of bodily weight over the foot, whether the rest of the body is above the foot, reaches forward, stays behind or is a mixture of all three. None of these relationships holds still. They give rise to further relations depending upon the corporeal play of forces.

This is one illustration of the sense in which dance consists of a succession of activities, of movements, each of which could be seen as the momentary formation of a body. The production of movement arises from relations of force which enable ever new, changing bodily forms. The will to power represents the determining, shaping dynamic inherent in the production of each bodily moment – it is that which enables movement to be movement. Forces within the dancing body contend with each other to produce new bodies out of old ones.

It is possible to conjecture a range of related forces at work in the activity of dancing. For example, the torso can lengthen upwards and backwards by reaching away from a pair of legs pushing into the ground. Length can be created along the spine through softening certain muscles and allowing gravity to be felt by the bones of the pelvis, through a head floating towards the ceiling as the lower end of the spine drops towards the ground. One part of the dancer's body may be held firm so that another part can soften. The multiple qualities and movements engendered in dancing very often require tensile distinctions of quality or direction, working with and against gravity, producing differences within the (dancer's) body and differentiation or cooperation between the dancer's body and other regions of contact.

Rebecca Skelton gives one account of dynamic difference through the activity of counter-balancing. She writes:

> As I understand it counter balance is effected through forces. It is a being drawn and expanded somehow, with equal force, in differing directions, which can be, I suggest, experienced as a multi-directional experience, as opposed to a conflict between polar opposites. I suggest, that this is a supple state of counter balance, where an aligning of the subject through many different directions and comings and goings of energy, is a multi-directional process of change. In essence, I see this as a state of flux, where nothing is fixed and where there is no holding on in any one area, no emphasis on one over the other but a continual process of change and growth; adjustment and re adjustment. (Skelton 2002)

The notion of the counter-balance in dancing recognises the multiplicity of forces at play and in flux within the body of the dancer. These 'comings and goings of energy' could be seen as a succession of bodies which form the plurality of bodies we discern in the dancer's body. Counter-balances occur in numerous ways. They are commonly performed as a duet between two dancers, where the weight of one body and its directions finds a response in the weight and direction of another. This dynamic balance changes all the time, requiring complex micro-adjustments on both sides. Counter-balancing is often made visible to the audience by creating poses that neither dancer alone could achieve. Counter-balances within the one body (of the dancer) are more subtle but equally dynamic. The play between distinct (differentiating) flows of movement (felt as the pouring of weight) allows the dancing body to play with the rhythmic emergence of the dancing. For example, the torso and head may pour backwards as the pelvis and sacrum fall forwards. This distinction of directions holds at bay (attenuates) the commitment to move in any one direction. Eventually, one flow will give way to another or combine to take the body elsewhere, mutating into something else. The notion of the counter-balance plays with the weights of the body, the bones, flesh, their multiplicity of directions *in* movement. The term, counter, suggests a vectorial flow of activities (forces) super-imposed upon one another to produce a corporeal event. Even standing 'still' involves a series of interrelated directions, muscular tonalities and weights.

The dancer's body can consist of a multiplicity of bodies, each with its own formative relations of force, quality of interaction and inherent dynamic. By the same token, larger bodies may be formed from the mingling of forces across a range of bodies, including bodies corporate such as companies or audience, social bodies and institutions of evaluation and learning.

To be in movement is to generate a series of shifts or changes, manifested through the flow of sensible becomings. Dancing is the movement from state to state, body to body, the passage of the passing moment.[8] The dancer's body, like posture itself, must be conceived as a mobile state of affairs, a plurality of bodies that make and re-make themselves through the passage of time.

Although there is a sense of resolution once a movement comes about – that is, becomes sensible, the passing moment is redolent with possibility. Deleuze notes that the sensibility of force, the capacity for being affected is 'necessarily fulfilled and actualized at each moment' (1983: 62). But it is nevertheless and simultaneously a capacity, a matter of 'feeling and sensibility' (62). The sensibility implicit in all becomings is 'the capacity for being affected' (62). This capacity is a feature of the will to power. It is informed by those forces that relate to a body at any given moment. The more ways a body can be affected, the more power a body has. This Spinozist conception 'is actualized at every moment by the bodies to which a given body is related' (62). Deleuze takes Spinoza's conception into Nietzsche's terrain by discussing the sensibility of forces and the qualities of 'sensibilia' of the will to power. Although we only encounter sensibility in the actualisation of movement, the greater the power of a body (in the Spinozist sense), the more forces are able to be brought into relation to a given body.

Such a conception could be extended to the notion of virtuosity in dance. Virtuosity is a capacity for fine differentiations of movement found in the moment of dancing. Virtuosity has become visibly coded within spectacular forms of balletic display but it can also pertain to the selective cultures of numerous kinaesthetic traditions. Different styles of dancing espouse distinct nuances of virtuosity. What they share is a plurality of 'working thoughts', each consisting of multiple relationships of force. I refer to the moment of becoming sensible as redolent with possibility. In Deleuzian terms this inheres in the passing moment. Skill, virtuosity and technical facility can be discerned in this passing moment. I want to say that virtuosic dancing both suggests and utilises a breadth of related forces. This is the feeling of power inherent in the will to power. Feeling pertains to a capacity that derives from its plasticity with respect to the field of related force. It is mobile but also wilful, an aspect of cultivated application that emerges as skilful dancing. This account of virtuosity avoids the attribution of knowledge to a subject and locates it in the passing moment. Its measure is conceived as the extent to which other bodies are brought into relation to this body: that is, through a complex multiplicity of sensible becomings. The corporeal power of suggestion, though dependent upon actual utilisation of force, evokes more than what is, via the *becoming* of movement: through its passing but also without beginning or end – 'precisely as what could not have started, and cannot finish, becoming' (Deleuze 1983: 48). Virtuosic breadth of power can be discerned in different kinds of dancing, through distinct evaluations, selections and manifestations of culture.

The field of virtuosity comes about, then, through a culture's values, established via training and selection. Taken together, these invoke the forces that feature in particular modes of dancing. Thomas DeFrantz writes about the interplay of specific forces utilised and suggested in African American expressions of culture. In a piece entitled 'Performing the Breaks, Notes on African American Aesthetic Structures', DeFrantz depicts a relational difference between rhythm and its disruption as key to African American artistic practices (DeFrantz 2010). The establishment of rhythmic force – via communal audience awareness or through backing vocals or the DJ – allows the performer to institute singular disruptive moments, the creation of a new body through a combination of sensitivity (to rhythm) and creativity (departure from it). The break signals a dynamic utilisation of force that generates an opening up of possibility as it relates itself to the forces of established rhythm. DeFrantz affirms the active role that African American audiences play in establishing rhythmic force, a role which white outsider audiences may be ill equipped, culturally and corporeally, to play. He evokes

Aretha Franklin's virtuosic engagement with the forces of musical arrangement and the supposed cadences of the lyrics, which enabled a counterpoint with her own sonorous departures, formed 'at her breath's will and according to her own creative sensibility' (2010). According to DeFrantz, the break emerges only through itself giving way to a return to rhythmic forces, through a passage into difference. Like the counter-balance, flows in one direction are in dynamic tension with other tendencies, ultimately yielding the generation of further differences from one body to the next.

For DeFrantz, the generative power of black social dance is an amalgam of performative, quotidian, historical and social elements that do not inhere in the body of the dancer alone, but nevertheless enable the circulation of tangible relations and affects between dancer, music and audience.[9] Different audiences enable different qualities of force, some actionable, others inert by way of immobile (white outsider) audience tendencies. DeFrantz writes of spiritual, rhythmic forces that drive the dance whereby the dancing body disappears in the dancing. The power of this dancing lies between the dancer and the collaborating audience, its virtuosity arising from the interstices and incitements generated in the larger body.

There is a suggestion that the break is more than that which exists – it is a 'flash of spirit' or an 'apparition of excess'. The break *suggests* by way of becoming other than itself. In another context, Russell Dumas speaks of 'becoming movement', through the suggestion of movement which is never ultimately completed, which is only ever forming. In this instance, the emergent body is juxtaposed with another body, ultimately giving way to that which emerges, the different, like the break's requisite return to rhythm, one utilisation of force overlapping the other. The suggestion is a feeling of power, a breath of Spinozan corporeal force, indicated but not exhausted. Aretha Franklin's dual evocation and departure from Obama's inaugural anthem could be seen as a virtuosic suggestion of becoming other, while maintaining a relation to an originary musical body.

Dance and the Reactive Apparatus

Thus far, dancing has been explicated as an activity which involves and produces a multiplicity of bodies which become sensible in the passing moment. The successive production of bodies is due to the domination of active force according to which a variety of reactions are variously acted: 'When force is affected by superior forces which it obeys, its

affects are made to submit, or rather, they are acted' (Deleuze 1983: 63).
Reactions are those related forces that adapt and respond to the impos-
ing authority of active forces which prevail in the given moment. There
are, however, other bodies which are also produced within all human
activity. These operate in a distinctively different manner. Deleuze and
Nietzsche were very much concerned to account for and critique the
many ways in which the forces of reaction have achieved prominence.
Drawing on the conceptual work of Nietzsche in *On the Genealogy of
Morality*, Deleuze theorises subjectivity as a parasitic formation whose
crowning achievement and necessary condition is the sabotage of active
force. While reactive force is qualitatively inferior, it gets the better of
active force by taking something away from it, that is, by separating
it from what it can do, thereby provoking it to become-reactive. This
involves the work of negation, nihilism and the spirit of *ressentiment*.

Deleuze explains the triumph of reactive force by way of the 'topical
hypothesis' originally found in Freud (1983: 112). The topical hypothesis posits consciousness as the product of two systems: conscious and
unconscious. The unconscious works in part through the formation of
lasting imprints and traces, reactions to external modes of excitation.
The topical approach depicts consciousness as a constructed response
to the unconscious trace. According to this process, the trace becomes
something else so as to become an object of consciousness: '*Thus,
there are two simultaneous processes: reaction becomes something
acted because it takes conscious excitation as its object and reaction to
traces remains in the unconscious, imperceptible*' (1983: 113; original
emphasis). Because consciousness functions as an experiential mode
of availability to 'new' excitations, there must be a means by which
consciousness comes to be renewed at each and every moment of experience. This is where Nietzsche's account of forgetting enters, to ensure
the character of conscious experience as we find it.

The topical hypothesis depicts a complex interplay between the unconscious and the construction of conscious perspective. Consciousness
arises at the border between the inside and the outside, between interiority and the external world (112). It (re)presents those excitations that
accumulate in the unconscious through the influx of exterior provoca-
tions. Although we think of interiority as given, this account explains its
manufacture via the two systems and the good offices of reactive force.[10]
The topical hypothesis shows how it is that consciousness and bodily
activity exemplify two entirely different modes of production. The
body's activities are superior and unconscious, while consciousness is no
more than a symptom of active force which has become frozen, viewed

through the lens of reaction. The dancer's corporeal feelings or experiences are a manifestation of this reactive turnaround. Consciousness transforms the active potential of force into a specific means of relating:

> *Thus at the same time as reaction to traces becomes perceptible, reaction ceases to be acted.* The consequences of this are immense: no longer being able to act a reaction, active force deprived of the material conditions of their functioning, they no longer have the opportunity to do their job, *they are separated from what they can do.* We can thus finally see in what way reactive forces prevail over active forces: when the trace takes the place of the excitation in the reactive apparatus, reaction itself takes the place of action, reaction prevails over action. (114; original emphasis)

Dance's superiority is to be found in its affirmation of active force's acting its reactions. This is an expression of what Deleuze calls 'the master type' (117). Dance is a corporeal activity wherein active force prevails and reactions are simply acted. This activity bypasses consciousness altogether. Corporeal experience is a parasitic reaction towards the alien world of bodily activity. It is a product or symptom of the body, an inert perspective upon its activities. Experience is a reaction that feeds off active force as it momentarily neutralises it. Although the triumph of reactive force is real, it never becomes active. Its power is purely negative.

Between Dance and Philosophy

Deleuze approaches the eternal return in Nietzsche's thought through affirming the reproduction of diversity and the repetition of difference (46). This is a selective thought, one that depends upon the transmutation of reaction and negation into affirmation writ large. Culture is also a mode of selection, whose violence seizes 'upon thought to make it affirmative and active' (108). I want to conclude by outlining an affinity between a certain perspective on dancing and the philosophical valorisation of affirmation. The affinity lies in those working thoughts of a heterogeneous field which encounters subjectivity as a problem. I introduce this field of dance for its initial proximity to Deleuze's Nietzsche around the question of difference. Deleuze elaborates a notion of the eternal return in Nietzsche's work which emphasizes the ongoing reproduction of difference (in contrast to the return of the same). The eternal return is the return of 'that which differs' (46).

While all dancing harnesses the changing character of corporeality – *qua* the ongoing self-differentiation of movement – there are two senses in which the dancer's subjectivity confronts the demand for difference in the body: firstly, with respect to the dancer, who needs to acquire and reproduce new movement materials; and secondly, in relation to the choreographic requirement for the production of difference. This occurs when choreography operates beyond any kind of codification such as exists in, for example, classical ballet. In both instances, bodies need to adapt, to change, towards unfamiliar, non-habitual movements. This calls for the production of new, unfamiliar bodies – unfamiliar, that is, from the dancer's reactive point of view. The challenge for dancers in this cultural milieu is not to fall into bad habits, when all repetition is liable to the habit of subjectivity – the practice of bad habits. In such a context we might remember Deleuze's claim that 'what is said of consciousness must also be said of memory and habit' (41).

It is possible to look at certain postmodern strategies of cutting and pasting or reversing movement materials as addressing the problem of familiarity and habit as a problematic tendency towards the same. These reassemblages call for the production of difference in the passage of their reformulation: that is, in the movement *between* new assemblages. Certain bodywork strategies such as ideokinesis try to occupy the subject with imagery as a means to winkle new bodies out of habitual tendencies. Other movement practices, such as Alexander and Feldenkrais techniques, also grapple with the weight of habitual tendencies as they engender new movement patterns. These practices aim to allow a body, or multiplicity of bodies, to extend its relational affectivity, creating an increase of corporeal power in the Spinozan sense. They illustrate a variety of attempts to move beyond the value of, and tendency towards, subjectivity. The choreographic commitment to the production of non-lexicon-based movement materials immediately raises a problem for those habitual tendencies embedded in the dancer's movement subjectivity. Bodywork techniques also engage the problem of movement habits when trying to create new movement pathways. Other cultural domains of the movement arts doubtless have their own strategies for the provocation and production of new bodies. This is as much a problem for traditional dance forms as for modern and postmodern styles of movement, though the problem may be felt in distinct ways. What the various cultures share is the Nietzschean sense in which training and selection 'brings the whole unconscious of the thinker into play': the sense in which acculturation is productive in the gaps between conscious experience (1983: 108). The issue is to support the extension of forces to which a body is related in the passing moment and thereby increase the power of the body, the feeling of power in the body.

Nietzsche knew he had an ally in dance. As a domain which affirms bodily activity, dance more readily supports the critique of subjectivity. Deleuze began his account of the body in Nietzsche by citing Spinoza's dictum that we do not know what a body can do (1983: 39). The body's superiority is a sign of its good health. Even reaction has its healthy side, for when reaction is acted, reaction comes along for the ride. According to Deleuze, dance is the spirit of lightness – 'Dance affirms becoming and the being of becoming' (194). Dance has the power to transform heaviness into lightness, to transmute the weight of human thought into something other than itself. In this sense, it treads lightly on the page, while pressing firmly against the floor.

Acknowledgements

I would like to thank Jon Roffe for commenting on an earlier draft of this chapter. Such as they are, the physical insights articulated here are informed by the understanding and generosity of those artists and practitioners with whom I have worked over many years. Russell Dumas, in particular, has shared his extensive experience and depth of understanding. Russell Dumas has been Artistic Director of Dance Exchange, Australia, since 1976. Before then he performed with Twyla Tharp and Dancers (USA), Trisha Brown and Company (USA), the Royal Ballet (UK), London Festival Ballet (UK), Ballet Rambert (UK) and Nederlands Dans Theater (Holland). His physical and artistic clarity underlies the philosophical articulations of this chapter.

References

Bataille, G. (1992), *On Nietzsche*, trans. B. Boone, London: Continuum.
Bourdieu, P. (1990), *The Logic of Practice*, trans. R. Nice, Stanford, CA: Stanford University Press.
DeFrantz, T. (2004), 'The Black Beat Made Visible: Body Power in Hip Hop Dance', in *Of the Presence of the Body: Essays on Dance and Performance Theory*, ed. A. Lepecki, Middletown, CT: Wesleyan University Press, pp. 64–81.
DeFrantz, T. (2010), 'Performing the Breaks, Notes on African American Aesthetic Structures', *Theatre* 40:1, pp. 31–7.
Deleuze, G. (1983), *Nietzsche and Philosophy*, trans. Hugh Tomlinson, New York: Columbia University Press.
Foster, S. (1992), 'Dancing Bodies', *Incorporations*, ed. J. Crary and S. Kwinter, New York: Zone, pp. 480–9.
Foucault, M. (1977), 'Nietzsche, Genealogy, History', in *Language, Counter-Memory, Practice*, ed. D. Bouchard, trans. D. Bouchard and S. Simon, Ithaca, NY: Cornell University Press.
Lingis, A. (1985), 'The Will to Power', in *The New Nietzsche*, ed. D. Allison, Cambridge, MA: MIT Press.

222 Deleuze and the Body

Nietzsche, F. (1967), *The Will to Power*, trans. W. Kaufmann, New York: Vintage.
Nietzsche, F. (1994), *On the Genealogy of Morality*, trans. C. Diethe, Cambridge: Cambridge University Press.
Nietzsche, F. (2001), *The Gay Science*, trans. J. Nauckhoff, Cambridge: Cambridge University Press.
Rainer, Y. (1998), '"No" to Spectacle . . .', in *Routledge Dance Studies Reader*, ed. A. Carter, London: Routledge, p. 35.
Rothfield, P. (2010), 'Differentiating Phenomenology and Dance', *Routledge Dance Studies Reader*, 2nd edition, ed. A. Carter and J. O'Shea, London: Routledge, pp. 303–18.
Skelton, R. (2002), 'Counter Balance: Aligning the roles of Dance Artist, Educator and Researcher within Higher Education', http://www.skinnerreleasing.com/articles/exploring_counter_balance.html (accessed 12 May 2009).

Notes

1. See Deleuze 1983: xiii.
2. Bear in mind, however, that in Nietzsche's thought the artist is not the source of cultural production but is rather the facilitator or midwife who is herself a product of cultural training and selection. He writes: 'This seems to me to be almost the norm among fertile artists – nobody knows a child less well than his parents' (Nietzsche 2001: 215 (§356)).
3. See Rothfield 2010.
4. In 'Nietzsche, Genealogy, History', Foucault describes the emergence (*Herkunft*) of the body in Nietzsche's work as a complex encounter with history: 'descent attaches itself to the body. It inscribes itself in the nervous system, in temperament, in the digestive apparatus; it appears in faulty respiration, in improper diets, in the debilitated and prostrate body of those whose ancestors committed errors.' Later he writes 'the body – and everything that touches it: diet, climate and soil – is the domain of the *Herkunft*. The body manifests the stigmata of past experience' (Foucault 1977: 148). Dance is an historical practice of acculturation (in the Nietzschean sense of culture), and is one manner of emergence in this Foucauldian form of *Herkunft*. It arises as a specific, historical emergence of a body which is marked by its encounter with a history and practice of dancing. Along with Foucault, this is a determinate, historical matter, marked by specificity, and constitutes the means by which the body emerges. There is no universal dancing body so much as a series of historically constituted bodies. See also Foster 1992.
5. Deleuze writes: 'any proposition is itself a set of symptoms expressing a way of being or a mode of existence of the speaker . . . In this sense, a proposition always reflects a mode of existence, a "type"' (1983: x). This is the sense in which Nietzsche often writes of the good health or otherwise of philosophy.
6. 'For in fact there is no "medium", no field of forces or battle. There is no quantity of reality, all reality is *already* quantity of force' (Deleuze 1983: 39). Nietzsche writes, similarly, 'If we eliminate these additions, no things remain but only dynamic quanta in a relation of tension to all other dynamic quanta' (Nietzsche 1967: 339, §635).
7. I owe this insight to Russell Dumas, Director of Dance Exchange, Australia (see Acknowledgements).
8. According to Deleuze, we need to think of the present moment – found in this body or multiplicity of bodies – also in terms of its passing. He writes: 'That the present moment is not a moment of being or of present "in the strict sense",

that it is the passing moment, *forces* us to think of becoming, but to think of it precisely as what could not have started, and cannot finish, becoming' (1983: 48).

9. In the case of hip hop, DeFrantz analyses the global circulation of affect beyond its origins within working-class black culture (DeFrantz 2004).

10. Deleuze writes: 'This is a strange subterranean struggle which takes place entirely inside the reactive apparatus, but which nevertheless has consequences for the whole of activity' (1983: 114).

Notes on Contributors

Ella Brians
Ella Brians completed her MA in Philosophy at the New School for Social Research. Her MA thesis examines the interrelation of the ethical and aesthetic in Deleuze's ontological critique, with a focus on *Difference and Repetition*. She is currently completing her PhD in Comparative Literature at Princeton University.

Claire Colebrook
Claire Colebrook is Edwin Erle Sparks Research Professor at Penn State University. She has written books and articles on Deleuze, literary theory, feminist theory, poetry and literary criticism. Her most recent book is *Deleuze and the Meaning of Life* (2010).

Rebecca Coleman
Rebecca Coleman is Lecturer in Media and Cultural Studies and Sociology in the Department of Sociology, Lancaster University, UK. Her research is centred on empirical and theoretical explorations of the relations between bodies and images. Her book, *The Becoming of Bodies: Girls, Images, Experience* (Manchester University Press, 2009), is based on empirical research with teenage girls and develops a feminist Deleuzian perspective for understanding how bodies become through images. She is currently working on a book on the affectivity and materialisation of popular cultural images of self-transformation and on an edited collection on Deleuzian-inspired research methodologies.

Anna Cutler
Anna Cutler is Director of Learning at Tate. Recent publications include 'What Is To Be Done, Sandra? Learning in Cultural Institutions of the Twenty-First Century'.

Laura Guillaume
Laura Guillaume holds a PhD in International Politics from Aberystwyth University. Her thesis uses insights from Deleuze and Guattari to illuminate the study of war by mobilising a particular understanding of the body. It is to be published with Routledge under the title *War on the Body: Rethinking the Ethics of War* in 2012. She is the co-editor of a special theme issue of *Theory and Event* on 'Deleuze and War'.

Joe Hughes
Joe Hughes is a Lecturer in English Literature at the University of Minnesota, Twin Cities. He is the author of *Deleuze's* Difference and Repetition and *Deleuze and the Genesis of Representation*.

Patricia MacCormack
Dr Patricia MacCormack is Reader in English, Communication, Film and Media at Anglia Ruskin University Cambridge. She has published extensively in Continental philosophy, queer and perversion theory, teratology, body modification and posthuman ethics. Her work has appeared in *Queering the Non-Human*, *Deleuze and Law*, *Deleuze and Queer Theory*, *Body and Society*, *New Formations*, *Afterimage*, *Angelaki* and others. She is the author of *Cinesexuality* and co-editor of *The Schizoanalysis of Cinema*.

Iain MacKenzie
Iain MacKenzie is a Lecturer in Political Thought. Recent publications include 'What is a Political Event?' and *The Idea of Pure Critique* (Continuum, 2004).

Peta Malins
Peta Malins is a Lecturer in Legal Studies at La Trobe University, Melbourne. Her work looks at the ethico-aesthetics of various forms of consumption with a focus on the ways in which sensory environments impact upon bodies and their capacities to form relations with others. Her areas of interest include drug and alcohol use, stencil art, urban space, advertising and the media, public memorials, food and animal ethics, corporate crime, activism and criminal justice. She has published in *Janus Head*; *Gender, Place and Culture*; and *Continuum: Journal of Media and Cultural Studies*, and is co-editor, with Anna Hickey-Moody, of *Deleuzian Encounters: Studies in Contemporary Social Issues* (Palgrave Macmillan, 2007).

John Protevi
John Protevi is Professor of French Studies at Louisiana State University in Baton Rouge, Louisiana. He is the author of *Time and Exteriority: Aristotle, Heidegger, Derrida* (Bucknell, 1994); *Political Physics: Deleuze, Derrida and the Body Politic* (Athlone, 2001); and co-author, with Mark Bonta, of *Deleuze and Geophilosophy: A Guide and Glossary* (Edinburgh, 2004). In addition, he is editor of the *Edinburgh Dictionary of Continental Philosophy* (Edinburgh, 2005). His latest book is *Political Affect: Connecting the Social and the Somatic* (Minnesota, 2009).

Philipa Rothfield
Philipa Rothfield is a Senior Lecturer in Philosophy at La Trobe University, Melbourne, Australia. She writes on philosophy of the body, largely in relation to dance. She has looked at the work of Merleau-Ponty, Nietzsche, Klossowski and Deleuze, to see what each of these philosophers can bring to dance and also to see what dance brings to philosophy. Alongside these commitments, she has engaged in an ongoing but intermittent performance project with Russell Dumas (director Dance Exchange, Australia). She also reviews dance for *RealTime*, an Australian arts magazine.

Nathan Widder
Nathan Widder is a Reader in Political Theory and Head of the Department of Politics and International Relations at Royal Holloway, University of London. He is author of *Genealogies of Difference* (University of Illinois Press, 2002), *Reflections on Time and Politics* (Penn State University Press, 2008) and numerous chapters and articles on aspects of Deleuze's thought and his relation to ancient, early Christian and medieval philosophy. He is currently working on *Deleuze and Political Theory* for Continuum Press.

Index